Senior Mathem[...]

Tony Gardiner

CAMBRIDGE UNIVERSITY PRESS

PUBLISHED BY THE PRESS SYNDICATE OF THE UNIVERSITY OF CAMBRIDGE
The Pitt Building, Trumpington Street, Cambridge, United Kingdom

CAMBRIDGE UNIVERSITY PRESS
The Edinburgh Building, Cambridge CB2 2RU, UK
40 West 20th Street, New York, NY 10011-4211, USA
477 Williamstown Road, Port Melbourne, VIC 3207, Australia
Ruiz de Alarcón 13, 28014 Madrid, Spain
Dock House, The Waterfront, Cape Town 8001, South Africa

http://www.cambridge.org

© Cambridge University Press 2002

This book is in copyright. Subject to statutory exception and to the provisions of relevant collective licensing agreements, no reproduction of any part may take place without the written permission of Cambridge University Press.

First published 2002

Printed in the United Kingdom at the University Press, Cambridge

Typeset by Mathematical Composition Setters Ltd, Salisbury, Wiltshire

Typeface Times   *System* QuarkXPress®

A catalogue record for this book is available from the British Library

ISBN 0 521 66567 1 paperback

The publisher has used its best endeavours to ensure that the URLs for external websites referred to in this book are correct and active at the time of going to press. However, the publisher has no responsibility for the websites and can make no guarantee that a site will remain live or that the content is or will remain appropriate.

Contents

A	Introduction	1
B	Resources for students aged 15–18	5
C	National Mathematics Contest problem papers	13
	1996	13
	1995	18
	1994	23
	1993	28
	1992	33
	1991	38
	1990	42
	1989	47
	1988	53
D	Ten short problem papers	59
E	Multiple-choice answers to all problem papers	77
F	Solutions to the National Mathematics Contest problems	79
	1996	79
	1995	94
	1994	105
	1993	113
	1992	123
	1991	130
	1990	140
	1989	153
	1988	166

A

Introduction

This book contains:

(i) the 1988–96 question papers from the National Mathematics Contest (NMC);
(ii) a collection of short (ten-question) problem papers in the same spirit;
(iii) a listing of the multiple-choice answers to (i) and (ii);
(iv) a section containing full written solutions to (i);
(v) a list of other available resources for students aged 15–18.

All the problems in this book are intended to be tackled *without a calculator*. My aim has been to make the problems in (i) available both as a historical record and as part of a valuable resource for stretching mathematics students in their last three years at school or college.

Multiple-choice mathematical 'challenge' papers for secondary pupils in the UK now involve around 450 000 pupils from 2700 schools and colleges each year. The problems set on these papers involve curriculum material, though sometimes in a slightly unfamiliar guise. The questions therefore challenge students to develop the flexibility to 'use what they know'. Participation is voluntary, but teachers and pupils alike recognise that these problems:

- introduce large numbers of youngsters to the pleasures and frustrations of using elementary techniques to tackle harder problems;
- encourage pupils' interest in mathematics;
- cultivate the kind of thinking which contributes to their long-term mathematical development.

Thus, participation can provide a valuable supplement to ordinary curriculum work in mathematics.

Part of the art of learning mathematics is to increase the number of situations which one can handle routinely. But it is important at the same

Introduction

time to learn to live dangerously, in the sense of being willing to tackle problems which at first sight look unfamiliar, but can, on close inspection, be solved relatively easily by combining familiar routines in unfamiliar ways. The only way to learn this elusive art is to spend the necessary time and effort struggling to solve problems for which you do not know any routine method of solution – there is no short cut.

The challenge papers depend on mastery of routine skills; but they are primarily designed to encourage a willingness to use these routine skills to solve unfamiliar problems. It would therefore contradict the spirit of these challenge papers to try to remove all uncertainty by excessive practice. However, the style of the problems is sufficiently different from ordinary classwork to warrant the publication of a collection of past papers in a convenient form.

The problems and the solutions

Section C comprises the 1988–96 problem papers (in reverse chronological order). Some of the original questions have been mildly edited – to eliminate errors and repeats, to clarify ambiguities and to fit the format of a book (as opposed to a question paper which is sat on a specified date in a particular year). To provide some additional material, Section D contains a new collection of short papers, each of which has ten questions chosen from the many excellent problems which were never used for the main papers. As on the NMC papers, the questions are roughly graded – with early questions intended to be easy and later questions hard. In order to help teachers and students check their answers quickly, Section E lists the correct multiple-choice answers (A, B, C, D, or E) for each question on both the NMC papers and the additional short papers.

Section F is devoted to full written solutions to the problems from the 1988–96 papers. This section occupies the most space, and is perhaps the most important part of the book. My aim has been to encourage teachers and students to use the collection as an elementary introduction to mathematical problem solving. Thus I have tried to make these solutions clear and simple, and to use them as a vehicle for emphasising key strategies and techniques, with a view to persuading as many readers as possible that they themselves could have solved each problem using only the techniques they already know. This has sometimes meant that I have deliberately chosen not to present a slick solution, or have given a short solution only as an 'alternative'. Slick solutions have a genuine appeal for experienced *cognoscenti*, but they can easily discourage beginners, who infer (wrongly) that since they cannot imagine 'discovering' such a solution for themselves, they probably do not have what it takes to become a good mathematician! In reality, any solution is a good solution – provided you always remember that you can learn from other approaches.

Historical background

The National Mathematics Contest was the predecessor of the present UK Senior Mathematical Challenge. The NMC had its roots in an initiative taken in 1961 by F. R. (Joe) Watson (then a mathematics teacher at Manchester Grammar School), who arranged for UK schools to use the challenging American problem paper the Annual High School Mathematics Examination (AHSME). For the first two years only a handful of schools were involved, but by 1963 there were nearly 1000 entries. This number grew to around 10 000 by 1967; entries increased slightly in the 1970s before falling back in the 1980s. (Sample AHSME papers covering the years 1950–94 are published by the Mathematical Association of America – see references [1–6] in the resources listed in Section B). In 1970 The Mathematical Association became formally involved in helping to run the NMC, and assumed full responsibility for running the event from 1975 until 1996, when responsibility passed to the United Kingdom Mathematics Trust.

Until 1988, there was no UK-produced popular national mathematics competition. By 1987, after the demise of 'seventh-term entrance' to Oxford and Cambridge, and with changes in UK school mathematics (stemming, for example, from the 1982 Cockcroft report), it became clear that a home-produced paper was needed to match local conditions.

The move towards a locally produced paper was started by Paul Woodruff. While there are no official records of all those who contributed to the NMC papers over the next ten years, contributors during part or all of this period included Steve Abbott, Greg Attwood, Colin Davis, John Deft, Colin Dixon, Stan Dolan, Tony Gardiner, Colin Goldsmith, Howard Groves, Aileen Ker, Nigel Oates, Peter Ransom, Tony Robin, Peter Thomas and Malcolm Wilson.

The 1987 paper was compiled using published questions selected from papers used in other countries. Thus the 1988 paper marks the first

Introduction

home-grown UK multiple-choice paper. The 1988–96 problem papers in Section C are the copyright of The Mathematical Association and I am grateful to them for permission to use them as the centrepiece of this book. I am also grateful to Bill Richardson for his support in numerous ways in helping to get this project off the ground, and in helping to bring it to fruition.

For the first three years (1988–90), the paper remained in the old AHSME format: 30 questions in 90 minutes. This may once have been an excellent way of identifying a small number of potential olympiad candidates, but proved to be unsuitable for a popular multiple-choice paper, designed to attract a large entry in the modern UK context. Most of the subsequent changes (such as the reduction to 25 questions, and the adoption of a lighter style of problem) were intended to make the event attractive to all interested A level candidates and to good students in Year 11. In particular, the aim is now to set a paper in which the technical demands of the first 15–20 questions might be summarised as 'GCSE + ε' – with predictable debates about the meaning of '+ ε'.

Participation has increased markedly – though there is still a long way to go, particularly in raising the number of entries from colleges. In 1988, there were around 8000 entries from 340 schools. By 1997, this had risen to 40 000 entries from nearly 900 schools and colleges.

In 1996–97, the massive expansion of national mathematics competitions led to a further reorganisation, with the United Kingdom Mathematics Trust taking over responsibility for the whole pyramid of secondary level national mathematics competitions. (See the references 11, 12 and 13 listed in Section B for resources based on some of the other UK national competitions.)

It is the privilege and responsibility of all mathematics teachers to present mathematics as a much more profound discipline than that which features in official syllabuses and exams. This book is dedicated to all those teachers who continue to contribute to the tradition of devising and using elementary problems which capture the essence of the Mathematics with a capital 'M' – problems which reach the parts no national curriculum can ever reach. May their spirit live on long after they are gone.

B

Resources for students aged 15–18

There are several difficulties in compiling a useful collection of resources.

- Although good mathematics problems have a shelf-life of many decades (or even centuries), many perennial classics are no longer easily available. Publishers like their lists of 'popular' titles to always appear fresh, so old titles are continually replaced by new ones. Hence good problem books are often allowed to go out of print long before they reach their 'sell by' date.

- Most books which claim to present mathematics and mathematical problems in an appealing way are written for, and are most effective with, experienced adults, so may not be easily accessible to interested students aged 15–18.

While the last ten years or so has seen a remarkable blossoming of public interest in mathematics – an interest greatly enhanced by the original heroic research and the subsequent popularisation of Andrew Wiles' proof of *Fermat's last theorem* (see reference [40] in the list of books below) – most of the books produced have been written for adults, rather than for students. Moreover, most are in prose format – for those who want to 'read about' mathematics, rather than those who want to get their hands dirty solving problems.

The wide range of new books being published (including some very interesting fiction) makes it hard for one person to know first hand which of the newer books can be used most effectively with interested 15–18 year olds. Hence this short list is only offered as a 'starter', and readers are strongly encouraged to supplement it with their own selection.

Resources

- Many of the excellent collections of problems which remain in print have to be ordered from specialist outlets in other countries.

Thus the three basic requirements of availability, accessibility and proven quality, combined with the limited experience of the author, make the list given here surprisingly short. However, as long as the reader understands its limitations, the shortness of the list may make it more, rather than less, useful.

In an attempt to help the reader, I distinguish two kinds of resources:

B1 books of problems and puzzles on a level similar to those in this book;
B2 books which explore related mathematical content in a readable way.

B1 Books of problems and puzzles on a level similar to those in this book

(a) American High School Mathematics Examination

The excellent problems used in this examination over the years have been well documented and are still available (see the Mathematical Association of America's website at www.maa.org).

[1] C. T. Salkind (ed.), *Contest problem book I*, Mathematical Association of America 1961 (ISBN 0 88385 605 0)
[2] C. T. Salkind (ed.), *Contest problem book II*, Mathematical Association of America 1966 (ISBN 0 88385 617 4)
[3] C. T. Salkind and J. M. Earl (eds.), *Contest problem book III*, Mathematical Association of America 1973 (ISBN 0 88385 625 5)
[4] R. A. Artino, A. M. Gaglione and Niel Shell, *Contest problem book IV*, Mathematical Association of America 1983 (ISBN 0 88385 629 8)
[5] George Berzsenyi and Stephen B. Maurer, *The contest problem book V*, Mathematical Association of America 1997 (ISBN 0 88385 640 0)
[6] Leo J. Schneider (ed.), *The contest problem book VI*, Mathematical Association of America 2000 (ISBN 0 88385 642 5)

(b) Australian Mathematics Competition

Lots of other excellent multiple-choice problems from the Australian Mathematics Competition can be ordered via the Australian Mathematics Trust website (see www.amt.canberra.edu.au).

[7] W. J. Atkins, J. D. Edwards, D. King, P. J. O'Halloran and P. J. Taylor

(eds.), *Australian Mathematics Competition, Book 1, 1978–1984*, AMT Publishing
[8] P. J. O'Halloran, G. H. Pollard and P. J. Taylor (eds.), *Australian Mathematics Competition, Book 2, 1985–1991*, AMT Publishing
[9] W. J. Atkins, J. E. M. Munro and P. J. Taylor (eds.), *Australian Mathematics Competition, Book 3, 1992–1998*, AMT Publishing
[10] W. J. Atkins, *Problem solving via the AMC*, AMT Publishing

(c) Canadian Mathematics Competitions

Similar material from the (older) Canadian Mathematics Competitions can be located and ordered from their website (see http://cemc.uwaterloo.ca).

(d) UK multiple-choice papers

A useful collection of the multiple-choice papers set in the UK for ages 12–15 is available in book form.

[11] Tony Gardiner, *Mathematical challenge*, Cambridge University Press 1996 (ISBN 0 521 55875 1)

(e) Olympiad problems

These two books are valuable introductions to learning to solve written 'olympiad' problems (as opposed to multiple-choice questions) – the first for lower secondary, the second for upper secondary.

[12] Tony Gardiner, *More mathematical challenges*, Cambridge University Press 1997 (ISBN 0 521 58568 6)
[13] A. Gardiner, *The mathematical olympiad handbook: an introduction to problem solving*, Oxford University Press 1997 (ISBN 0 19 850105 6)

(f) Puzzle books with a light touch – but a strictly mathematical focus

[14] A. Gardiner, *Mathematical puzzling*, UK Mathematics Foundation 1996 (ISBN 0 7044 17545), or Dover Publications 1999 (ISBN 0 486 40920 1)
[15] Martin Gardner, *Riddles of the sphinx and other mathematical puzzle tales*, Mathematical Association of America 1987 (ISBN 0 88385 632 8)
[16] Boris A. Kordemsky, *The Moscow puzzles*, Dover Publications 1992 (ISBN 0 486 27078 5)
[17] Charles W. Trigg, *Mathematical quickies: 270 stimulating problems with solutions*, Dover Publications 1985 (ISBN 0 486 24949 2)

(g) Puzzle books with a wider appeal

These are a few examples of the many puzzles books written for a wider audience.

[18] Brian Bolt, *Amazing mathematical amusement arcade*, Cambridge University Press 1984 (ISBN 0 521 26980 6)
[19] Brian Bolt, *Mathematical funfair*, Cambridge University Press 1989 (ISBN 0 521 37743 9)
[20] Martin Gardner, *My best mathematical and logic puzzles*, Dover Publications 1994 (ISBN 0 486 28152 3)
[21] Martin Gardner and Anthony Ravielli, *Entertaining mathematical puzzles*, Dover Publications 1986 (ISBN 0 486 25211 6)

The many other Martin Gardner books (including *Mathematical circus* and *Mathematical puzzles and diversions*, which are still available from Penguin Books) contain a vast reservoir of mathematical gems. They are written with a wonderfully light touch, if mainly for an adult audience.

[22] R. Smullyan, *The lady or the tiger and other logic puzzles*, Times Books 1992 (ISBN 0 812 92117 8)
[23] R. Smullyan, *What is the name of this book?*, Penguin Books 1990 (ISBN 0 14 013511 1)
[24] R. Smullyan, *Alice in puzzleland*, Penguin Books 1984
(ISBN 0 14 007 056 7)
The last of these Smullyan gems is unfortunately out of print, but well worth hunting down.
[25] Ian Stewart, *Game, set and math: enigmas and conundrums*, Penguin Books 1991 (ISBN 0 14 013237 6)
A wonderful collection of problems written in Stewart's racy – but always seriously mathematical – style.

(h) Problems from the Scottish Mathematical Challenge

The second, third and fourth of a series of collections of lovely problems from this annual take-home event – with solutions – are available from The Mathematical Association (www.m-a.org.uk) or The Scottish Mathematical Council (www.scot-maths.co.uk).

[26] *Mathematical challenges II, III, IV*, Scottish Mathematical Council

(i) Resources designed for classroom use with upper secondary students

[27] Charlie Stripp and Steve Drape (eds.), *Problem pages: a photocopiable book of thought-provoking mathematics problems for sixth forms and upper secondary school students* (with solutions), The Mathematical Association 2000 (ISBN 0 906588 45 6)

B2 Books which explore related mathematical content in a readable way

(a) General resources

[28] R. Courant and H. Robbins (revised by Ian Stewart), *What is mathematics? An elementary approach to ideas and methods*, Oxford University Press 1996 (ISBN 0 19 510519 2)
[29] W. W. Rouse Ball and H. S. M. Coxeter, *Mathematical recreations and essays*, Dover Publications 1987 (ISBN 0 486 25357 0)
Every mathematician's first reference for recreational mathematics.
[30] Fred Schuh, *The master book of mathematical recreations*, Dover Publications 1969 (ISBN 0 486 22134 2)
Another standard reference for elementary recreational mathematics.
[31] David Wells, *The Penguin dictionary of curious and interesting numbers*, Penguin Books 1997 (ISBN 0 14 026149 4)
Everything you ever wanted to know about your favourite numbers.
[32] David Wells, *You are a mathematician*, Penguin Books 1995 (ISBN 0 14 017480 X)
A gentle invitation to you, dear reader, to engage in problem solving.

(b) School 'extension work' texts for ages 14–16

[33] Tony Gardiner, *Maths challenge book 2*, Oxford University Press 2000 (ISBN 0 19 914778 7)
[34] Tony Gardiner, *Maths challenge book 3*, Oxford University Press 2000 (ISBN 0 19 914779 5)
Twenty one sections, including extension work on algebra, congruence and similarity, percentages, divisibility, fractions, Pythagoras and Pythagorean triples, fractions and decimals, the art of counting, and geometry through paper folding.
[35] *SMP 11–16 Book YE2*, Cambridge University Press 1993 (ISBN 0 521 31002 4)
Some serious content including sections on surds, rational/irrational numbers and decimals, logic puzzles, polyhedra, logarithms, curves and surfaces.

(c) Books covering specific subject material

[36] John H. Conway and Richard K. Guy, *The book of numbers*, Copernicus 1996 (ISBN 0 387 97993 X)
A unique introduction to the fascinating elementary mathematics which lies just behind the facade of the familiar positive integers.

The next two books focus on infinity and infinite processes. The first contains a detailed, hands-on analysis of the development and the mathematics of infinite processes arising in elementary mathematics. The second is a beautifully written and produced survey for the general interested reader.

[37] A. Gardiner, *Understanding infinity: the mathematics of infinite processes*, Dover Publications 2002 (ISBN 0 486 42538 X)
[38] Eli Maor, *To infinity and beyond: a cultural history of the infinite*, Princeton University Press 1991 (ISBN 0 691 02511 8)

The following three books are examples of the many excellent popular books on mathematics for the general reader which have been published in recent years.

[39] Robert Kanigel, *The man who knew infinity*, Abacus 1992 (ISBN 0 349 10452 2)
[40] Simon Singh, *Fermat's last theorem*, Fourth Estate 1998 (ISBN 1 85702 669 1)
[41] Simon Singh, *The code book: the secret history of codes and code-breaking*, Fourth Estate 2000 (ISBN 1 85702 889 9)

The next four books come from the Gelfand School Outreach Program, and present elementary mathematics in a way that brings out those features which are of most significance for higher mathematics.

[42] I. M. Gelfand and A. Shen, *Algebra*, Birkhäuser Boston 1995 (ISBN 0 8176 3677 3)
[43] I. M. Gelfand, E. G. Glagoleva and A. A. Kirilov, *The method of coordinates*, Birkhäuser Boston 1996 (ISBN 0 8176 3533 5)
[44] I. M. Gelfand, E. G. Glagoleva and E. E. Shnol, *Functions and graphs*, Birkhäuser Boston 1996 (ISBN 0 8176 3532 7)
[45] I. M. Gelfand and M. Saul, *Trigonometry*, Birkhäuser Boston 2001 (ISBN 0 8176 3914 4)

The next five books come from the Mathematical Association of America's New Mathematical Library, and are available via the MAA website (www.maa.org).

[46] I. Niven, *Numbers: rational and irrational*, Mathematical Association of America 1961 (ISBN 0 88385 601 8)
[47] I. Niven, *Mathematics of choice: how to count without counting*, Mathematical Association of America 1965 (ISBN 0 88385 615 8)
[48] O. Ore, *Graphs and their uses*, Mathematical Association of America 1963 (revised 1990) (ISBN 0 88385 635 2)
[49] O. Ore, *Invitation to number theory*, Mathematical Association of America 1967 (ISBN 0 88385 620 4)
[50] E. Packel, *The mathematics of games and gambling*, Mathematical Association of America 1981 (ISBN 0 88385 628 X)

(d) Books taking an unusual look at elementary mathematics

[51] A. Gardiner, *Discovering mathematics: the art of investigation*, Oxford University Press 1987 (ISBN 0 19 853265 2)
[52] H. Steinhaus, *Mathematical snapshots*, Dover Publications 1999 (ISBN 0 486 40914 7)

The National Mathematics Contest problem papers

National Mathematics Contest, 1996

1 Which of the following is an odd number?

  A 1^4+1 **B** 3^4+2 **C** 5^4+3 **D** 7^4+5 **E** 11^4+7

2 The solid shown rests on a flat surface. It is made from one-centimetre cubes placed, but not glued, together. Some of the cubes may be hidden. What is the minimum number of such cubes required to made such a solid?

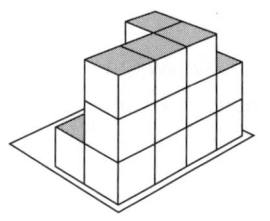

  A 12   **B** 13   **C** 14   **D** 15   **E** 16

3 How many square numbers between 1 and 1001 are divisible by 2?

  A 15   **B** 16   **C** 30   **D** 32   **E** 500

4 Which expression does not equal 1996?

  A $500^2 - 498^2$ **B** $2^2(500-1)$ **C** $\dfrac{50\,000 - 100}{25}$

  D $500 - 1 \times 4$ **E** $5 \times 20^2 - 2^2$

5 The line AB shown has a gradient of $-\dfrac{1}{k}$ ($k>1$). The y coordinate of the point B is k. What is the x coordinate of the point A?

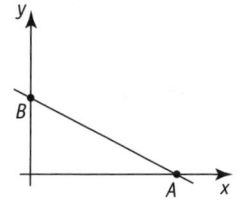

  A $\dfrac{1}{k^2}$ **B** $\dfrac{1}{k}$ **C** 1   **D** k **E** k^2

13

6 Your bone marrow makes approximately two hundred thousand million new red blood cells every day. To keep the total number constant, the same number of 'worn out' red blood cells are destroyed every day by your spleen. About how many new red blood cells will you produce during the 90 minutes you are sitting this paper?

A 1×10^7 **B** 1×10^{10} **C** 1×10^{11} **D** 2×10^{11} **E** 3×10^{12}

7 The number n is a perfect square. What is the next perfect square above it?

A $n + \sqrt{n}$ **B** $n + 2\sqrt{n} + 1$ **C** $n^2 + 1$ **D** $n^2 + n$ **E** $n^2 + 2n + 1$

8 A regular hexagon *ABCDEF* has sides of length 2 cm. The mid-point of *AB* is *M*. Which of the following line segments has length $\sqrt{13}$ cm?

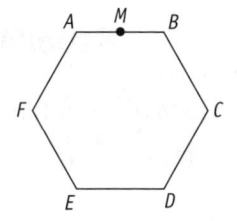

A *BD*   **B** *BE*   **C** *EM*
D *FM*   **E** none of these

9 Arthur Weekly sold two quality used cars for £9999 each. On one he made a 10% profit and on the other a 10% loss. What was his overall profit or loss over the two transactions?

A loss of £202   **B** loss of £101   **C** broke even
D profit of £101   **E** profit of £202

10 In the equation $\dfrac{1}{f} = \dfrac{1}{u} + \dfrac{1}{v}$, if f and u are both halved, what is the effect on v?

A quadrupled   **B** doubled   **C** unchanged   **D** halved   **E** quartered

11 The solid *ABCDEFGH* is a cube. The point *P* is the mid-point of *BC* and the point *Q* is the mid-point of *EF*. Which of the following best describes the figure *APHQ*?

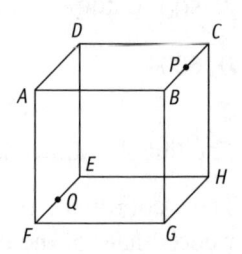

A quadrilateral   **B** parallelogram   **C** square
D rhombus   **E** rectangle

12 During an experiment the radius of a circular metal disc expands by 3%. What is the approximate percentage expansion in its area?

A 0.09% **B** 6% **C** 9% **D** 3π% **E** 9π%

13 If two non-zero numbers, x and y, are such that their product is twice their sum, which of the following equations is correct?

A $\dfrac{1}{x} + \dfrac{1}{y} = 2$ **B** $\dfrac{1}{x+y} = 2xy$ **C** $y = \dfrac{2x}{x+2}$

D $x = \dfrac{2y}{2-y}$ **E** $\dfrac{1}{x} + \dfrac{1}{y} = \dfrac{1}{2}$

14 The diagram on the right shows the speed–time graph of a train between two stations on its route. Which of the following graphs may describe the relationship between the distance travelled and the time elapsed during the same journey?

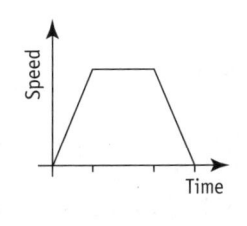

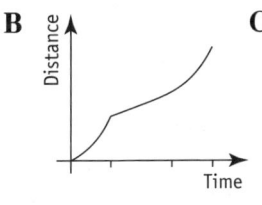

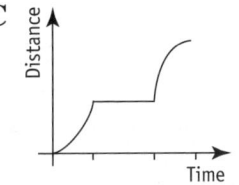

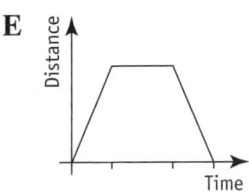

15 What is the middle digit of the product of 968 880 726 456 484 032 and 875?

A 2 **B** 4 **C** 5 **D** 6 **E** 9

16 The centre of the circle is O and $EF = FC$. If B is the mid-point of the arc AC, what is the size of the angle ABC?

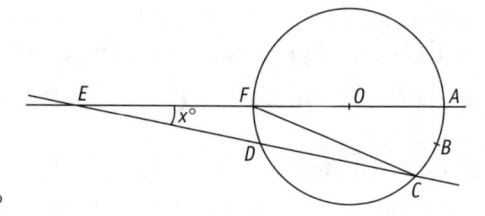

A $180° - 2x°$ **B** $180° - x°$
C $180° - \dfrac{x°}{2}$ **D** $90° + x°$
E $90° + 2x°$

17 If $x + \dfrac{1}{x} = 8$, what is the value of $x^4 + \dfrac{1}{x^4}$?

A 8^4 **B** $8^4 + 2$ **C** $8^4 - 2^8 + 2$ **D** $8^4 + 2^8 - 2$ **E** $8^4 + 2^8$

18 Observe that $98 + 76 + 5 + 4 + 3 + 2 + 10 = 198$.
In how many other ways can the digits 9, 8, 7, 6, 5, 4, 3, 2, 1, 0, in that order, with only addition signs placed between them, make a total of 198?

A 0 **B** 1 **C** 2 **D** 3 **E** 4

19 Tamara was walking along a straight coastline at 4 km/hour from east to west. Meanwhile, a small fishing boat was travelling parallel to the shore. When Tamara first sighted the boat it was on a bearing of 060°. Two hours later she could still see the boat, but by then it was on a bearing of 330° from her new position. The distance from the boat to the shore was always 1500 m. What was the average speed of the boat in km/hour?

A $4 + \sqrt{3}$ **B** $8 - \sqrt{3}$ **C** $4 + 2\sqrt{3}$ **D** $8 + \sqrt{3}$ **E** $8 + 2\sqrt{3}$

20 In a fairground game, balls are rolled down a chute and bump into equally spaced pins. When they hit a pin, they are equally likely to go left or right. At the bottom, the balls fall into boxes with the scores shown in the diagram. If three balls are rolled, what is the probability that the total score is 6?

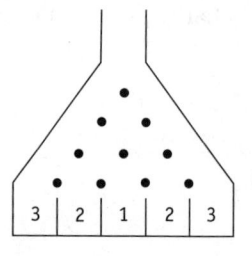

A $\dfrac{11}{512}$ **B** $\dfrac{7}{128}$ **C** $\dfrac{17}{256}$ **D** $\dfrac{41}{256}$ **E** $\dfrac{17}{64}$

National Mathematics Contest, 1996

21 A cube has its vertices removed by slicing a tetrahedron off each corner in such a way that each square face is changed into a regular octagon of side a. What is the volume of the new solid?

A $(6+4\sqrt{2})a^3$ **B** $(7+\frac{13}{3}\sqrt{2})a^3$ **C** $7(1+\frac{2}{3}\sqrt{2})a^3$
D $(7+\frac{19}{4}\sqrt{2})a^3$ **E** $\frac{77}{3}a^3$

22 How many of the equations listed below could be the equation for the sketch shown on the right?

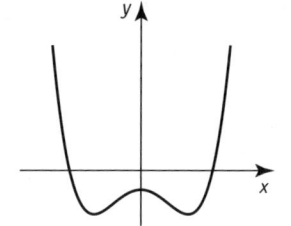

$y = x^4 - 2x^2 - 3$ $y = 3x^4 + 2x^2 - 1$
$y = x^4 + 3x^2 - 3$ $y = x^4 + 2x^2 - 3$
$y = 3x^4 - 2x^2 - 1$

A 1   **B** 2   **C** 3   **D** 4   **E** 5

23 A pair of tangents is drawn to a circle of radius R, such that the angle between them is 60°. An infinite sequence of smaller circles is then drawn such that the two straight lines are tangent to each circle. If each circle touches the next one, what is the total area of all the circles?

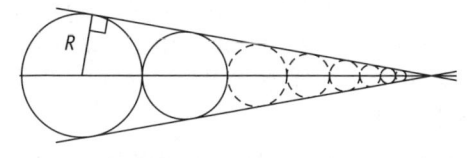

A $\dfrac{27\pi R^2}{26}$ **B** $\dfrac{9\pi R^2}{8}$ **C** $\dfrac{4\pi R^2}{3}$ **D** $\dfrac{3\pi R^2}{2}$ **E** none of these

24 What is the area of the largest equilateral triangle which fits inside a square of side a?

A $\dfrac{\sqrt{3}a^2}{4}$ **B** $(2\sqrt{3}-3)a^2$ **C** $\dfrac{\sqrt{3}a^2}{2}$ **D** $\sqrt{3}a^2$ **E** $(3\sqrt{3}-3)a^2$

25 A square $BCDF$ of side 6 is drawn in the triangle ACE such that F lies on AE. If AE is of length 20, what is the perimeter of the triangle ACE?

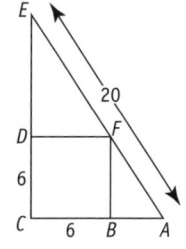

A $26 + 2\sqrt{109}$ **B** $26 + 2\sqrt{118}$ **C** 48
D $32 + 2\sqrt{109}$ **E** $32 + 2\sqrt{118}$

17

National Mathematics Contest, 1995

1 What is the seventh prime number?

   A 7   **B** 11   **C** 13   **D** 15   **E** 17

2 Which of the following hexominoes is not a possible net for a cube?

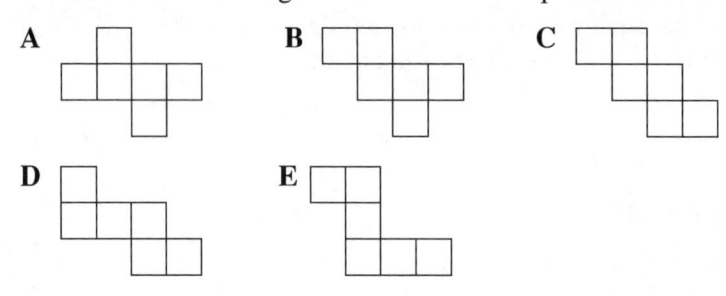

3 The first 'Match of the Day' programme in 1964 was watched by fifty thousand people. The thirtieth anniversary programme in 1994 had an audience of five million people. What percentage increase did this represent?

   A 100   **B** 990   **C** 5000   **D** 9900   **E** 10 000

4 The houses in a street are spaced so that each house is directly opposite another house. The houses are numbered 1, 2, 3, ... and so on up one side, continuing in order back down the other side. Number 37 is opposite number 64. How many houses are there?

   A 98   **B** 100   **C** 102   **D** 104   **E** 106

5 One-half of a year group obtained grade A; one-third of the rest obtained grade B; one-quarter of the remainder obtained grade C; one-fifth of the others obtained grade D. What fraction of the year group obtained grade E or worse?

   A $\frac{1}{10}$ **B** $\frac{1}{9}$ **C** $\frac{1}{6}$ **D** $\frac{1}{5}$ **E** $\frac{1}{4}$

6 In the diagram, $AC = AB$ and $CX = XY = YB$.
Which of the following statements is true?

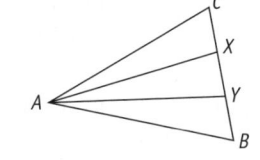

A none of the statements B, C, D, E is correct
B $AC = AX = AY = AB$
C $\angle CAX = \angle XAY = \angle YAB$
D perimeter($\triangle CAX$) = perimeter($\triangle XAY$) = perimeter($\triangle AYB$)
E area($\triangle CAX$) = area($\triangle XAY$) = area($\triangle YAB$)

7 How many factors, including 1 and 1995, does 1995 have?

A 4 B 6 C 8 D 14 E 16

8 In this competition you may attempt 25 questions. You receive 4 points for each correct answer, −1 for each incorrect answer and 0 for each question left unanswered. Twenty-five marks are then added to this total to give your overall score. Which of the following scores could not be obtained under this system?

A 113 B 114 C 115 D 116 E 117

9 How many axes of rotational symmetry does a cylinder have?

A 1 B 2 C 3 D 360 E infinitely many

10 London and Bern are in different time zones. An airline flight schedule using local times shows:

| Bern | dep. | 10:00 | London | dep. | 11:30 |
| London | arr. | 10:40 | Bern | arr. | 14:10 |

What is the flying time, in minutes, between these airports?

A 40 B 100 C 140 D 160 E 205

11 If x lies in the range $0 < x < 1$, which of the following has the smallest value?

A x^2 B x^{-1} C $x^{\frac{1}{2}}$ D x^{-2} E x

12 Four cogwheels mesh together as shown in the diagram. The cogwheels have 18, 17, 16 and 15 teeth respectively. How many revolutions must the largest cogwheel make before all the cogwheels first return to their original positions?

A 66 **B** 306 **C** 680 **D** 4080 **E** 73 440

13 Chris has an unusual dice. It is weighted in such a way that the probability of obtaining a score of n when it is rolled once is equal to $1/n$. The numbers on five of the faces are 4, 6, 8, 12 and 24 respectively. What number is on the sixth face?

A 2 **B** 3 **C** 16 **D** 48 **E** 49

14 A circular disc of radius a is rolled without slipping around the outside of an n-sided polygon. The perimeter of the polygon is p. What is the length of the path traced out by the centre of the disc?

A p **B** $p + \pi a$ **C** $p + 2\pi a$ **D** $p + n\pi a$ **E** $p + 2n\pi a$

15 $ABCDE$ is a regular pentagon. P is the point inside $ABCDE$ such that PED is an equilateral triangle. What is the size of angle APB?

A 72° **B** 84° **C** 90° **D** 96° **E** 108°

16 What is the sum of all the three-digit numbers that can be formed using three different digits chosen from 1, 2, 3, 4 and 5?

A 1080 **B** 1180 **C** 19 980 **D** 20 180 **E** 21 080

17 Peter Piper is purchasing pounds of pickled peppers. He notices that with the amount of money he has available he could buy six pounds more if the current price was reduced by 10p per pound, but four pounds less if the current price was increased by 10p per pound. How much does he have available to spend?

A £6 **B** £8 **C** £10 **D** £12 **E** £14

18 What is the diameter of the inscribed circle of the triangle with sides 8, 15 and 17?

A $4\sqrt{2}$ B $5\frac{2}{3}$ C 6 D $2\sqrt{10}$ E $\dfrac{3\sqrt{17}}{2}$

19 If $a \neq 0$ and $a \neq \pm 1$, then $\dfrac{a(a^3 + 2a^2 - a - 2) + (a^2 - 1)}{a(a^2 - 1)}$ equals:

A $\dfrac{(a+1)^2}{a}$ B $a + 2$ C $a^3 + 2a^2 - a - 1$

D $a^3 + 2a^2 - a - 2$ E $\dfrac{a^3 + 3a^2 - a - 3}{(a^2 - 1)}$

20 A point P is chosen at random in a square $ABCD$. What is the probability that the angle APB is obtuse?

A $\dfrac{1}{4}$ B $\dfrac{1}{3}$ C $\dfrac{3}{8}$ D $\dfrac{\pi}{8}$ E $\dfrac{\sqrt{3}}{4}$

21 A cube of side 1 has a cube of side $\frac{1}{2}$ stuck on top of it; this in turn has a cube of side $\frac{1}{4}$ stuck on top of it; and so on, each cube having side half the previous one. If this is continued for ever, what is the total surface area of the resulting solid?

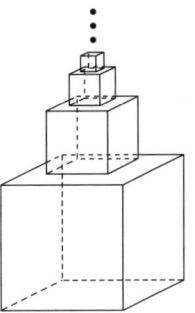

A 2 B 6 C $6\frac{2}{3}$ D $7\frac{1}{3}$ E $7\frac{11}{16}$

22 A sphere of radius r sits on a table. A point source of light is positioned directly above the centre of the sphere at a height h above the table top. The shadow of the sphere has area equal to the surface area of the sphere. Which of the following gives the height h in terms of the radius r?

A $2r$ B $\dfrac{4r}{\sqrt{3}}$ C $\dfrac{8r}{3}$ D $3r$ E $\dfrac{8r}{\sqrt{3}}$

23 I can go to work on either a number 17 bus or a number 29 bus. Number 17 buses run every 15 minutes; number 29 buses run every 12 minutes. The first number 17 bus leaves x minutes after the first number 29 bus, where $0 < x < 3$. If I arrive at the bus stop at random and catch the first available bus, what is the probability that it is a number 17 bus?

A $\dfrac{27-x}{60}$ B $\dfrac{12-x}{27}$ C $\dfrac{15-x}{27}$ D $\dfrac{2x+9}{30}$ E $\dfrac{4}{9}$

24 Nine identical spheres fit tightly in a cube whose edges have length 10. Four spheres fit in the corners of the base, one sphere is in the centre of the cube, and the others are placed in the four corners above the centre sphere. What is the radius of each sphere?

A $5(2\sqrt{3}-3)$ B $\dfrac{30\sqrt{3}-5\sqrt{6}}{17}$ C $\dfrac{5\sqrt{2}}{3}$ D 2.5   E $\dfrac{5\sqrt{3}}{3}$

25 Given that $5 \cos x + 12 \cos y = 13$, find the maximum value of $5 \sin x + 12 \sin y$.

A 7   B $\sqrt{119}$ C $\sqrt{120}$ D 12   E 13

National Mathematics Contest, 1994

1 The average of x and $8x$ is 18. What is the value of x?

A $1\frac{1}{2}$ B 2   C 4   D $4\frac{1}{2}$ E 9

2 Which of the following figures does not have six lines of symmetry?

A   B 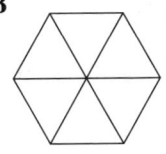   C

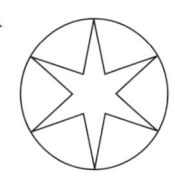

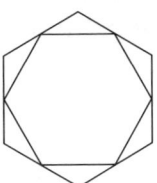

D 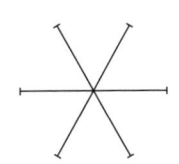   E

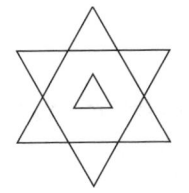

3 I write out the numbers from 1 up to 30 *in words*. If N denotes the number of times I write the letter 'n', M denotes the number of times I write the letter 'm', and C denotes the number of times I write the letter 'c', then $N + M + C$ equals:

A 27   B 28   C 29   D 30   E 31

4 Which of the following five numbers shares a common factor (> 1) with exactly one of the other four numbers?

A 91   B 52   C 39   D 35   E 24

5 $ABCD$ is a quadrilateral with $AB = AD = 25$ cm, $CB = CD = 52$ cm and $DB = 40$ cm. How long is AC in cm?

A 32.5   B 48   C 52   D 60   E 63

6 The number of pounds of pickled peppers that Peter Piper purchased for £59 is equal to the number of pounds Peter would pay for two hundred and thirty-six pounds of peppers. How much would he pay for twenty pounds of pickled peppers?

A £5   B £10   C £20   D £40   E £80

7 Which expression has the smallest value when $x = -0.5$?

  A $2^{\frac{1}{x}}$ **B** $-\frac{1}{x}$ **C** $\frac{1}{x^2}$ **D** 2^x **E** $\frac{1}{\sqrt{-x}}$

8 Over an average lifetime in the UK, roughly how many times does a person's heart beat?

  A 4×10^7 **B** 5×10^7 **C** 2×10^8 **D** 3×10^9 **E** 2×10^{10}

9 What is the sum of the reciprocals of the first six triangular numbers 1, 3, 6, 10, etc.?

  A 10   **B** $\frac{12}{7}$ **C** 56   **D** $\frac{3}{2}$ **E** $\frac{49}{21}$

10 A rope 15 m long and 5 cm in diameter is coiled in a flat spiral as shown. What is the best estimate for the diameter of the 'circle' (in cm)?

  A 10   **B** 100   **C** 150   **D** 200   **E** 300

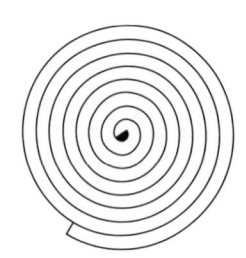

11 If $a \otimes b = \dfrac{(ab + a + b + 1)}{a}$, then $19 \otimes 94$ equals:

  A 95   **B** 100   **C** 208   **D** 1882   **E** 1994

12 The diagram shows a semicircle with radius 1 cm and centre O. If C is an arbitrary point on the semicircle, which of the following statements may be false?

  A $\angle ACB$ is a right angle
  B $\triangle AOC$ is isosceles
  C area($\triangle ABC$) ≤ 1 cm^2
  D area($\triangle AOC$) = area($\triangle OBC$)
  E $AO^2 + OB^2 = AC^2 + BC^2$

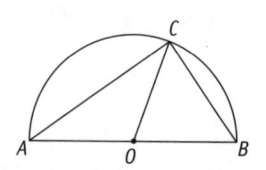

13 A giant marrow in my garden weighed 50 pounds and was 98% water. During a rainy day it then absorbed water so that it became 99% water. What was its new weight (in pounds)?

  A 50.01   **B** 50.5   **C** 98   **D** 99   **E** 100

National Mathematics Contest, 1994

14 A solid cuboid has edges of lengths a, b, c. What is its surface area?

  A $(a+b+c)^2 - (a^2+b^2+c^2)$ **B** abc
  C $2(a^2+b^2+c^2)$ **D** $(a+b+c)^2$ **E** $ab+bc+ca$

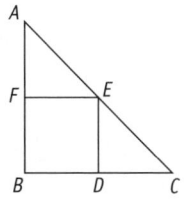

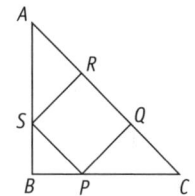

15 Given two copies of an isosceles right-angled triangle ABC, squares $BDEF$ and $PQRS$ are inscribed in different ways as shown.
What is the ratio area($PQRS$) : area($BDEF$)?

  A $8:9$ **B** $2:3$ **C** $1:1$ **D** $\sqrt{2}:\sqrt{3}$ **E** $9:8$

16 What is the last digit of $1994^{(1995+1996+1997+1998+1999+2000)}$?

  A 0 **B** 2 **C** 4 **D** 6 **E** 8

17 When two dice are thrown the probability that the total score is a multiple of 2 is $\frac{1}{2}$. For how many other values of n is it true that, when two dice are thrown, the probability that the total score is a multiple of n is equal to $\frac{1}{n}$?

  A 1 **B** 2 **C** 3 **D** 4 **E** 5

18 How many digits are there in the smallest number which is composed entirely of fives (e.g. 5555) and which is divisible by 99?

  A 9 **B** 10 **C** 18 **D** 36 **E** 45

19 The price of a second-hand car is displayed (in pounds) on four cards on the windscreen. Each card shows one digit. If the card with the thousands digit blew off in the wind, the apparent price of the car would drop to one forty-ninth of the intended value. What number is on that card?

  A 5 **B** 6 **C** 7 **D** 8 **E** 9

20 The graph of y − x against y + x is as shown on the right. The same scale has been used on each axis. Which of the following shows the graph of y against x?

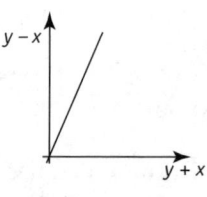

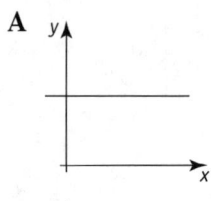

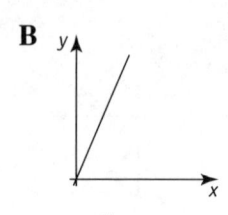

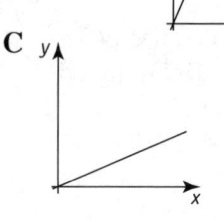

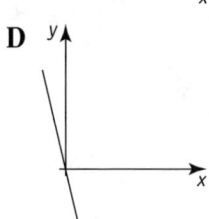

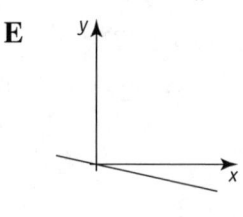

A   B   C   D   E

21 Which is smallest?

A $5 + 6\sqrt{7}$ B $7 + 6\sqrt{5}$ C $6 + 5\sqrt{7}$ D $7 + 5\sqrt{6}$ E $6 + 7\sqrt{5}$

22 A train leaves London at 06:00 and arrives in Newcastle at 09:30. Another train leaves Newcastle at 07:00 and arrives in London at 09:30. If both trains use the same route and each travels at a constant speed, at what time would they meet?

A $07:57\tfrac{1}{2}$ B $08:02\tfrac{1}{2}$ C $08:07\tfrac{1}{2}$
D $08:27\tfrac{1}{2}$ E more information required

23 The triangle ABC has a right angle at A. The hypotenuse BC is trisected at M and N so that BM = MN = NC. If AM = x and AN = y, then MN is equal to:

A $\dfrac{x+y}{2}$ B $\dfrac{\sqrt{y^2 - x^2}}{2}$ C $\sqrt{y^2 - x^2}$ D $\dfrac{\sqrt{x^2 + y^2}}{3}$ E $\sqrt{\dfrac{x^2 + y^2}{5}}$

24 Susan has a fixed time to get to work. If she drives to work at x mph she will be one minute late; if she drives at y mph she will be one minute early. How far does she drive to work (in miles)?

A $\dfrac{xy}{30(y-x)}$ B $\dfrac{2xy}{y-x}$ C $\dfrac{x+y}{y-x}$ D $\dfrac{x+y}{3}$ E $\dfrac{x+y}{60(y-x)}$

25 The octagonal figure shown is obtained by fitting eight congruent isosceles trapezia together. If the three shorter sides of each trapezium have length 1, how long is each outer edge?

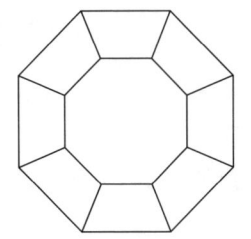

A $1 + \sqrt{2}$ **B** $\dfrac{1+\sqrt{2}}{2}$ **C** $\sqrt{2}$
D 2 **E** $1 + \sqrt{2 - \sqrt{2}}$

National Mathematics Contest, 1993

1. How many ancestors can most people claim as their great-great-grandparents if relations are not allowed to intermarry?

   A 2   B 4   C 12   D 16   E 32

2. George Green was one of the finest English mathematicians of the nineteenth century. He was entirely self-taught. Early in July 1993, we celebrated the two hundredth anniversary of his birth by unveiling a plaque to his memory in Westminster Abbey. Green died in May 1841. How old was he when he died?

   A 34   B 47   C 48   D 49   E 52

3. In a department store, items are always priced at 'so many pounds and ninety-nine pence'. If the total bill a shopper pays is £36.72, how many items have been bought?

   A 28   B 36   C 37   D 72   E can't be sure

4. The value of $(1 + \frac{1}{2})(1 + \frac{1}{3})(1 + \frac{1}{4})(1 + \frac{1}{5})$ is:

   A $\frac{1}{120}$ B $1\frac{1}{120}$ C 3   D $4\frac{1}{30}$ E $5\frac{17}{60}$

5. The faces of a cuboid have areas 48 cm², 54 cm² and 72 cm². What is the length of the longest edge in cm?

   A 8   B 9   C 12   D 18   E 72

6. If $x \otimes y = \sqrt{xy}$, what is the value of $(3 \otimes 48) \otimes 9$?

   A $6\sqrt{3}$ B $6\sqrt{\sqrt{3}}$ C 6   D 36   E 108

7. I have sixty-four candle stubs. I can make one full new candle using the wax from four stubs. A full candle burns for one hour and then goes out, leaving a stub. If I only light full candles, what is the maximum number of hours I can have candlelight?

   A 16   B 20   C 21   D 64   E 80

8 Which one of these solids *cannot* be cut into two pieces so that the cross-section exposed is an equilateral triangle?

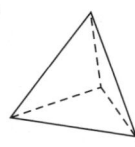

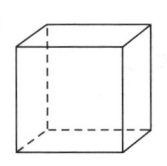

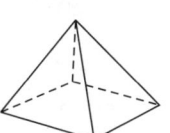

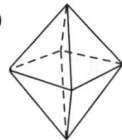

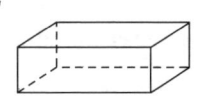

A B C

D E

9 w wabbits can dig a warren in w weeks. How many weeks would it take $w + 3$ wabbits to dig an identical warren?

A $\dfrac{w^2}{w+3}$ **B** $w+3$ **C** $\dfrac{w}{w+3}$ **D** $w-3$ **E** $\dfrac{w-3}{2w}$

10 How many times between midday and midnight do the hour hand and minute hand of a clock point in exactly opposite directions?

A 1   **B** 3   **C** 10   **D** 11   **E** 12

11 The number of elves in Bri-tain.
Is six digits long, I main-tain.
It's a cube. It's a square.
If six elves went elsewhere,
A prime number of them would re-main.

A 558 003   **B** 279 643   **C** 117 649   **D** 108 144   **E** 21 025

12 The equilateral triangle BPC is drawn inside the square $ABCD$ and angle $APD = x°$. What is the value of x?

A 60   **B** 75   **C** 90   **D** 135   **E** 150

13 It takes me an hour and a quarter to walk into town from home. Buses run every fifteen minutes from town to home, taking fifteen minutes for the journey. How many buses can I expect to meet coming towards me on a typical walk?

A 5   **B** 6   **C** 8   **D** 9   **E** 10

14 Which of the following cubes cannot be made from the given net?

A   B   C

D   E

15 A certain convex polygon has 119 distinct diagonals. How many sides does it have?

   A 14   **B** 17   **C** 60   **D** 118   **E** 120

16 For how many integral values of n is the fraction $\dfrac{n+13}{n-4}$ an integer?

   A 0   **B** 1   **C** 2   **D** 3   **E** 4

17 The number of ways of arranging all the letters of the alphabet is $26! = 26 \times 25 \times 24 \times \ldots \times 2 \times 1$. If a computer prints these arrangements at a rate of 1000 arrangements per second, approximately how long will it take to print them all?

   A 12 days   **B** 7 months   **C** 5 years   **D** 200 years
   E longer than the age of the universe (~10 000 000 000 years)

18 In a family of father, mother and two children, what is the probability that at least two birthdays fall in the same month of the year? (Assume a birth in any month is equally likely.)

   A $\dfrac{1}{20\,736}$ **B** $\dfrac{55}{96}$ **C** $\dfrac{2}{3}$ **D** $\dfrac{14\,641}{20\,736}$ **E** $\dfrac{41}{96}$

19 If $\dfrac{a}{b} + \dfrac{c}{d} = \dfrac{a+c}{b+d}$ and a, b, c, d are non-zero integers with $b + d \neq 0$, which of the following statements is true?

   A a and c must be opposite in sign
   B a and c must both be even
   C b and d must be equal
   D b and d must have a common factor
   E there are no values of a, b, c, d for which this is correct

National Mathematics Contest, 1993

20 The square shown has sides of length 2 units. What is the radius of the circle?

A 1   B $\frac{4}{5}$ C $\frac{5}{4}$ D $\sqrt{\frac{5}{4}}$ E $\sqrt{\frac{4}{5}}$

21 From the first 1993 positive integers certain integers are excluded. The arithmetic mean of the excluded integers is equal to the arithmetic mean of the integers remaining. The sum of the excluded elements must be a multiple of:

A 2   B 5   C 1001   D 997   E 1993

22 Triangle ABC is such that its three angles $\angle A$, $\angle B$, $\angle C$ are in the ratio $3:4:5$. What is the ratio of its three sides $BC:CA:AB$?

A $\sqrt{3}:\sqrt{4}:\sqrt{5}$ B $(1+\sqrt{2}):\sqrt{6}:(1+\sqrt{3})$ C $2:\sqrt{6}:(1+\sqrt{3})$
D $3:4:5$ E $\sqrt{6}:(1+\sqrt{3}):(\sqrt{2}+\sqrt{3})$

23 The diagram shows part of a hockey pitch with goal posts A and B, 5 m apart. Sandy is running along the line DC where $AC = 4$ m. Sandy chooses to hit the ball towards the goal from the point P, where the angle APB is as large as possible. What is the distance CP in metres?

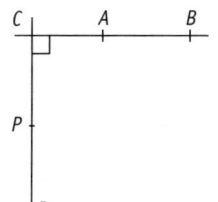

A 5   B 6   C 7   D $4\sqrt{2}$ E $3\sqrt{3}$

24 What is the sum to infinity of the series:

$$\frac{1}{2\sqrt{2}+3}+\frac{1}{5\sqrt{2}+7}+\frac{1}{12\sqrt{2}+17}+\cdots$$

where, if $\dfrac{1}{a\sqrt{2}+b}$ and $\dfrac{1}{c\sqrt{2}+d}$ are successive terms, $c = a+b$ and $d = c+a$?

A $1-\dfrac{1}{\sqrt{2}}$ B $1+\sqrt{2}$ C $\dfrac{1}{\sqrt{2}}$ D $\sqrt{2}$ E $\dfrac{\sqrt{2}-1}{2}$

25 If x is a real number, $[x]$ is defined to be the greatest integer less than or equal to x (e.g. $[6.9] = 6$). How many positive values of x are there with $[x] \neq 0 \neq [3x]$ such that $\dfrac{1}{[x]} + \dfrac{1}{[3x]} = x - [x]$?

A 0   B 1   C 2   D 3   E infinitely many

National Mathematics Contest, 1992

1. Which of these numbers is not a prime number?

   A $3^2 - 2$ **B** $5^2 - 2$ **C** $7^2 - 2$ **D** $11^2 - 2$ **E** $13^2 - 2$

2. A calculator displays the digits 1.23456   78, representing the number 1.23456×10^{78}. What does the calculator show if 20 is added to this number?

   A 21.23456   **B** 1.23456   78   **C** 1.23476   78
   D 21.23456   78   **E** 1.23456   98

3. How many different triangles can be made from five rods of length 2, 3, 4, 5 and 6 cm if they are taken three at a time?

   A 6   **B** 7   **C** 10   **D** 20   **E** 60

4. The digit 1 is placed after a three-digit number whose hundreds digit is h, tens digit is t and units digit is u. What is the value of the new number?

   A $h + t + u + 1$ **B** $10h + 10t + 10u + 1$ **C** $1000h + 100t + 10u + 1$
   D htu **E** $100h + 10t + u + 1$

5. What is the probability that the next person you meet has an above average number of arms?

   A 0   **B** nearly 0   **C** 0.5   **D** nearly 1   **E** 1

6. Suppose UN maps to DEUX, DEUX to QUATRE, QUATRE to SIX, SIX to TROIS and TROIS to CINQ. What does CINQ map to?

   A UN   **B** DEUX   **C** TROIS   **D** QUATRE   **E** CINQ

7. The population of the UK is approximately 50 million. It stays roughly constant. Approximately how many births are there each year?

   A 20 000   **B** 70 000   **C** 200 000   **D** 700 000   **E** 2 000 000

8. $M(x)$ means 'the mother of x', and $M(M(x))$ is abbreviated to $M^2(x)$. What relation is Alan to Betty if M^2 (Alan) = M (Betty) and M (Alan) ≠ Betty?

   A nephew   **B** uncle   **C** son   **D** father   **E** cousin

9 The diagram shows a shape made from four identical cubes stuck together. Its surface area (in cm^2) is numerically equal to its volume (in cm^3). What is the length (in cm) of the edge of each cube?

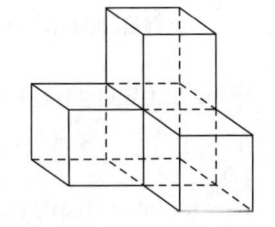

A $\frac{9}{4}$ B $\sqrt[3]{6}$ C $\frac{15}{4}$ D $\frac{9}{2}$ E 6

10 Gill's elder sister, Lill, is a chip off the old block. Coming from the same family they are mathematically similar, their heights being in the ratio of their ages. Gill is currently 4 and Lill is 5 years old. Gill's mass is 16 kg. What is Lill's mass in kg?

A $12\frac{4}{5}$ B 17   C 20   D 25   E $31\frac{1}{4}$

11 Square sheets of overlapping paper are pinned on a notice board with the minimum number of drawing pins. Each sheet has a pin close to each corner. In the diagram, 20 pins are required in total. If n sheets of paper are arranged to form a square on the notice board, how many pins are required?

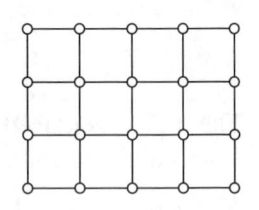

A $4n$ B $2(n+1)$ C $n+2\sqrt{n}+1$ D n^2 E $(n+1)^2$

12 Margaret (M) and Neil (N) were paid the same in 1989. On 1 January 1990, Margaret had a 10% pay rise whilst Neil had an 8% rise. On 1 January 1991, Neil had a 10% rise whilst Margaret had an 8% rise. Which of the following statements is true?

A M earned more than N in both years 1990 and 1991
B M earned more than N in 1990 but less than N in 1991
C the total earnings for each person over the three years were equal
D N earned more altogether than M
E N earned less than M in 1990, but they both earned the same in 1991

13 An alarm clock was correct at midnight but then began to lose 12 minutes each hour. The next morning I noticed that it showed 1 am but it had in fact stopped ten hours earlier. At what time did I look at the clock?

A 10:45   B 10:48   C 11:00   D 11:12   E 11:15

14 How many planes of symmetry does a regular octahedron possess?

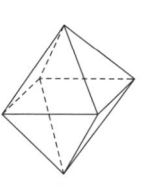

  A 3   B 5   C 8   D 9   E 12

15 My granny and her sisters all got married in the 1940s, and both they and their husbands are still going strong. Like most people in those days, they all got married on a Saturday. Which of the following statements about their silver, ruby and golden wedding anniversaries is true? (A silver anniversary celebrates 25 years, a ruby anniversary celebrates 40 years and a golden anniversary celebrates 50 years of marriage.)

  A all the anniversaries must have occurred at a weekend
  B the golden anniversaries must have been at a weekend, the ruby and silver anniversaries cannot have been at a weekend
  C the ruby anniversaries must have been at a weekend, the golden may have been, but the silver anniversaries cannot have been
  D golden, ruby and silver anniversaries may have occurred at a weekend, but need not have done
  E not enough information to decide whether any particular kind of anniversary did, or did not, occur at the weekend

16 The angles at A and B in a parallelogram are trisected as shown. How big is angle MCN?

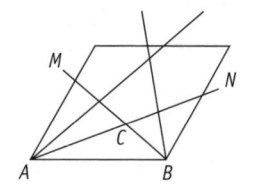

  A 110°   B 120°   C 130°
  D 135°   E 150°

17 A rally driver travels an average of k miles a day for the first d days in a race and m miles a day for the next b days. Her car uses x litres of petrol per 100 miles. How many litres of petrol does her car use altogether?

  A $\dfrac{x(kd + mb)}{100}$ B $\dfrac{(k + m)x}{100}$ C $\dfrac{100(k + m)}{x}$

  D $\dfrac{100(kd + mb)}{x}$ E $\dfrac{bdkmx}{100}$

18 The sections of rail on a railway are 10 m long. As the train passes over each place where the rails are joined, there is an audible click. The speed of the train in miles per hour is approximately the number of clicks heard in:

A 10 minutes **B** $1\frac{2}{3}$ minutes **C** 1 minute
D $\frac{1}{2}$ minute **E** $\frac{3}{8}$ minute

19 C, E, M, N all represent different digits in the range 0 to 9 inclusive, the same letter representing the same digit consistently. What digit could E represent?

```
  N M C
-   9 2
  -----
  4 M E
```

A 0 or 1 **B** 2 or 3 **C** 4 or 5 **D** 6 or 7 **E** 8 or 9

20 $|x| = \begin{cases} x & \text{for } x \geq 0 \\ -x & \text{for } x < 0 \end{cases}$. For example, $|7| = 7, |-2.1| = 2.1$.

What is the area (in square units) of the region enclosed by the graph $|x| + |y| = 1$?

A 1 **B** $\sqrt{2}$ **C** 2 **D** π **E** 4

21 ABCDE is a pentagon inscribed in a circle, with AC parallel to ED and $\angle ABE = 20°$. If AD and CE cross at X, what is the size of angle AXC?

A 100° **B** 120° **C** 135° **D** 140° **E** 160°

22 Two bicycle wheels, with diameters 28 inches and 26 inches, are fitted with correctly calibrated cyclometers. (A cyclometer measures the distance travelled by counting the number of revolutions of one wheel.) The cyclometers are swapped over and the bicycles travel a certain distance; the difference in the cyclometer readings is then 27 miles. What was the actual distance, in miles, travelled by each bicycle?

A 54 **B** 169 **C** 182 **D** 196 **E** 392

23 At a carnival, circular coins of radius r cm are rolled onto a board covered by non-overlapping squares of side x cm. If the probability that a coin lies completely inside a square is 0.64, what is the value of $\frac{r}{x}$?

A 0.1 **B** 0.18 **C** 0.2 **D** $1 - \frac{0.64}{\pi}$ **E** $\frac{0.8}{\sqrt{\pi}}$

24 Three identical snooker balls of unit radius lie on a table, all touching each other. After they are fixed in this position, a fourth identical ball is placed on top so that all four are in contact with each other. How high above the table is the centre of the fourth ball?

A $1 + \dfrac{2\sqrt{6}}{3}$ **B** $1 + \sqrt{3}$ **C** $1 + \sqrt{2}$ **D** $\sqrt{2} + \sqrt{\dfrac{3}{2}}$ **E** $1 + \sqrt{6}$

25 If $x = \sqrt{1 + 1992^2 + \dfrac{1992^2}{1993^2}} + \dfrac{1992}{1993}$, then which statement is true?

A $1992 < x < 1993$ **B** $x = 1993$ **C** $1993 < x < 1994$
D $x = 1994$ **E** $x > 1994$

National Mathematics Contest, 1991

1. Which of the following is not a prime number?

   A $2^2 - 2 + 1$ **B** $2^3 - 2^2 + 2 - 1$ **C** $2^4 - 2^3 + 2^2 - 2 + 1$
   D $2^5 - 2^4 + 2^3 - 2^2 + 2 - 1$ **E** $2^6 - 2^5 + 2^4 - 2^3 + 2^2 - 2 + 1$

2. When $1991^2 - 1991$ is worked out, what are the tens and units digits in your answer?

   A ...00   **B** ...10   **C** ...81   **D** ...90   **E** ...91

3. You start with the diagram on the right. You want to finish with a pattern of three grey and four white hexagons which does not have exactly one line of symmetry. Which additional cell must be shaded?

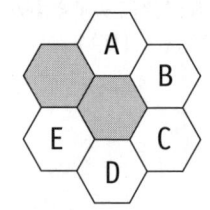

   A A   **B** B   **C** C   **D** D   **E** E

4. Three days ago, yesterday was the day before Sunday. What day will it be tomorrow?

   A Monday   **B** Tuesday   **C** Wednesday   **D** Thursday   **E** Friday

5. In this addition, different letters stand for different digits, but each letter represents the same digit each time it appears. If the letter O stands for 7, what digit must U represent?

   ```
     T W O
   + T W O
   -------
   F O U R
   ```

   A 1   **B** 3   **C** 5   **D** 7   **E** 9

6. Which of the following events is most likely?

   A four ordinary coins tossed together all show the same side
   B an ordinary dice thrown once shows a six
   C your first child will be born on a Friday
   D two ordinary dice thrown together show a total of nine
   E a whole number chosen at random is a multiple of five

7. One day I noticed that my newspaper had twenty-six pages and that page 6 and page 20 were on the same double sheet. Which other two pages were also on this sheet?

   A 5 and 19   **B** 5 and 21   **C** 7 and 19   **D** 7 and 21   **E** can't be sure

National Mathematics Contest, 1991

8 In 1971, the UK adopted its present decimal money system. Before that date, the pound (£) was divided into twenty shillings (s) and each shilling into twelve pence (d). In 1970, a family bought two cups of coffee at 1s 6d each and three cups of tea at 1s 3d each. How much change did they get from £1?

    A 13s 11d   **B** 12s 9d   **C** 13s 1d   **D** 12s 11d   **E** 13s 3d

9 Between 1981 and 1986, the number of items in a certain mathematics syllabus increased by 40%. Between 1981 and 1991, the number of items in this syllabus increased by 100%. By how much did the number of items increase between 1986 and 1991 (to the nearest per cent)?

    A 60%   **B** 53%   **C** 50%   **D** 43%   **E** 40%

10 Hadrian's Wall runs 80 miles from Bowness-on-Solway to Wallsend. Some people think that it was built as a defence against the Picts. If the Romans had decided to keep out the Picts by lining up shoulder to shoulder along the line of the Wall, roughly how many men would they have needed?

    A 7000   **B** 20 000   **C** 70 000   **D** 200 000   **E** 700 000

11 In the diagram, the sloping line divides the area of the rectangle in the ratio $1:4$. What is the ratio $a:b$?

    A $1:1$ **B** $1:2$ **C** $1:3$ **D** $1:4$ **E** $2:3$

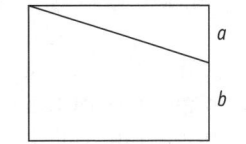

12 A micrometer screw gauge was set up to measure the diameter of a metal bar. Five pupils then took turns to read the scale. Each pupil recorded their measurement to a different level of accuracy. Their recorded measurements are given below in millimetres. One is inconsistent with the others. Which is it?

    A 80   **B** 77   **C** 76.5   **D** 76.48   **E** 76.482

13 At which of these times is the angle between the two hands of a clock equal to 170°?

    A 12:30   **B** 6:02   **C** 8:10   **D** 9:15   **E** 10:20

14 The sequence '22' is self-describing because it contains precisely two 2s. Similarly, the sequence '31 12 33 15' is self-describing because it contains precisely three 1s, one 2, three 3s and one 5. Which of the following sequences is *not* self-describing?

   A 21 32 23 16   **B** 31 12 33 18   **C** 31 22 33 17 19
   D 21 32 33 24 15   **E** 41 32 23 24 15 16 18

15 O is the centre of the circle. If $BC = OA$, which of the following must be true?

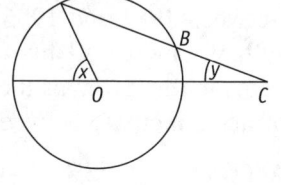

   A $x = 3y$ **B** $x = 60°$ **C** $x + y = 90°$
   D $x = 2y$ **E** $x = 4y$

16 What type of a number is $(\sqrt{50}^{\sqrt{50}})^{\sqrt{50}}$?

   A an irrational number   **B** perfect fifth power   **C** a perfect square
   D a triangular number   **E** a perfect cube

17 A car travels steadily at k km/h. If it uses l litres of petrol per 100 km, how many litres will it use in m minutes?

   A $\dfrac{klm}{6000}$ **B** $\dfrac{6lm}{10k}$ **C** $\dfrac{klm}{100}$ **D** $\dfrac{lm}{6000k}$ **E** $\dfrac{6klm}{10}$

18 Begin with a unit square. Then shade two quarters as shown; then shade two quarters of the bottom right quarter; then shade two quarters of the bottom right quarter of that; and so on for ever. What is the limiting value of the total shaded area?

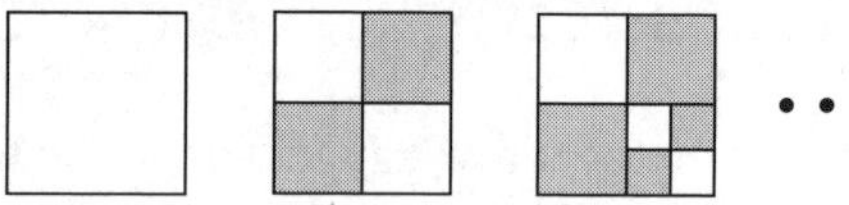

   A $\dfrac{1}{2}$ **B** $\dfrac{3}{5}$ **C** $\dfrac{5}{8}$ **D** $\dfrac{2}{3}$ **E** $\dfrac{1}{\sqrt{2}}$

19 Aileen walked from B to C and back by the same path without stopping. The round trip took six hours. She averaged 4 km/h on level ground, 3 km/h whenever she went uphill and 6 km/h downhill. How far (in km) did she walk?

   A 12   **B** 13   **C** 24   **D** 27   **E** can't be sure

20 Unlike many infinitely long expressions, $\sqrt{6 + \sqrt{6 + \sqrt{6 + \sqrt{6 + \sqrt{6 + \cdots}}}}}$ has a finite value. What is that value?

    A 3   **B** π **C** $\sqrt{10}$ **D** $\frac{22}{7}$ **E** 6

21 I recently set one of my classes this task:

> *Shade one quarter of this rectangle.*
> *You may shade whole squares only.*

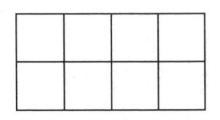

I was delighted when everyone responded correctly! I knew they hadn't cheated because they all had different answers. Curiously, no-one produced a solution in which two shaded squares had a common side, though I saw every other possible solution. How many pupils were in the class?

    A 14   **B** 16   **C** 18   **D** 20   **E** 36

22 A cube has edges of length $2a$. Each corner of the cube is removed by a plane cut through the mid-points of the three edges meeting at that corner. What is the volume of the remaining solid?

    A $\frac{4}{3}a^3$ **B** $\frac{47}{6}a^3$ **C** $\frac{1}{6}a^3$ **D** $\frac{20}{3}a^3$ **E** $2\sqrt{2}a^3$

23 The function f is defined on ordered pairs (x, y) of positive integers and has the following properties for all permissible values of x and y:

$$f(x, x) = x, \quad f(x, y) = f(y, x), \quad (x + y)f(x, y) = (2x + y)f(x, x + y).$$

What is the value of $f(19, 91)$?

    A $\frac{1}{50}$ **B** $\frac{1}{53}$ **C** 2   **D** $\frac{2}{91}$ **E** $\frac{1}{55}$

24 N is a positive integer and $N^2 - 1991$ is a perfect square. How many possible values are there for N?

    A 0   **B** 1   **C** 2   **D** 3   **E** 4

25 Triangle XYZ has sides of lengths 3, 4, 5. P is a point within the triangle for which $\angle XPY = \angle YPZ = \angle ZPX$. The distances from P to X, Y and Z are l, m and n respectively. What is the value of $l^2 + m^2 + n^2$?

    A $25 - 4\sqrt{3}$ **B** 50   **C** $\frac{25}{2} + 4\sqrt{3}$ **D** $10\sqrt{3}$ **E** $10 + 4\sqrt{3}$

National Mathematics Contest, 1990

1 The picture shows me holding a large square notice up to the class. If I rotate the notice through 180° about the diagonal axis joining my two thumbs, which of the following will I then be able to see?

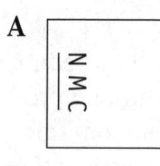

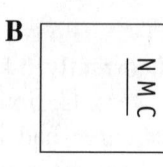

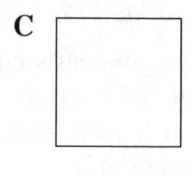

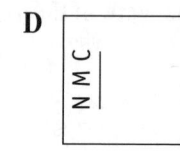

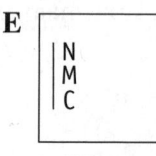

A ☐ (N M C sideways)   B ☐ (N M C sideways)   C ☐

D ☐ (N M C sideways)   E ☐ (N M C vertical)

2 The sum of two whole numbers is 8 and the sum of their cubes is 152. What is the product of the original numbers?

A 0   B 7   C 12   D 15   E 16

3 How many letters are there in the correct answer to this question?

A one   B two   C three   D four   E five

4 $0.\dot{3}$ multiplied by itself is equal to:

A $0.0\dot{9}$ B $0.0\ddot{9}$ C $0.\dot{1}$ D $0.\dot{9}$ E none of these

5 *ABCD* is a square, and *P* is a point inside the square such that triangle *ADP* is equilateral. How big is angle *PBC*?

A 15°   B 20°   C 25°   D 30°   E 75°

6 On simple weighing scales, seven golden dollrs exactly balance thirteen silver nickls, and seven silver dims exactly balance thirteen golden dollrs. How many silver coins do you need to balance one hundred golden dollrs?

A 7   B 13   C 40   D 91   E 100

National Mathematics Contest, 1990

7 A square peg just fits in a round hold. What fraction of the hole is occupied by the peg?

   A $\dfrac{2}{\pi}$ B $\dfrac{\pi}{2} - 1$ C $\dfrac{2}{\pi - 2}$ D $1 - \dfrac{2}{\pi}$ E none of these

8 Four numbers are written in a row. The average of the first two numbers is 7; the average of the middle two numbers is 2.3; and the average of the last two numbers is 8.4. What is the average of the first number and the last number?

   A 5.9   B 7.7   C 13.1   D 15.4   E can't be sure

9 A mathematics competition charges each school an entry fee of 35p per pupil for the first eight candidates and 25p per pupil for each extra pupil. A school pays an average entry fee of 29p per pupil. How many pupils did it enter?

   A 10   B 12   C 20   D 24   E 30

10 A debate is raging in the Shire as to whether the Hobbits should introduce metal coinage. One proposal is that all coins should be circular, that they should all have the same thickness, and that their face value should be directly proportional to their volume. If an Arkenstone has diameter a and is worth twice as much as a Baggins, of diameter b, what is the value of the ratio $\dfrac{b}{a}$?

   A exactly $\tfrac{1}{4}$ B roughly $\tfrac{1}{2}$ C exactly $\tfrac{1}{2}$
   D roughly $\tfrac{7}{10}$ E roughly $\tfrac{8}{10}$

11 Each letter stands for a different digit, but where a letter occurs more than once it always stands for the same digit. What digit does H stand for?

   ```
     S I X T H
   +ardo F O R M
   ─────────────
     M A T H S
   ```

   A 1   B 3   C 8   D 9   E can't be sure

12 A, B, C, D, E, F, G, H are the vertices (in order) of a regular octagon. The diagonals AD and BH cross at I. How big is angle BID?

   A 45°   B 67.5°   C 90°   D 112.5°   E none of these

13 In the expansion of $\frac{1}{7000}$ as a decimal, the digit in the 7000th decimal place is:

A 1   B 2   C 4   D 7   E 8

14 'The sum of any N consecutive integers is always odd' is a true statement when $N = 2$. What is the next value of N for which the statement is true?

A 3   B 4   C 5   D 6   E none of these

15 Four of the lines below have a common point which does not lie on the other line. Which is the odd line out?

A $x + y = 5$ B $x = 2y + 1$ C $y = x - 2$
D $x = 3y - 1$ E $y = 3x - 9$

16 As I arrived home at my local station one night at twenty minutes and twelve seconds past one, I noticed instantly that the first three digits on the platform clock were the same as the last three, and in the same order. How many times in twenty four hours does this happen?

A 96   B 108   C 180   D 600   E 1000

17 If $f(x) = 2^x$, then 16^8 is equal to:

A $f(7)$ B $f(12)$ C $f(f(5))$ D $f(f(3))$ E $f(f(f(f(3))))$

18 How many positive integers from 1 up to 1990 do *not* have either 3 or 5 as a factor?

A 663   B 929   C 1061   D 1327   E 1858

19 The triangle ABC is isosceles with $AB = AC$ and $\angle BAC = 2\theta$. AE and BD are altitudes which intersect at P. The ratio $PE : AE$ is equal to:

A $\frac{1}{4}$ B $\frac{1}{3}$ C $\sin \theta$ D $\dfrac{1}{\cos \theta}$ E $(\tan \theta)^2$

20 A small square is cut out of the corner of a large square leaving an L-shape. Given that the side length of each square is a whole number of centimetres and that the L-shape has area 60 cm², how many possible values are there for the area of the original large square (in cm²)?

A 1   B 2   C 3   D 6   E 12

21 The triangles OAB and OPQ are similar. If $\dfrac{OA}{OQ} = 3$ and $\dfrac{OB}{OP} = 2$, then $\dfrac{AB}{PQ}$ equals:

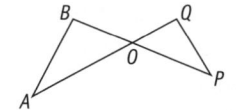

A $2\frac{1}{4}$ B $\sqrt{6}$ C $2\frac{1}{2}$ D $\dfrac{3\sqrt{3}}{2\sqrt{2}}$ E 6

22 Starting with a large circle of pastry, I used two pastry cutters to cut out four touching circles as shown to form the bases and tops of two identical pies. What fraction of the pastry remained unused?

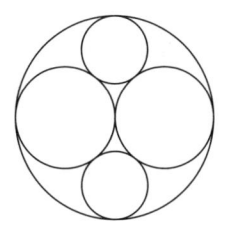

A $\frac{1}{2}$ B $\frac{7}{18}$ C $\frac{1}{3}$ D $\frac{5}{18}$ E $\frac{2}{9}$

23 A wall of length a and height b is papered with vertical strips of plain wallpaper of width x. If a is not an exact multiple of x and if $[y]$ denotes the largest integer $\leq y$, then the length of wallpaper required is:

A $\left(\left[\dfrac{a}{x}\right]+1\right)b$ B $\left[\dfrac{a}{x}\right]b$ C $\dfrac{ab}{x}$ D $\dfrac{[a]}{x}b$ E $\dfrac{a}{[x]}b$

24 Let b be a real number satisfying $b^3 = b + 1$. Which of the following is *not* true?

A $b^4 = b^2 + b$ B $b^5 = b^4 + 1$ C $b^4 = b^3 + b^2 - 1$

D $b^2 + b + 1 = 1 + \dfrac{1}{b-1}$ E $b^4 + b^3 = b^2 + 1$

25 x men work x hours a day for x days to dig an x metre length of tunnel. If y men work y hours a day for y days what length (in metres) of the same tunnel would you expect them to dig?

A $\dfrac{x^2}{y^3}$ B $\dfrac{y^2}{x^3}$ C y D $\dfrac{x^3}{y^2}$ E $\dfrac{y^3}{x^2}$

26 Two different numbers x and y are such that $x \leq 1$ and $y \geq 1$. If S is the sum of x and y and P is their product, then $S - P$ is:

A always >1   B always <1   C always ≥ 1
D always = 1   E sometimes <1

27 Steffi and Boris are playing tennis. In the current game, they have just reached 'deuce': the winner of the game will now be the first player to get two clear points ahead of the other. Steffi is serving and for each point the probability that she wins is $\frac{3}{5}$, whereas the probability that Boris wins is $\frac{2}{5}$. What is the probability that Steffi will win the game?

A $\frac{9}{25}$ **B** $\frac{7}{13}$ **C** $\frac{3}{5}$ **D** $\frac{16}{25}$ **E** $\frac{9}{13}$

28 A 'turtle' on a computer screen obeys the pair of instructions 'Walk 10 units, turn left through 20°' five times in succession. What is the direct distance between its starting and finishing positions?

A $80 \sin 25°$ **B** $\dfrac{10 \sin 50°}{\sin 10°}$ **C** $80 \sin 40° \cos 10°$

D $40 \cos 20° \cos 10°$ **E** $\dfrac{50 \cos 40°}{\cos 10°}$

29 If $a = \dfrac{xy}{x+y}$, $b = \dfrac{yz}{y+z}$, $c = \dfrac{zx}{z+x}$, where $a, b, c \neq 0$, then x equals:

A $\dfrac{abc}{ab + bc + ca}$ **B** $\dfrac{2abc}{ab + bc + ca}$ **C** $\dfrac{2abc}{ab - bc + ca}$

D $\dfrac{2abc}{-ab + bc + ca}$ **E** $\dfrac{2abc}{ab + bc - ca}$

30 In the diagram, area x equals:

A 22   **B** 16   **C** 7   **D** 4   **E** can't be sure

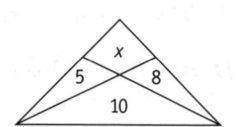

National Mathematics Contest, 1989

1 The diagram shows a magic square in which the sum of the numbers in any row, column or diagonal is the same. What is the value of n?

   A 10   **B** 3   **C** 7   **D** 11   **E** 6

		8
5		9
	n	4

2 I have an unlimited number of 1p, 2p, 3p, 4p and 5p stamps. How many different combinations of stamps are there which total 6p?

   A 12   **B** 9   **C** 6   **D** 8   **E** 10

3 When the cap is on the bottle and the bottle is upright, how far from the top of the table is the bottom of the brush?

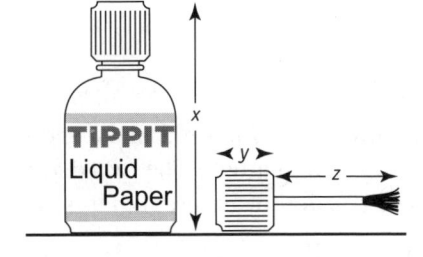

   A $x - y - z$ **B** $x - y + z$
   C $x + y + z$ **D** $x + y - z$
   E $-x + y + z$

4 Which statement is *false*?

   A any equilateral triangle can be divided into four congruent triangles
   B any isosceles triangle can be divided into two congruent triangles
   C when both diagonals are drawn, any square is divided into four congruent triangles
   D when both diagonals are drawn, any rectangle is divided into four congruent triangles
   E when both diagonals are drawn, any rhombus is divided into four congruent triangles

5 How many prime numbers are there between 110 and 120?

   A 1   **B** 2   **C** 3   **D** 4   **E** 5

47

6 FITCAT biscuits altered the size of their packs, so there are now seven biscuits in a pack instead of six. The price of each FITCAT biscuit has dropped by:

WAS 6 FOR 55p **NOW ONLY 61p for 7** FITCATS

A $\dfrac{19}{61 \times 55}$ p **B** $\dfrac{1}{7}$ p **C** $\dfrac{19}{42}$ p **D** $\dfrac{6}{7}$ p **E** 1p

7

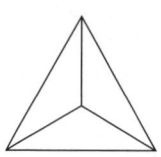

Figure 1 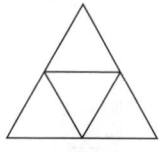   Figure 2 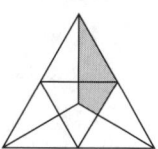   Figure 3

Figure 1 and Figure 2 show the same equilateral triangle divided into thirds and quarters. The two dissections are combined to form Figure 3. The fraction of Figure 3 that is shaded is:

A $\dfrac{2}{7}$ **B** $\dfrac{2}{9}$ **C** $\dfrac{1}{4}$ **D** $\dfrac{5}{24}$ **E** $\dfrac{1}{5}$

8 This chart shows a prediction for the 1989 NMC entry in thousands for each area (North, South, East and West) by age. To the nearest per cent, what percentage of 17-year-olds taking the NMC are expected to come from the East?

	N	S	E	W
18 years	4.2	5.2	5.7	3.5
17 years	2.5	3.6	1.5	0.4
16 years	0.1	0.1	0.1	0.3
15 years	0.1	0.1	0.2	0.4

A 5% **B** 19% **C** 20% **D** 23% **E** 25%

9 The 12 digits in a credit card number are to be written in the boxes below. The sum of any three consecutive digits is 15.

| | 7 | | | x | | | 5 | | |

The value of x is:

A 3 **B** 4 **C** 5 **D** 6 **E** 7

48

10 The smallest three-digit product of a one-digit prime and a two-digit prime is:

A 102 **B** 103 **C** 104 **D** 105 **E** 106

11 Let n be a positive whole number. The units digit of the sum $1 + 2 + 3 + \cdots + n$ *cannot* be equal to:

A 0 **B** 2 **C** 5 **D** 6 **E** 8

12 A shopkeeper increases the price of an article by $x\%$. Some time later he reduces the new price by $y\%$ and notices that the price is now the same as it was originally. The value of $\dfrac{1}{y} - \dfrac{1}{x}$ is:

A $-\frac{1}{100}$ **B** 0 **C** $\frac{1}{100}$ **D** none of these
E not uniquely determined by the given information

13 A sequence $x_1, x_2, x_3, \ldots$ is defined by:

$$x_1 = 4, \qquad x_{n+1} = 3 - \frac{3}{x_n} \quad \text{for } n \geqslant 1$$

Then x_{46} is:

A $\frac{1}{2}$ **B** $\frac{43}{46}$ **C** $1\frac{1}{5}$ **D** $1\frac{2}{3}$ **E** 4

14 It is known that all plinks are plunks and that some plonks are plinks. Which of the following statements is/are necessarily true?

    I   Some plunks are plonks.
    II Some plinks are not plonks.
    III No plonks are plunks.

A all three **B** I and II only **C** II and III only
D I only **E** III only

15 Two circular discs A and B, of radii 3 units and 5 units respectively, are held against a vertical wall. Disc B is in contact with horizontal ground.

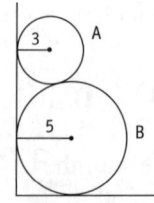

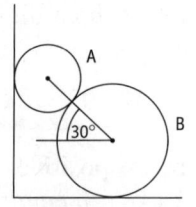

Both discs lie in the same vertical plane perpendicular to the wall (see Figure 1). B is slowly moved directly away from the wall and A falls vertically so that it is always in contact with B (see Figure 2).

When the line joining the centres of the discs is inclined at 30° to the horizontal, the distance that the centre of disc B has moved is:

A $3 + \sqrt{2}$ B $4 + \sqrt{2}$ C $2\sqrt{3} + 1$ D $2\sqrt{3} - 1$ E $4\sqrt{3} - 2$

16 An insect crawls from one corner of a solid 1-metre cube to the diagonally opposite corner. The shortest route, in metres, that it can take is of length:

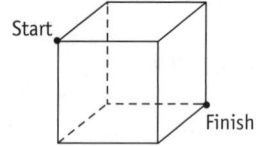

A $\sqrt{2}$ B $\sqrt{3}$ C $\sqrt{5}$
D $1 + \sqrt{2}$ E 3

17 All the terms of a certain arithmetic sequence are positive integers. The sum of the first ten terms of the sequence is equal to the 58th term. The smallest possible value of the first term is:

A 1   B 2   C 3   D 4   E 12

18 There are two paths up a hill, one of gradient $\frac{3}{4}$ and the other of gradient $\frac{5}{12}$. A person uses the first path to walk up the hill and the second path to walk back down again. What fraction of the total distance covered is uphill?

A $\frac{9}{14}$ B $\frac{25}{64}$ C $\frac{1}{2}$ D $\frac{5}{14}$ E none of these

(In this question, the *gradient* of a straight path is the vertical height climbed divided by the horizontal distance covered.)

19 1989 can be expressed in the form $n(n+4)(n+8)$ where n is a whole number. The next number after 1989 for which this is true is:

A 1990   B 2000   C 2048   D 2250   E 2520

National Mathematics Contest, 1989

20 A circle is divided into four unequal sectors. Each sector is to be painted so that no two adjacent sectors have the same colour. If four colours are available, then the number of different ways this can be done is:

    A 24   **B** 64   **C** 84   **D** 108   **E** 256

21 In the diagram, the value of $\sin \alpha$ is:

    A $\frac{25}{169}$ **B** $\frac{100}{169}$ **C** $\frac{120}{169}$ **D** $\frac{10}{13}$ **E** $\frac{12}{13}$

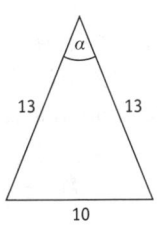

22 The medians drawn from the two acute angles of a right-angled triangle are of lengths $\sqrt{2}$ and $\sqrt{3}$. The length of its hypotenuse is:

    A 2   **B** $\sqrt{5}$ **C** $\sqrt{6}$ **D** $2\sqrt{2}$ **E** $2\sqrt{3}$

(A *median* of a triangle is a line joining a vertex to the mid-point of the opposite side.)

23 If $x^9 + 512 = (x + 2)(a_8 x^8 + a_7 x^7 + \cdots + a_1 x + a_0)$, then $a_8 + a_7 + \cdots + a_1 + a_0$ equals:

    A 1   **B** 19   **C** 57   **D** 17   **E** 171

24 Rectangle *PQRS* is inscribed in triangle *ABC* with side *SR* along *BC*. The length of *PS* is one-third the length of the perpendicular from *A* to *BC*.
Then area(*PQRS*) : area($\triangle ABC$) is:

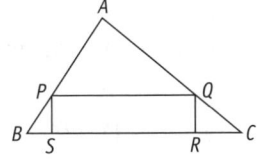

    A 1 : 3   **B** 2 : 3   **C** 2 : 9   **D** 4 : 9   **E** 5 : 9

25 The graphs with these equations are drawn:

    I $y = |x + 1|$
    II $x^2 - y^2 = 0$
    III $x^2 + xy = 2x + 2y$
    IV $y^2 = |x|$

Which of them does not/do not consist entirely of straight lines or half-lines?

    A all of them   **B** IV only   **C** III only   **D** II, III and IV only
    E III and IV only

26 Ten points are taken on a circle and are joined, in pairs, by straight lines. The greatest possible number of crossing points inside the circle is:

A 160   B 184   C 200   D 208   E 210

27 $ABCDEFGH$ is a regular octagon. $AB = 1$. $ABB'A'$ etc. are squares. The shaded area equals:

A $\dfrac{1}{9}$ B $\dfrac{\sqrt{2}-1}{2}$ C $3 - 2\sqrt{2}$ D $\dfrac{1}{8}$ E $\sqrt{5} - 2$

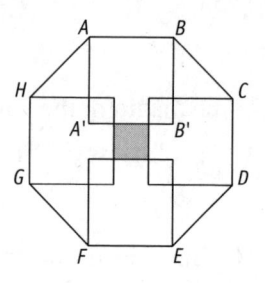

28 What is the smallest value of k such that every integer n can be expressed in the form:

$$n = a_1^2 \pm a_2^2 \pm \cdots \pm a_k^2$$

where $a_1, a_2, \ldots, a_k$ are integers?

A 2   B 3   C 4   D 5   E no such k can be found

29 The functions f, g and h are defined as follows:

$f(x, 0) = x$
$f(x, y + 1) = f(x, y) + 1$

$g(x, 0) = 0$
$g(x, y + 1) = f(x, g(x, y))$

$h(x, 0) = 1$
$h(x, y + 1) = g(x, h(x, y))$

The value of $h(2, 3)$ is:

A 2   B 4   C 6   D 8   E none of these

30 How many ordered pairs (a, b) of rational numbers are there with $a + b \geq 2$ and such that $\dfrac{3a + 1}{b}$ and $\dfrac{3b + 1}{a}$ are both positive integral powers of 2?

A 1   B 2   C 3
D a finite number greater than 3   E infinitely many

National Mathematics Contest, 1988

1. The angle between the two diagonals shown on the faces of this cube is:

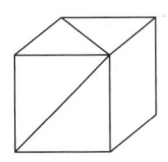

   A 45° B 60° C 75° D 90° E 135°

2. Which of the following is the greatest?

   A 2^{31} B 4^{15} C 8^{11} D 16^{8} E 32^{6}

3. The prices of 20 articles are 1p, 2p, 3p, ..., 20p. I could pay for most of them using the coins in my pocket, but for some of them I will need change. In my pocket I have a 1p, a 2p, a 5p, a 10p and a 20p coin. The number of articles needing change is:

   A 1 B 2 C 3 D 4 E 5

4. 434 is a *palindromic* number, reading the same from right to left as from left to right. The number of palindromic numbers between 100 and 1000 is:

   A 64 B 81 C 90 D 100 E none of these

5. This figure is to be drawn without taking the pencil off the paper, starting at one of the points shown and drawing each line only once. The number of possible starting points is:

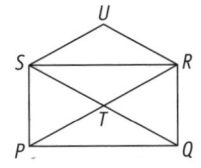

   A 1 B 2 C 4 D 5 E 6

6. If $a+b-c = b+c-d = c+d-a = d+a-b = 6$, then $a+b+c+d$ equals:

   A 6 B 12 C 18 D 24 E 30

7. For $x \geq 0$, $|x| = x$; for $x < 0$, $|x| = -x$. The number of real solutions of the equation $x^2 - 3|x| + 2 = 0$ is:

   A 4 B 3 C 2 D 1 E 0

8 A square has centre $(2, 1)$. One vertex is at $(5, 6)$. Points P, Q, R have coordinates $P := (-3, 4)$, $Q := (-1, -4)$, $R := (5, -4)$. Which of the following are vertices of the square?

A P, Q and R B P only C P, R only D Q only E P, Q only

9 In the diagram, the triangle is equilateral. The ratio of the area of the inscribed circle to the area of the circumscribed circle is:

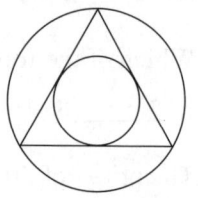

A $1:6$ B $1:4$ C $1:2\sqrt{3}$
D $1:3$ E $1:2$

10 If d hungry dogs eat s kg of steak in m minutes, then, assuming all dogs eat at the same constant rate, the amount of steak in kg consumed by s hungry dogs in d minutes equals:

A m B $d^2 m^2 s$ C $\dfrac{d^2}{m}$ D $\dfrac{ms^2}{d^2}$ E $\dfrac{s^2}{m}$

11 $ABDF$ is a rectangle.
$\angle FEA + \angle DEC$ equals:

A $120°$ B $125°$ C $130°$
D $135°$ E $140°$

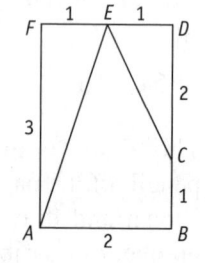

12 The angles of a cyclic quadrilateral, in clockwise order, are given in degrees by $3x + 2y$, $5x + 3y$, $4x + 5y$ and $6y - 8x$. The ordered pair (x, y) is equal to:

A $(\frac{30}{7}, \frac{150}{7})$ B $(10, 20)$ C $(\frac{135}{7}, \frac{45}{7})$ D $(0, \frac{45}{2})$ E $(\frac{720}{37}, \frac{180}{37})$

13 The number of axes of rotational symmetry of a cube is:

A 4 B 6 C 7 D 12 E 13

14 The number of pairs of integers (x, y) satisfying $2^x + 2^y = 2^{x+y}$, or $3^x \times 3^y = 3^{xy}$, or both, is:

A 0 B 1 C 2 D 3 E infinite

National Mathematics Contest, 1988

15 Dad gave Mum a 4-minute start for their 9 km jog. Each ran at a constant speed. Dad ran 1.5 km/h faster than Mum, who started at 2 pm, and they finished together. When did they finish?

   A 2:35 pm **B** 2:36 pm **C** 2:40 pm **D** 2:44 pm **E** 2:48 pm

16 Two equal circles are to be cut from a 1-metre square piece of paper. The radius in metres of the largest possible circles is:

   A $\dfrac{1}{2+\sqrt{2}}$ **B** $\dfrac{2+\sqrt{2}}{8\sqrt{2}}$ **C** $\dfrac{2\sqrt{2}-1}{7}$ **D** $\dfrac{\sqrt{2}}{4}$ **E** $\dfrac{1+\sqrt{2}}{8}$

17 The complete set of real values of x for which the inequality

$$x(x-1)^2 < (x-1)x^2$$

holds is:

   A all real x **B** $x > 0$ **C** $x < 1$ **D** $0 < x < 1$ **E** $x < 0$ or $x > 1$

18 O is the centre of the circle ABC. If $AB = BC = 3$ cm and the area of quadrilateral $OABC$ is 6 cm^2, then the radius of the circle in centimetres is:

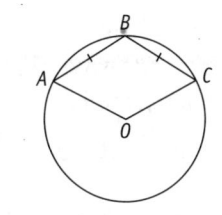

   A 2 **B** $2\tfrac{1}{2}$ **C** 3 **D** $\dfrac{3\sqrt{3}}{2}$ **E** 4

19 In the figure, AB, EF and DC are perpendicular to BC. AEC and BED are straight lines. $AB = x$, $EF = h$, $DC = y$. Then h is:

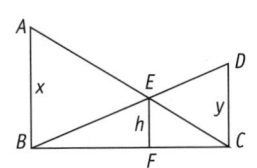

   A $\dfrac{xy}{x+y}$ **B** $\dfrac{x^2+y^2}{2(x+y)}$ **C** $\dfrac{x^3+y^3}{4xy}$

   D $\dfrac{x+y}{xy}$ **E** not enough information

20 The smallest integer of the form $p^r q^q r^p$, where p, q and r are distinct primes is:

   A 2700 **B** 21 600 **C** 121 500 **D** 225 000
   E greater than 10^{10}

55

21 In triangle PQR, $PQ = PR = 12$ cm. T lies on QR and PT is perpendicular to QR. S lies on PT and $ST = 1$ cm. S is equidistant from P, Q and R. The length of PS in centimetres is:

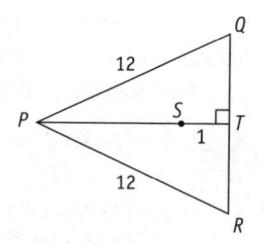

A $6\sqrt{3} - 1$ B 10 C $\sqrt{140} - 1$ D 8 E $4\sqrt{3}$

22 The number of three-digit positive integers which are 12 times the sum of their digits is:

A 0 B 1 C 5 D 9 E none of these

23 The real number k lies between 0 and 1. The area of the quadrilateral bounded by the lines $y = kx$, $y = kx + 1$, $x = ky$, $x = ky + 1$ is:

A $\dfrac{1}{1-k}$ B $\dfrac{k}{1-k}$ C $\dfrac{1}{1-k^2}$ D $\dfrac{k}{1-k^2}$ E $\dfrac{k^2}{1-k^2}$

24 The vertices of a regular octahedron can be labelled A, B, C, D, E, F in $6! = 720$ ways. The number of these ways in which $ABCD$, in that order, is a square is:

A 8 B 12 C 24 D 48 E 120

25 The number of prime values of the polynomial $n^3 - 10n^2 - 84n + 840$ where n is an integer, is:

A 0 B 1 C 2 D 4 E infinite

26 Triangle ABC is isosceles with $AB = AC$; E and F lie on AB and AC respectively with $AE = 2EB$ and $AF = 2FC$; EC and FB meet at G. Then area($\triangle ABC$) : area($\triangle EFG$) is equal to:

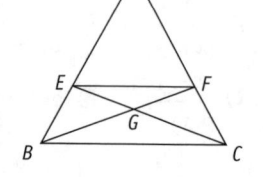

A $45 : 8$ B $45 : 7$ C $15 : 2$
D $9 : 1$ E $45 : 4$

27 If n is a positive integer, then the last two digits of n^{10} cannot be equal to:

A 01 B 25 C 36 D 49 E 76

28 The set of points (x, y) in the plane which satisfy the equation

$$|2y - 1| + |2y + 1| + 2|x| = 4$$

looks like:

A B 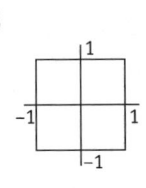 C

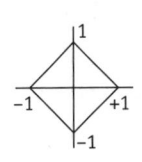

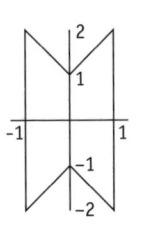

D 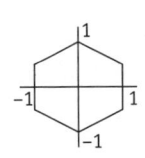 E

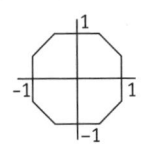

29 Triangle ABC is right-angled at B and angle ACB is α radians. The semicircle with diameter BC cuts AC at D. The area of the region bounded by AB, AD and the arc BD is equal to the area of the region bounded by the line DC and the arc DC. Which of the following is true?

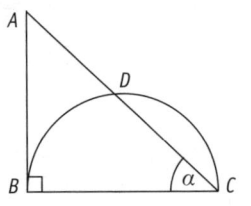

A $\tan \alpha = \dfrac{\pi}{4}$ **B** $\alpha = \dfrac{\pi}{4}$ **C** $\alpha = 1$

D $\sin 2\alpha = \dfrac{\pi}{4}$ **E** $\tan \alpha = \dfrac{1}{2}$

30 How many real-valued functions $f(x)$ of a real variable satisfy

$$f(x)f(y) = f(x + y) + xy$$

for all real numbers x, y?

A 0 **B** 1 **C** 2
D a finite number greater than 2 **E** infinitely many

D

Ten short problem papers

Short paper 1

1. What is the value of $\sqrt{1 + \sqrt{2 + \sqrt{4}}}$?

   A $\sqrt{2}$ **B** $\sqrt{3}$ **C** 2   **D** $\sqrt{7}$ **E** 4

2. The two-digit integer n is such that, if a decimal point is placed between its two digits, the resulting number is one-quarter of the sum of the two digits. What can you say about n?

   A $10 \leqslant n \leqslant 27$ **B** $28 \leqslant n \leqslant 45$ **C** $46 \leqslant n \leqslant 63$
   D $64 \leqslant n \leqslant 81$ **E** $82 \leqslant n \leqslant 99$

3. Which of the following integers has the smallest number of factors?

   A 2^6 **B** 3^5 **C** 4^4 **D** 5^3 **E** 6^2

4. The boundary of the region shown is made up of four circular arcs, each one-third of a circle of radius 10 cm. What is the area of the shaded region (in cm^2)?

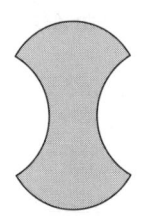

   A 100   **B** $\dfrac{80\pi}{3}$ **C** 200   **D** 80π **E** 300

5. If we ignore the usual convention, then the expression $a^{b^{c^d}}$ can be bracketed in five different ways to give five different algebraic expressions. How many different values do these five algebraic expressions yield when $a = b = c = d = 2$?

   A 5   **B** 4   **C** 3   **D** 2   **E** 1

6 Huggy the slug crawls d centimetres in t minutes. How many hours would it take her to cover a distance of d metres?

A $\dfrac{t}{100}$ B $\dfrac{t}{60}$ C $\dfrac{5t}{3}$ D $\dfrac{3t}{5}$ E $100t$

7 Let $y = \dfrac{0.2x}{x+1}$. If x takes all values ≥ 1, what range of values does y take?

A $0.1 \leq y < 0.2$ B $0 < y \leq 0.1$ C $0 < y < 0.2$
D $0 \leq y \leq 0.1$ E $0.1 \leq y \leq 0.2$

8 In a regular tetrahedron, the centroids of the four faces form the vertices of a smaller tetrahedron. What fraction of the original tetrahedron is occupied by the smaller tetrahedron?

A $\frac{1}{3}$ B $\frac{1}{4}$ C $\frac{1}{8}$ D $\frac{1}{9}$ E $\frac{1}{27}$

9 The value of $\sqrt{1.009} - \sqrt{0.991}$ to 5 decimal places equals:

A $0.003\,00$ B $0.006\,00$ C $0.009\,00$ D $0.012\,00$ E $0.018\,00$

10 In triangle ABC the bisector of the angle BAC meets BC at Y. The point X lies between A and Y. Which of the following is not necessarily equal to $\dfrac{BY}{YC}$?

A $\dfrac{\sin ACY}{\sin ABY}$ B $\dfrac{BX}{XC}$ C $\dfrac{\text{area}(\triangle ABX)}{\text{area}(\triangle AXC)}$ D $\dfrac{AB}{AC}$ E $\dfrac{\cos ABY}{\cos ACY}$

Short paper 2

1 IX multiplied by IV equals:

A IXXIV B LIV C IVXIX D LXVI E XXXVI

2 For the simultaneous equations

$3x - 4y = 2$ and $8y - 6x = 5$:

A $x = 2, y = 1$ B $x = 0, y = \frac{5}{8}$ C $x = 0, y = 0$
D there is no solution E there are infinitely many solutions

3 What is the smallest number of coins needed to be able to make every amount from 1p up to £1?

A 6   B 7   C 8   D 9   E 10

4 The Earth has radius of 6400 km. If all twenty-five million cars in Britain were lined up nose-to-tail around the equator, roughly how many times would the line encircle the Earth?

A 1   B 3   C 10   D 20   E 50

5 When Peter was purchasing pounds of pickled peppers he noticed that the cost in pence of one pound was exactly eight times the sum of the two digits of the cost (in pence) per pound. He purchased as many pounds as he could with £5. How much change did he receive?

A 10p   B 50p   C 56p   D 68p   E 72p

6 You are given a wooden regular hexagon sitting comfortably in a hexagonal hole. Let **R** denote an anticlockwise rotation of the wooden regular hexagon about its centre through 60°, and let **V** denote the reflection in the vertical axis of symmetry. **RR** denotes the operation obtained by doing **R** twice in succession, etc. Four of the following expressions represent the same symmetry operation. Which is the odd one out?

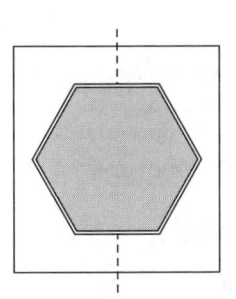

A VRVR   B RVRV   C VRRVRR
D VRVRVR   E RRVRRRVR

7 How many real numbers have the property that the sum of x and the reciprocal of x^2 is equal to the sum of x^2 and the reciprocal of x?

A 0   B 1   C 2   D 3   E 4

8 A triangle has sides of lengths x, 28, 31. Another triangle has sides of lengths y, 28, 31. Both triangles have an angle of 60° opposite the side of length 28. If $x \neq y$, which of the following is true?

A $x + y = 31$ B $xy = 59$ C $2(x + y) = 59$
D $xy = 155$ E $x + y = 28$

9 Three cubes X, Y, Z are such that cube X circumscribes a given sphere $\mathcal{S}$, and cube Y has all its edges tangent to the same sphere $\mathcal{S}$, and cube Z is inscribed inside the sphere $\mathcal{S}$. What is the ratio of the edge lengths of the three cubes X : Y : Z?

A $\sqrt{6}:\sqrt{3}:\sqrt{2}$ **B** $2:\sqrt{3}:1$ **C** $3:2:1$
D $\sqrt{3}:\sqrt{2}:1$ **E** $2:\sqrt{2}:1$

10 An infinite number of 2p coins are fitted together to cover the whole plane as shown. What fraction of the plane remains uncovered?

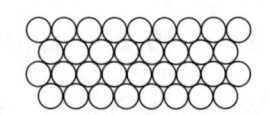

A $\dfrac{1}{4}$ **B** $\dfrac{\pi-3}{\pi}$ **C** $\dfrac{4-\pi}{4}$ **D** $\dfrac{1}{3}$ **E** $\dfrac{2\sqrt{3}-\pi}{2\sqrt{3}}$

Short paper 3

1 The units digit of a perfect cube:

A is never 0   **B** is never 2   **C** is never 3
D is never 9   **E** can be any digit 0–9

2 What is the value of $((-3)^{-2})^{-1}$?

A -6 **B** -3 **C** $-\frac{1}{9}$ **D** $\frac{1}{9}$ **E** 9

3 A circle has circumference 10 cm. What is its area (in cm²)?

A 10π **B** $\dfrac{25}{\pi}$ **C** $2\pi\sqrt{10}$ **D** $\dfrac{5}{\pi}$ **E** 25π

4 The speed of sound at sea level is approximately 1200 km/h. At a height of 8 km the speed of sound is approximately $\frac{9}{10}$ of the speed at sea level. A plane's speed is often described in terms of its *Mach number*; this is equal to the plane's speed divided by the speed of sound at the height at which the plane is flying. What is the approximate speed (in km/h) of a plane flying with Mach number 0.65 at a height of 8000 m?

A 700   **B** 750   **C** 780   **D** 870   **E** 2050

> Ernst Mach (1838–1916) was a German physicist who also made a profound analysis of the methodology of science. Some of his work had a considerable influence on Einstein.

5 What is the arithmetic mean (or average) of the reciprocals of the prime factors of 1001?

   A $\frac{31}{3003}$ **B** $\frac{311}{3003}$ **C** $\frac{1001}{3099}$ **D** $\frac{1033}{3003}$ **E** $\frac{1313}{3003}$

6 *ABCDEFGH* is a cube. What is the cosine of the angle *CFH*?

   A $\frac{1}{\sqrt{3}}$ **B** $\frac{\sqrt{2}}{3}$ **C** $\sqrt{\frac{2}{3}}$ **D** $\frac{\sqrt{3}}{2}$ **E** $\frac{1}{\sqrt{2}}$

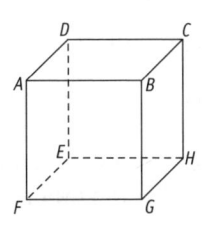

7 How many different ordered arrangements can be made using all seven letters of the word ORDERED each time?

   A 24   **B** 56   **C** 315   **D** 630   **E** 5040

8 A square *n* by *n* array of dots has a triangular array pointing outwards on each side: the array for *n* = 3 is shown in the diagram on the right. How many dots will there be altogether in the array for general *n*?

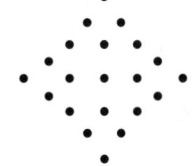

   A $n(3n-2)$ **B** $n^2 + 4n$ **C** $2n^2 + n$
   D $(n+2)^2 - 4$ **E** $2n^2 + 3n - 6$

9 Each letter stands for one of the digits 0–9. Different letters stand for different digits. How many possible values are there for the letter F?

   A 0   **B** 1   **C** 2   **D** 3   **E** 4

   ```
     F O U R
   + F I V E
   ---------
     N I N E
   ```

10 A semicircle is inscribed in an equilateral triangle as shown. What fraction of the triangle lies inside the semicircle?

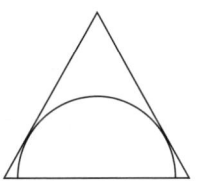

   A $\frac{\pi}{4}$ **B** $\frac{2\pi}{5}$ **C** $\frac{\pi}{2}$ **D** $\frac{\pi\sqrt{3}}{8}$ **E** $\frac{4\pi}{9}$

Short paper 4

1 $\sqrt{8} + \sqrt{18}$ equals:

   A $\sqrt{13}$ **B** $\sqrt{20}$ **C** $\sqrt{26}$ **D** $\sqrt{28}$ **E** $\sqrt{50}$

2 The number '1212' is multiple of 2, and a multiple of 3, and a multiple of 4. How many of the five positive integers

   123 123,   234 234,   345 345,   456 456,   567 567

are multiples of 7, and of 11, and of 13?

A 5   B 4   C 3   D 2   E 1

3 Let $\mathscr{C}$ and $\mathscr{C}'$ be non-intersecting circles in the plane. Neither circle is inside the other. How many circles can be drawn which are tangent both to $\mathscr{C}$ and to $\mathscr{C}'$?

A 1   B 2   C 4   D 6   E infinitely many

4 Which of the following is equivalent to the algebraic fraction $\dfrac{6a+b+10}{6a+b-5}$?

A -2 B $\dfrac{15}{6a+b-5}$ C 15 D $1+\dfrac{15}{6a+b-5}$ E -1

5 What is the value of $(\sqrt[7]{\sqrt[6]{\sqrt[5]{\sqrt[4]{\sqrt[3]{(\sqrt{3})}}}}})^{20\,160}$

A $\sqrt{3}$ B 3 C 27 D 81 E 343

6 What is the value of $\sin 75°$?

A $\dfrac{1+\sqrt{3}}{2\sqrt{2}}$ B $\dfrac{1}{2}+\dfrac{1}{\sqrt{2}}$ C 0.966 D $\dfrac{3}{4}$ E $\dfrac{\sqrt{3}+1}{3}$

7 A caterpillar is crawling due north at c m/s on a southbound train travelling at s km/h. A boy is walking due south at b m/min on a northbound train travelling at n km/h. How fast is the caterpillar moving relative to the boy (in km/h)?

A $n-s+c-b$ B $n-s+\dfrac{36c}{10}-\dfrac{6b}{100}$ C $n+s$

D $n-s+\dfrac{6c}{10}-\dfrac{36b}{100}$ E $n+s+\dfrac{6c}{10}-\dfrac{36b}{100}$

8 Triangle *PQR* has a right angle at *Q*. *S* is the mid-point of *PR*. If
   QS = *QP*, how big is angle *QPR*?

   A $67\frac{1}{2}°$ **B** 60° **C** 55° **D** 45° **E** 30°

9 On Monday, the school cadet corps did its square-bashing arranged in a
   square formation – i.e. in rows, with the number of cadets in each row
   equal to the number of rows. The next day 203 cadets reported 'sick'
   with blisters and were excused square-bashing. Fortunately, the remaining cadets could still be arranged in a square formation for another dose
   of square-bashing. How many fewer rows were there compared with the
   previous day?

   A 3 **B** 5 **C** 7 **D** 9 **E** 11

10 A bug crawls from *S* to *F* on the outside of this
   Rubik's cube, keeping to the grid lines. How
   many different shortest paths are there from *S* to
   F?

   A 54 **B** 132 **C** 148 **D** 168 **E** 384

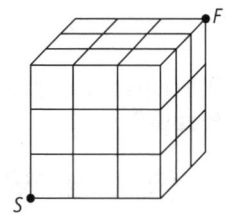

Short paper 5

1 When you roll a single ordinary dice, which of the following is most
   likely to be true about your score?

   A it is odd   **B** it is a factor of 18   **C** it is prime
   D it is a factor of 12 **E** it is even

2 Of the six integers formed by permuting the digits of the number 137,
   how many are prime numbers?

   A 2 **B** 3 **C** 4 **D** 5 **E** 6

3 I have ten cards numbered 0, 1, 2, ..., 9. How many different ways are
   there to select three different cards whose numbers total 18?

   A 6 **B** 7 **C** 8 **D** 9 **E** 10

4 The Earth is roughly a sphere of radius 6400 km. Given that four-fifths of its surface is covered with water, what is the total area of land (in millions of km²)?

  A 50   B 100   C 400   D 1000   E 4000

5 $\dfrac{\sqrt{2}+1}{\sqrt{3}+2} - \dfrac{2-\sqrt{3}}{\sqrt{2}-1}$ equals:

  A −2   B −1   C 0   D 1   E 2

6 An isosceles trapezium $ABCD$ has $AB = BC = CD = 1$ and $\angle ADC = \theta$. Which of the following expressions is equal to the area of $ABCD$?

  A $1 + \cos \theta$
  B $(1 + \sin \theta) \cos \theta$
  C $1 + \cos \theta \sin \theta$
  D $(1 + \cos \theta) \sin \theta$
  E $1 + \sin \theta$

7 If h hens lay e eggs in d days, how many days would it take H hens to lay E eggs?

  A $\dfrac{Hde}{Eh}$ B $\dfrac{EHd}{he}$ C $\dfrac{Ehe}{Hd}$ D D E $\dfrac{Ehd}{He}$

8 Emily (Em) and her Aunt Emm are playing the 'Smarties Game'. Two piles of Smarties contain seven and twelve Smarties respectively. Em and Emm take turns. A 'turn' requires the player to choose a pile and then to remove one, two or three Smarties from that pile. The player to take the last Smartie wins. Em goes first. Precisely one of the following statements is true. Which is it?

  A there is no way to know in advance who will win
  B no matter what Em does on her first move, Aunt Emm can always win
  C Em is bound to win
  D if Em makes a random first move, she can expect to win roughly half of the time
  E if Em plays carefully, she can always win

9 Ottawa (Canada) and Rijeka (Croatia) both have latitude 45°N. Ottawa has longitude 76°W and Rijeka has longitude 14°E. If the equator has length 40 000 km, which of the following is the best estimate for the length in km of the shortest route (for a jet) from Ottawa to Rijeka?

A 5000   B $\dfrac{20\,000}{\pi}$ C 6666   D $\dfrac{10\,000}{\sqrt{2}}$ E 10 000

10 $\cos 30°\,(\sin 40° + \cos 50°) - \sin 70° - \cos 80°$ is closest to:

A −0.2   B −0.1   C 0   D 0.1   E 0.2

Short paper 6

1 $2^x - 2^{x-2} = 192$. What is the value of x?

A 5   B 6   C 7   D 8   E 9

2 *ABCDEFGH* is a cube with edges of length 2. *L* is the mid-point of *FE* and *M* is the mid-point of *GH*. What is the area of $\triangle ALM$?

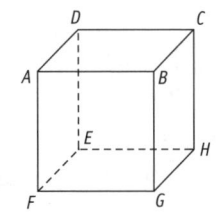

A $\dfrac{3\sqrt{2}}{2}$ B $\dfrac{3\sqrt{10}}{4}$ C $\sqrt{5}$ D 3   E $\dfrac{3\sqrt{5}}{2}$

3 The first two terms of a sequence are a, b. From then on, each term is equal to the negative of the previous term plus the term before that. What is the sixth term?

A $2b - 3a$ B $b - a$ C f D $5b - 3a$ E $-3a + b$

4 On Saturdays I work in Pete's Pizza Parlour. Employees get 40% off the price of any meal. On Monday night, prices are reduced by 30% for all customers. And as a special promotion this month, all prices have been cut by 25%. What is the most I can save altogether if I go for a meal at Pete's some time during this month?

A 95%   B 68.5%   C 55%   D 40%   E 31.5%

5 The area of the small square is one-third of the area of the large square. What is the value of $\frac{x}{y}$?

A $\frac{\sqrt{3}+1}{2}$ B $\frac{1}{\sqrt{3}}$ C $\frac{1}{9}$ D $\sqrt{3}$ E $\sqrt{3}-1$

6 A point P is chosen at random in an equilateral triangle ABC. What is the probability that angle APB is obtuse?

A $\frac{1}{\sqrt{3}}$ B $\frac{\pi}{6}+\frac{1}{2}$ C $\frac{\pi}{2\sqrt{3}}$ D $\frac{\pi}{6\sqrt{3}}+\frac{1}{2}$ E $\frac{3}{4}$

7 Two squares of side $2s$ overlap in a regular octagon. How long is each side of the regular octagon?

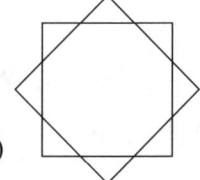

A $\frac{2s}{3}$ B $s(2-\sqrt{2})$ C s D $\frac{s\sqrt{2}}{2}$ E $2s(\sqrt{2}-1)$

8 $\cot\frac{\pi}{4} + \cot\frac{\pi}{6} + \cot\frac{\pi}{8}$ equals:

A $2+\sqrt{2}+\sqrt{3}$ B $\sqrt{2}-1$ C $1+\sqrt{3}+\sqrt{2}$
D $\sqrt{2}+\sqrt{3}$ E $1+\sqrt{3}+2\sqrt{2}$

9 A circle of radius r is surrounded by three circles of radius R, which touch each other externally. What is the value of $\frac{R}{r}$?

A 1   B $\sqrt{3}$ C 2   D $1+\sqrt{3}$ E $3+2\sqrt{3}$

10 An old edition of the *Highway Code* gives the 'total stopping distance' in feet for a vehicle travelling at v mph as $v + \frac{v^2}{20}$. A stream of traffic on the motorway is driving at a fixed speed v mph. If all cars are 15 feet long and each leaves a gap between it and the car in front equal to the total stopping distance for its speed, what value of the speed v gives rise to the greatest rate of flow of traffic?

A very slow (to make the gaps small)   B 17   C 30
D 47   E 70

Short paper 7

1 Which gives the biggest answer?

   A 20×20 **B** 21×19 **C** 22×18 **D** 23×17 **E** 24×16

2 Five girls want to sit side by side in a row. Auli refuses to sit next to Angela, and Angela refuses to sit next to Anna. Amy and Anita always sit together, and Anna insists on being at one end. How many ways are there for them to be seated?

   A 0   **B** 2   **C** 4   **D** 6   **E** more than 6

3 O is the centre of the circle. If $AB = OA$, which of the following must be true?

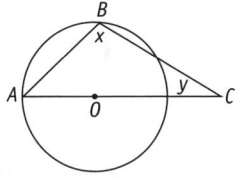

   A $x + y = 120°$ **B** $y = 30°$ **C** $x = 90°$
   D $x - y = 90°$ **E** $x + y > 120°$

4 As n ranges over all positive integers, what are the possible remainders when $2^{2n} + 3^{2n}$ is divided by 5?

   A 0 or 1   **B** 1 or 2   **C** 0   **D** 2 or 3   **E** 0 or 1 or 2 or 3 or 4

5 If a is the average of xy, y^2 and yz, b is the average of yz, z^2 and zx, and c is the average of zx, x^2 and xy, what is the average of x, y and z?

   A $a + b + c$ **B** $\sqrt{\dfrac{a+b+c}{3}}$ **C** $\dfrac{a+b+c}{3}$

   D $\dfrac{a+b+c}{\sqrt{3}}$ **E** $\sqrt{3(a+b+c)}$

6 A sequence begins 1, 3, 4, 7, 11, …. Each term (after the first two terms) is equal to the sum of the two previous terms. How many of the following statements are true?

     I   The 20th term is divisible by 2
     II The 30th term is divisible by 3
     III The 40th term is divisible by 4
     IV The 50th term is divisible by 5

   A 0   **B** 1   **C** 2   **D** 3   **E** 4

7 A two-digit number N is such that when you multiply it by 2 you get a two-digit number which is the same as the result of adding 2 to N and then interchanging the digits in the answer. What is the sum of the digits of N?

   A 7   B 8   C 9   D 10   E 11

8 Triangle ABC is inscribed in a circle with centre O and radius 1. The area of the minor sector bounded by the radii OB and OC is equal to $\dfrac{5\pi}{12}$. What is the approximate total area of the shaded region?

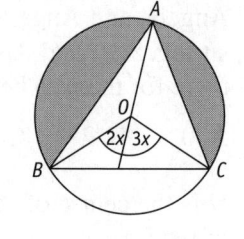

   A 0.6   B 0.7   C 0.8   D 0.9   E 1.0

9 Let

$$e(x) = \cos^4 x - \sin^4 x$$
$$f(x) = 1 - 2\sin^2 x$$
$$g(x) = (\cos x + \sin x)(\cos x - \sin x)$$
$$h(x) = (1 - \sin x)(1 + \tan x)(1 + \sin x)(1 - \tan x).$$

If I work out $e\left(\dfrac{\pi}{7}\right)$, $f\left(\dfrac{\pi}{7}\right)$, $g\left(\dfrac{\pi}{7}\right)$ and $h\left(\dfrac{\pi}{7}\right)$, how many different values do I get?

   A 1   B 2   C 3   D 4   E can't be done without a calculator

10 A sphere of radius 1 is cut by two parallel planes into three parts. The volume of the part between the two planes is exactly half the volume of the whole sphere. What is the smallest possible distance between the two planes?

   A $2\cos 40°$ B $2\cos 45°$ C $2\cos 60°$ D $2\cos 75°$ E $2\cos 80°$

Short paper 8

1 Here is a question from an old-fashioned arithmetic book: 'When the quotient is 1083 and the divisor 555, what is the dividend?'

   A 1717   B 44 928   C 56 115   D 601 065   E 601 145

2 A cube has surface area 216 cm^2. What is its volume (in cm^3)?

  A 6   **B** 36   **C** 162√6   **D** 125   **E** 216

3 When a dart is thrown at a dart-board the score can be zero (= miss), a single (1, 2, 3, ... or 20), a double (2 × 1, 2 × 2, 2 × 3, ... or 2 × 20), a treble (3 × 1, 3 × 2, 3 × 3, ... or 3 × 20), an inner (25) or a bull (50). What is the smallest possible total that *cannot* be scored with three darts?

  A 143   **B** 149   **C** 155   **D** 163   **E** 179

4 To the nearest whole number, what is the area (in square units) of the triangle with vertices at (1, 6), (2, 9) and (7, 4)?

  A 9   **B** 10   **C** 11   **D** 12   **E** 13

5 1995 is equal to the product of four prime numbers, each less than 20. How many years before 1995 was the previous year when the same was true?

  A 665   **B** 565   **C** 210   **D** 175   **E** 125

6 The circle and the square have the same centre and the same area. If the circle has radius 1, what is the length of *AB*?

  A $\sqrt{4-\pi}$ **B** $2\sqrt{1-\pi}$ **C** $4-2\sqrt{\pi}$
  D $2-\sqrt{\pi}$ **E** $4-\pi$

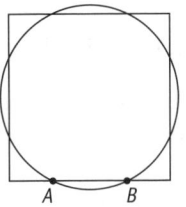

7 An *n* by *n* by *n* cube is constructed from n^3 unit cubes glued together, and the large cube is suspended in space. If I walk round the cube with one eye closed, what is the largest number of unit cubes I would ever be able to see at one time?

  A $3n^2$ **B** $3n^2 - 3n$ **C** $3n^2 - 3n + 1$ **D** $3n^2 - 1$ **E** $3n^2 - 9n + 1$

8 In a regular octagon, the ratio of the length of the shortest diagonal to the length of the longest diagonal is:

  A $1:\sqrt{2}$ **B** $(\sqrt{2}-1):1$ **C** $1:2$ **D** $2:(2+\sqrt{2})$ **E** none of **A–D**

Ten short problem papers

9 A square-based pyramid has all its edges of length 2. What is the radius of the largest sphere that will just fit inside the pyramid?

A $\dfrac{\sqrt{2}}{1+\sqrt{2}}$ B $\dfrac{1+\sqrt{2}}{3-\sqrt{3}}$ C $2-\sqrt{2}$ D $\dfrac{3-\sqrt{3}}{2}$ E $\dfrac{\sqrt{3}-1}{\sqrt{2}}$

10 In the Fibonacci sequence 1, 1, 2, 3, 5, 8, 13, 21, 34, 55, ... each term after the first two is the sum of the two previous terms. What is the sum to infinity of the series:

$$\tfrac{1}{2}+\tfrac{1}{4}+\tfrac{2}{8}+\tfrac{3}{16}+\tfrac{5}{32}+\tfrac{8}{64}+\tfrac{13}{128}+\tfrac{21}{256}+\tfrac{34}{512}+\tfrac{55}{1024}+\ldots$$

A $\tfrac{3}{2}$ B 2 C $\tfrac{5}{2}$ D 3 E impossible to calculate

Short paper 9

1 How many prime numbers between 10 and 99 remain prime when their digits are reversed?

A 9 B 10 C 11 D 12 E 13

2 Which speed is fastest?

A 1 mm/s   B 1 cm/min   C 1 m/h
D 1 furlong/fortnight   E 1 mile/month

3 A wedge (i.e. a triangular prism) of cheese is cut with a single vertical cut to remove a smaller wedge, leaving two-thirds of the cheese. What is length x (in cm)?

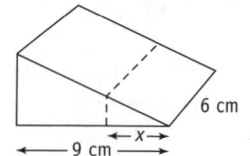

A 3 B $4\tfrac{1}{2}$ C $3\tfrac{2}{3}$ D $3\sqrt{3}$ E $3+\sqrt{3}$

4 $(2^{-\tfrac{1}{3}}+(\tfrac{1}{4})^{\tfrac{1}{6}})^3$ equals:

A $-\tfrac{3}{2}$ B $\tfrac{1}{2}$ C 1 D $2\tfrac{1}{2}$ E 4

5 Suppose that Meg rolls a dice three times, and that all you know about her three scores is that after two rolls her total score is more than 6, and after three rolls her total score is more than 12. What is her most likely final total after three rolls?

A 13 B 14 C 15 D 16 E 17

6 *ABCD* is a square. The shaded area is the overlap between two circular arcs, one centred at *A* and one centred at *C*. The area of the shaded region is 10 cm². What is the length of *AB* (in cm)?

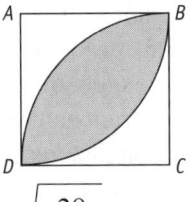

A $\dfrac{40}{\pi - 2}$ B $\sqrt{\dfrac{40}{\pi - 2}}$ C $\sqrt{30}$ D $\dfrac{20}{\pi - 2}$ E $\sqrt{\dfrac{20}{\pi - 2}}$

7 The French Revolution in 1789 led to many changes. In 1791, the French Academy of Sciences recommended a new 'metric' system of measures. This system was to be based on a 'natural' unit of length, called the metre, which was equal to one ten-millionth of the distance from the North Pole to the equator – measured along the circle of longitude through Paris! The system was adopted in 1795. What is the volume of the Earth in cubic metres – to the nearest power of 10?

A 10^{16} B 10^{21} C 10^{26} D 10^{31} E 10^{36}

8 A metal rod *AB* hangs vertically from a hinge at *A*, so that the end *B* just touches the horizontal ground 2 m from a vertical wall. While *A* stays fixed, the lower end *B* is pushed to one side until it touches the wall, 2 cm above the ground. How long is the rod (in m)?

A 100 B $\sqrt{3.9204}$ C 100.01 D 2 E 100.005

9 Let *R* be the circumradius of a regular decagon with sides of length 1. How many of the following four expressions are equal to *R*?

$\dfrac{\cos 18°}{\sin 36°}$, $\sqrt{\dfrac{3 + \sqrt{5}}{2}}$, $\sqrt{\dfrac{1}{2(1 - \cos 36°)}}$, $2 \sin 54°$

A 0 B 1 C 2 D 3 E 4

Ten short problem papers

10 A truncated octahedron is obtained by trisecting the edges of a regular octahedron, and then cutting a pyramid (with edges of length one-third the edges of the regular octahedron) off each of the six corners. The truncated octahedron has eight regular hexagons and six squares as faces. The solid is like a cube in that repeated copies fit together to fill space without any gaps. A net for the solid is shown here. The net just fits on a rectangular piece of card. What fraction of the card is 'wasted'?

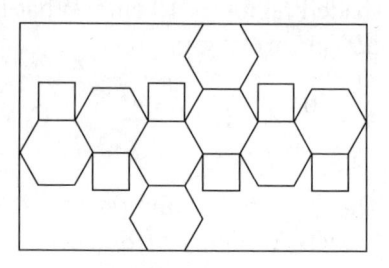

A $\dfrac{85 - 8\sqrt{3}}{133}$ B $\dfrac{73}{133}$ C $\dfrac{60}{133}$ D $\dfrac{8(6 + \sqrt{3})}{133}$ E $\dfrac{1}{2}$

Short paper 10

1 1 + 22 + 333 + 4444 + 55 555 + 666 666
+ 7 777 777 + 88 888 888 + 999 999 999 equals:

A 1 097 393 685   B 1 097 393 645   C 1 097 389 685
D 1 097 093 685   E 1 077 393 685

2 A drawer contains seven red socks, seven blue socks and seven white socks. Socks are selected one at a time without looking. How many socks must be selected to be sure of getting at least two pairs of the same colour?

A 4   B 7   C 9   D 10   E 12

3 When it is 12 noon in New York, it is 5 pm in London. A plane leaves New York and flies to London, and then returns to New York. It leaves London at 18:40 (local time) and arrives in New York at 19:55 (local time). If the plane originally left New York at 10:50 (local time) and both journeys take the same time, at what time did it arrive in London?

A 12:05   B 15:50   C 18:40   D 17:05   E 22:05

4 One-millionth of a second is called a *micro*second. Roughly how long is a *micro*century?

A 1 second   B 1 minute   C 1 hour   D 1 day   E 1 week

5 An equilateral triangle is initially completely black. First the middle quarter is painted white. Then the middle quarter of each of the three remaining black triangles is painted white, and so on. What fraction of the triangle ultimately remains black?

A 0   B $\frac{1}{4}$ C $\frac{1}{3}$ D $\frac{1}{2}$ E $\frac{9}{13}$

6 A video lasting three hours is wound on a spool whose solid centre has diameter 26 mm. The fully wound tape (including the central spool) has diameter 82 mm. The tape is partly used, and the remaining tape (plus the central spool) has diameter 46 mm. How much recording time (to the nearest minute) is left?

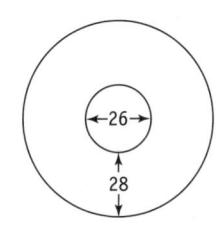

A 10   B 23   C 43   D 50   E 64

7 For each real number x, $[x]$ denotes the greatest integer which is less than or equal to x. What can be said about the following four equations?

(1) $[x + 3] = [x] + 3$
(2) $[x + y] = [x] + [y]$
(3) $[5x] = 5[x]$
(4) $[x.y] = [x].[y]$

A all four equations are satisfied for all real numbers x and y
B equations (1) and (3) are satisfied for all real numbers x
C the four equations are satisfied only when x and y are integers
D equations (1) and (2) are satisfied for all real numbers x and y
E equations (2), (3) and (4) are false for most values of x and y

8 A solid sphere of radius r fits snugly inside a cylinder, touching the sides, the top and the bottom. What fraction of the cylinder is empty?

A $\frac{2}{3}$ B $\frac{1}{3}$ C $\frac{1}{2}$ D $\frac{3}{4}$ E it depends on the value of r

9 *ABCD* is a rectangle. The diagonals *AC* and *BD* cross at *X*. *Z* lies on *CX* and *Y* is the foot of the perpendicular from *Z* to *BX*. If *XY* = 3, *YZ* = 4 and *ZX* = 5, then *AB* : *BC* equals:

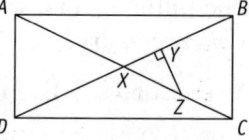

A 3 : 4   **B** 1 : 1   **C** 4 : $\sqrt{5}$ **D** 4 : 3   **E** 2 : 1

10 You are given a regular tetrahedron $\mathcal{T}$ with edges of length 2 and twelve congruent isosceles triangles with base of length 2. These triangles are then used in threes to erect a tetrahedron on each of the four faces of $\mathcal{T}$. Normally you would expect this to produce a solid with 12 faces. However, in this case the resulting polyhedron has six rhombic faces. What is the area of each of the isosceles triangles?

A $\sqrt{3}$ **B** $\sqrt{2}$ **C** $\dfrac{2}{\sqrt{3}}$ **D** 1   **E** $\dfrac{\sqrt{3}}{2}$

E

Multiple-choice answers to all problem papers

We list here the correct option for each question in the problem papers in Sections C and D.

C The NMC problem papers

1996
B D A D E B B C A D D B E D B A C E A E C B B B A
1995
E E D B D E E B E B A C B C B C D C A D D C D A C
1994
C E D D E B A D B B B E E A A C E C B D C B E A E
1993
D B A C B A C D A D C E B D B E E E A C D C B A E
1992
D B B C D D D A D E C E E D C B A E E C D C A A B
1991
D D C D B E A E D D E B E D A B A D C A C D E C A
1990
B D D C A E A C C D D B A D B A C C E B B D A E E C E B E A
1989
D E A D A C D B A E B C C D E C D B E C C A E D B E C B D C
1988
B C D C B D A E B E D A E D C A E B A B D B C D C E C D A C

D Ten short problem papers

1 B A D E D   C A E C E
2 E D C B D   D C A A E
3 E E B A B   C D A C D
4 E A E D D   A B B C E
5 D B B B C   D E E C C
6 D C D B A   D E A E B
7 A C A D B   B E D A E
8 D E D B C   A C A E B
9 A A D E A   E B C E D
10 A D E C A   C E B E D

F

Solutions to the National Mathematics Contest problems

1996

1 B In an easy problem involving numbers it is tempting to calculate without thinking about the underlying mathematics. Instead you should think about the *structure* of the calculations to see how much you can discover *without calculating at all*.

Odd times odd is odd; so any power of an odd number is odd.
∴ $1^4, 3^4, 5^4, 7^4, 11^4$ are all odd.
∴ The first term in each of the five options is odd.
∴ If the final answer is to be odd, you have to add an even number.
∴ $3^4 + 2$ is the only expression giving an odd answer.

2 D Each of the four blocks in the top (L-shaped) layer must sit at the top of a stack of three cubes – giving 4×3 cubes.

Adding the stack of two cubes on the right-hand end, and the single cube on the left-hand end gives a minimum possible total of 15 cubes.

3 A What is the largest integer N for which $N^2 \leq 1001$?
$30^2 = 900$ is close, and:
$$31^2 = (30+1)^2 = 30^2 + 2 \times 30 + 1 = 961 < 1001$$
$$32^2 = (30+2)^2 = 30^2 + 2 \times 2 \times 30 + 4 = 1024 > 1001$$
So you only need to count the *even* squares among $1^2, 2^2, \ldots, 31^2$.

Solutions to the National Mathematics Contest problems

4 D Again you must resist the temptation to 'multiply out'. Instead, use elementary algebra to find *effortless* ways of calculating each option.

    A $500^2 - 498^2 = (500 - 498)(500 + 498) = 2 \times 998 = 1996$
    B $2^2(500 - 1) = 2000 - 4 = 1996$
    C $\dfrac{(50\,000 - 100)}{25} = \dfrac{50\,000}{25} - \dfrac{100}{25} = 2000 - 4 = 1996$
    D $500 - 1 \times 4 = 500 - (1 \times 4) = 500 - 4 = 496$
    E $5 \times 20^2 - 2^2 = 5 \times 400 - 4 = 2000 - 4 = 1996$

5 E You are told that the y-coordinate of B is k; so $B := (0, k)$.
Let the x-coordinate of A be a; so $A := (a, 0)$.

$\therefore$ Gradient of line $AB = \dfrac{y_B - y_A}{x_B - x_A} = \dfrac{k - 0}{0 - a} = -\dfrac{k}{a}$

$\phantom{\therefore \text{Gradient of line } AB} = -\dfrac{1}{k}$ (given)

$\therefore a = k^2$

6 B Number of red blood cells made in 24 hours $\approx 200\,000\,000\,000$
$\phantom{\text{Number of red blood cells made in 24 hours}} = 2 \times 10^{11}$

Number of minutes in 24 hours $= 24 \times 60$

$\therefore$ Number of red blood cells made in 1 minute $\approx \dfrac{2 \times 10^{11}}{24 \times 60}$

$\therefore$ Number of red blood cells made in 90 minutes $\approx \dfrac{2 \times 10^{11}}{24 \times 60} \times 90$

$\phantom{\therefore \text{Number of red blood cells made in 90 minutes}} = \dfrac{2 \times 90}{60} \times \dfrac{10^{11}}{24}$

$\phantom{\therefore \text{Number of red blood cells made in 90 minutes}} = \dfrac{3 \times 10^{11}}{24} = \dfrac{10^{11}}{8} \approx 10^{10}$

Alternatively   90 minutes $= 1\tfrac{1}{2}$ hours, and $24 = 1\tfrac{1}{2} \times 16$

$\therefore$ Required number $\approx \dfrac{2 \times 10^{11}}{16} \approx 10^{10}$

7 B You are told that 'n is a perfect square'.
$\therefore n = k^2$ for some integer $k \geq 0$
$\therefore k = \sqrt{n}$
$\therefore k + 1 = \sqrt{n} + 1$
$\therefore (k + 1)^2 = (\sqrt{n} + 1)^2 = n + 2\sqrt{n} + 1$

8 C The only obvious way to identify the line segment with length $\sqrt{13}$ is to do several quick calculations to rule out four of the options.

(a) Notice first that:
$$3.5^2 = (\tfrac{7}{2})^2 = \tfrac{49}{4} = 12.25$$
∴ $\sqrt{13}$ is slightly bigger than 3.5.
This immediately rules out FM (since $FM < FA + AM = 2 + 1 = 3$).

Let O be the circumcentre of the regular hexagon.

(b) $\triangle BOC$ is equilateral of side 2
∴ $BX = \sqrt{3}$
∴ $BD = 2\sqrt{3}$
$< \tfrac{7}{2}$ (since $(2\sqrt{3})^2 = 48 < 49 = 7^2$)

(c) $BE = BO + OE = 2 + 2 = 4 > \sqrt{13}$

(d) This leaves only EM to be checked.
Use the cosine rule in $\triangle BME$ (with $\angle MBE = 60°$).
∴ $EM^2 = MB^2 + EB^2 - 2 \cdot MB \cdot BE \cdot \cos 60°$
$= 1 + 4^2 - 2 \cdot 1 \cdot 4 \cdot \tfrac{1}{2} = 13$
∴ $EM = \sqrt{13}$

Alternatively $MO = \sqrt{2^2 - 1^2} = \sqrt{3}$, by Pythagoras in $\triangle BMO$
∴ $MN = 2 \cdot MO = 2\sqrt{2^2 - 1^2} = \sqrt{12}$
∴ $EM = \sqrt{1^2 + 12} = \sqrt{13}$

9 A Each '10%' stands for '10% of the cost price'. And although the two cars had the same selling price, they had different cost prices. Hence the profit and loss are definitely not equal, so they do not cancel out! Since there is no easy solution, you have to do two calculations.

Let £x be the price Arthur paid for the first car.
∴ $9999 = \tfrac{110}{100}x$, so $x = 9090$, with a corresponding profit of £909

Let £y be the price Arthur paid for the second car.
∴ $9999 = \tfrac{90}{100}y$, so $y = 11\,110$, with a corresponding loss of £1111

Hence his overall loss was £1111 − £909 = £202.

Solutions to the National Mathematics Contest problems

10 D Suppose $\dfrac{1}{f} = \dfrac{1}{u} + \dfrac{1}{v}$

$\therefore \dfrac{1}{v} = \dfrac{1}{f} - \dfrac{1}{u}$

This expresses $\dfrac{1}{v}$ for all values of f and u.

If f and u are halved, then f is replaced by $\dfrac{f}{2}$ and u is replaced by $\dfrac{u}{2}$, so the RHS becomes:

$$\dfrac{1}{f/2} - \dfrac{1}{u/2} = \dfrac{2}{f} - \dfrac{2}{u} = 2\left(\dfrac{1}{f} - \dfrac{1}{u}\right) = 2\left(\dfrac{1}{v}\right) = \dfrac{1}{v/2}$$

11 D The answer to this question hinges on the word 'best'. The best description of $APHQ$ is the one that tells you the most about it. For example, $APHQ$ is certainly a quadrilateral – but it is much more than just a quadrilateral. You have to decide exactly 'how much more'.

Suppose the cube has side $2s$.

Let A be taken as origin, with AB as x-axis, AD as y-axis and AF as the *negative* z-axis.

Then A, P, H, Q have coordinates
$\quad A := (0, 0, 0), P := (2s, s, 0), H := (2s, 2s, -2s), Q := (0, s, -2s)$
$\therefore A, P, Q, H$ lie in the plane with equation $x - 2y - z = 0$.
$\therefore APHQ$ is a planar quadrilateral.

Note Mathematically this needs to be proved – even though in the context of the question paper it is more or less given since all five options are planar quadrilaterals!

AP and QH lie in parallel planes, so AP is parallel to QH.
Similarly AQ is parallel to PH.
$\therefore APHQ$ is a parallelogram.
$AP^2 = AB^2 + BP^2 = 5s^2$; and $PH^2 = PC^2 + CH^2 = 5s^2$
$\therefore APHQ$ is a rhombus.

Moreover, since:
$\quad PQ^2 = BF^2 = FA^2 + AB^2 = 8s^2$
$\quad AH^2 = AB^2 + BG^2 + GH^2 = 12s^2$
the two diagonals are unequal, so $APHQ$ is *not* a square.

Alternatively Having established that $APHQ$ is a parallelogram, observe that $AP = PH = HQ = AQ$, since these are the hypotenuses of the four congruent right-angled triangles $\triangle APB$, $\triangle HPC$, $\triangle HQE$ and $\triangle AQF$.
$AP = AQ = s\sqrt{5}$, $AH = 2s\sqrt{3}$, $PQ = 2s\sqrt{2}$, so the diagonals of $APHQ$ are not equal.

12 B The radius 'expands by 3%', so it increases from r to $r' = (1.03)r$.
∴ The original area $A = \pi r^2$ increases to $A' = \pi r'^2 = \pi(1.03r)^2$.

∴ The percentage increase $= \dfrac{A'}{A} \times 100 - 100 = \left(\dfrac{A' - A}{A}\right) \times 100$

$= 100[(1 + 0.03)^2 - 1]$
$= 100[(1 + 2 \times 0.03 + 0.03^2) - 1]$
$= 100(0.06 + 0.0009)$
$\approx 6\%$

13 E You are given two numbers, x and y, whose product is twice their sum.
∴ $xy = 2(x + y)$

∴ $\dfrac{1}{2} = \dfrac{x + y}{xy} = \dfrac{1}{y} + \dfrac{1}{x}$

14 D The graph has three distinct sections.
So the journey has three qualitatively different parts, or stages:
Stage 1 Speed increases uniformly at a constant rate.
    ∴ Total distance travelled increases more and more quickly.
Stage 2 Graph is flat, so speed remains constant.
    ∴ Total distance travelled increases uniformly at a constant rate.
Stage 3 Speed decreases uniformly to zero at a constant rate.
    ∴ Total distance travelled continues to increase, but increases more and more slowly.

Hence the middle part of the distance–time graph (Stage 2) must be a straight line with positive slope, so the answer is either **B** or **D**.

Both **B** and **D** have the correct shape for Stage 1, but **B** shows the 'total distance travelled' increasing more and more *quickly* during Stage 3.

Alternatively This informal reasoning can be put into exact mathematical form.
Let the three time intervals be $(0, t_1)$, (t_1, t_2), (t_2, t_3).

Solutions to the National Mathematics Contest problems

The speed–time graph indicates that if the slope of the graph from time 0 to time t_1 is $a > 0$, where a is in fact the *acceleration*, then the slope from time t_2 to time t_3 is almost exactly $-a$.

Hence: on the interval $(0, t_1)$, the speed increases linearly: $v = at$
on the interval (t_1, t_2), the speed remains constant: $v = at_1$
on the interval (t_2, t_3), the speed decreases linearly:
$$v = at_1 - a(t - t_2) = a(t_1 + t_2) - at$$

Setting $v = ds/dt$ and integrating with respect to time gives the equations of the separate parts of the distance–time graph:

- on $(0, t_1)$, $s = at^2/2$ (so the distance–time graph is part of an upward-curving parabola with apex at the origin);
- on (t_1, t_2), $s = at_1 t + at_1^2/2 = at_1(t + t_1/2)$ (so this part of the distance–time graph is a straight line with gradient at_1 starting at $(t_1, at_1^2/2)$);
- on (t_2, t_3), $s = at(t_1 + t_2) - at^2/2 + C$, where C is chosen to make $s = 0$ when $t = t_1 + t_2$ (so this part of the graph – though still rising – is part of a downwards-curving parabola with apex at $t = t_1 + t_2$).

15 B The problem has been deliberately made to look complicated in order to force you to look for *an idea*, and to discourage blind calculation.

Notice that:

(a) $875 = \frac{7}{8} \times 1000$;
(b) successive pairs of digits in the number:
96 88 80 72 64 56 48 40 32
are successive multiples of 8.

∴ 968 880 726 456 484 032 000 × 875
= 96 88 80 72 64 56 48 40 32 × ($\frac{7}{8}$ × 1000)
= (12 11 10 09 08 07 06 05 04 × 7) × 1000
= 84 77 70 63 56 49 42 35 28 × 1000
= 847 770 635 649 423 528 000

Reference [29, Chapter XIII] in Section B contains an interesting discussion of calculating prodigies and some of the methods they use.

16 A $EF = FC$ (given)

∴ $\triangle FEC$ is isosceles.

∴ $\angle FCE = \angle FEC = x°$

$\angle AFC = \angle FEC + \angle FCA = 2x°$ (exterior angle of $\triangle FEC$)

∴ $\angle ABC = (180 - 2x)°$ (opposite angles in a cyclic quadrilateral)

Alternatively If this property of cyclic quadrilaterals is not familiar, you could use the 'angles in the same segment theorem' and argue as follows.

B is the mid-point of arc AC (given)

∴ Chords AB and BC are equal.

∴ $\angle AFB = \angle BFC = \angle AFC/2 = x°$

$\angle ACB = \angle AFB = x°$ (angles subtended by chord AB)

$\qquad = \angle CAB$ (angles subtended by equal chords CB and AB)

∴ $\angle ABC = (180 - 2x)°$ (since the angles in $\triangle ABC$ add to 180°)

17 C You should know that $(a + b)^4 = a^4 + 4a^3b + 6a^2b^2 + 4ab^3 + b^4$.

Hence, since $x + \dfrac{1}{x} = 8$ (given)

$$8^4 = \left(x + \frac{1}{x}\right)^4 = x^4 + 4 \cdot x^3 \cdot \left(\frac{1}{x}\right) + 6 \cdot x^2 \cdot \left(\frac{1}{x}\right)^2 + 4 \cdot x \cdot \left(\frac{1}{x}\right)^3 + \left(\frac{1}{x}\right)^4$$

$$= x^4 + \left(\frac{1}{x}\right)^4 + 4\left[x^2 + \left(\frac{1}{x}\right)^2\right] + 6$$

So to work out the value of $x^4 + \left(\dfrac{1}{x}\right)^4$ you need to know the value of $x^2 + \left(\dfrac{1}{x}\right)^2$.

$\left(x + \dfrac{1}{x}\right) = 8$,

∴ $8^2 = \left(x + \dfrac{1}{x}\right)^2 = x^2 + 2 + \left(\dfrac{1}{x}\right)^2$

∴ $x^2 + \left(\dfrac{1}{x}\right)^2 = 8^2 - 2$

Solutions to the National Mathematics Contest problems

$$\therefore 8^4 = \left(x + \frac{1}{x}\right)^4 = x^4 + \left(\frac{1}{x}\right)^4 + 4\left(x^2 + \left(\frac{1}{x}\right)^2\right) + 6$$

$$= x^4 + \left(\frac{1}{x}\right)^4 + 4(8^2 - 2) + 6$$

$$\therefore x^4 + \left(\frac{1}{x}\right)^4 = \left(x + \frac{1}{x}\right)^4 - 4(8^2 - 2) - 6$$

$$= 8^4 - 4(8^2 - 2) - 6 = 8^4 - 4 \cdot 8^2 + 2 = 8^4 - 2^8 + 2$$

18 E Since only addition signs can be used, there can be *no three-digit numbers* on the left-hand side (since any three-digit number would have to be ≥ 210, and $210 > 198$).

> In a similar spirit, one may also observe that, since the answer has to be 198, there must be at least three two-digit numbers on the left-hand side (since the largest possible total with just two two-digit numbers is given by $98 + 76 + 5 + 4 + 3 + 2 + 1 + 0 = 189$).
> However, this observation is not needed in the solution that follows.

Start out with the triangular number:
$$9 + 8 + 7 + 6 + 5 + 4 + 3 + 2 + 1 + 0 = \frac{9 \times 10}{2} = 45 \quad (*)$$

To obtain an answer of 198, we need to increase the answer on the right hand side by $153 = 9 \times 17$.

Each two-digit summand in the final equation corresponds to omitting the '+' sign between (say) i and $i - 1$ on the LHS of (*). *This increases the answer (on the right-hand side) by $9 \times i$.*

To get an equation with sum 198, you have to increase the LHS of (*) by 9×17. This corresponds to choosing a set S of *non-adjacent digits* whose sum is equal to 17.

$\therefore S = \{9, 7, 1\}$ (which corresponds to the given expression
$$98 + 76 + 5 + 4 + 3 + 2 + 10 = 198)$$
or $\{9, 6, 2\}$ or $\{9, 5, 3\}$ or $\{8, 6, 3\}$ or $\{8, 5, 3, 1\}$

19 A In the given time of two hours, Tamara walks from A to B ('from east to west').

Initially, Tamara sights the boat on a bearing of 060°, at X. Two hours later, Tamara sees the boat on a bearing of 330°, at Y.

$AB = 8$ (given)
$\angle A'AX = 60°$ (given)
$\therefore \angle AXA' = 30°$
Similarly, $\angle B'BY = 30°$ (given)
$\therefore \angle BYB' = 60°$
$\therefore$ Distance XY travelled by boat (in km)
$= XA' + A'B' + B'Y$
$= 1.5 \tan 30° + 8 + 1.5 \tan 60°)$
$= \left(\dfrac{\sqrt{3}}{2} + 8 + \dfrac{3\sqrt{3}}{2}\right)$
$= 2(4 + \sqrt{3})$
$\therefore$ Average speed during two-hour journey $= (4 + \sqrt{3})$ km/h

20 E A total score of 6 from three balls means that the balls scored either
(a) 1, 2, 3 (in some order) or (b) 2, 2, 2.
(a) can occur in 3! different ways (since there are 3! possible orders in which the scores 1, 2 and 3 may occur).
(b) can occur in only one way.
(a) First calculate the probability of scoring a '1' or a '2' or a '3' with just one ball.
  - To score a '3' with one ball, the ball must either:
    (i) bounce left at each pin: probability $(\tfrac{1}{2})^4$; or
    (ii) bounce right at each pin: probability $(\tfrac{1}{2})^4$.
    $\therefore$ Total probability $= (\tfrac{1}{2})^4 + (\tfrac{1}{2})^4 = \tfrac{1}{8}$
  - To score a '2' with one ball, the ball must either:
    (i) bounce left at three pins and right at one pin (in any order): probability $\binom{4}{1} \times (\tfrac{1}{2})^4$ (where $\binom{4}{1} = {}^4C_1 = 4$); or
    (ii) bounce right at three pins and left at one pin (in any order): probability $\binom{4}{1} \times (\tfrac{1}{2})^4$.
    $\therefore$ Total probability $= 4 \times (\tfrac{1}{2})^4 + 4 \times (\tfrac{1}{2})^4 = \tfrac{1}{2}$
  - To score a '1' with one ball, the ball must bounce left at two pins and right at two pins (in any order), and so land up in the central box.
    There are $\binom{4}{2} = 6$ different ways of arranging four bounces, two of which are left and two of which are right.

Solutions to the National Mathematics Contest problems

$\therefore$ Probability of scoring a '1' $= 6 \times (\frac{1}{2})^4 = \frac{3}{8}$
Hence the probability of scoring a total of '6' as $1 + 2 + 3$ in some order is given by:

(number of different ways) × (probability of each way)
$= 3! \times (\frac{3}{8} \times \frac{1}{2} \times \frac{1}{8}) = \frac{9}{64}$

(b) The probability of scoring a total of 6 as $2 + 2 + 2 = \frac{1}{2} \times \frac{1}{2} \times \frac{1}{2} = \frac{1}{8}$

$\therefore$ Total probability of scoring 6 with three balls $= \frac{9}{64} + \frac{1}{8} = \frac{17}{64}$

Alternatively You may prefer to calculate directly:
prob$(1 + 2 + 3) = 3!$(prob$(1) \times$ prob$(2) \times$ prob$(3)) = 3!(\frac{6}{16} \times \frac{8}{16} \times \frac{2}{16})$
prob$(2 + 2 + 2) = (\frac{8}{16})^3$
$\therefore$ Total probability $= \frac{9}{64} + \frac{1}{8} = \frac{17}{64}$

You should recognise the number of different routes which a ball can follow from the top to each of the five boxes at the bottom $(1, 4, 6, 4, 1)$ as *binomial coefficients*. Among the references listed in Section B, see [13, Part I, 2.5], [28, Chapter I, 2.6], [30, pages 96–98], [36, Chapter 3], and [47, Chapter 3] for more on binomial coefficients; see [52, Chapter 13] for more on shortest routes and the link with the normal distribution.

21 C The resulting solid may be a bit hard to picture. It has six regular octagonal faces and eight equilateral triangular faces. At each vertex there are two octagons and one triangle – which is why the polyhedron is denoted by $8^2.3$.
You certainly do not know a formula for its volume. But:

- you do know how to calculate the volume of a cube;
- you should also know how to calculate the volume of each of the eight tetrahedra cut from the eight corners;
- you know how to subtract!

Let each octagonal face have sides of length a.
$\therefore$ Each isosceles right-angled triangle cut from the corner of each face of the cube has hypotenuse of length a and so has legs of length $h = \dfrac{a}{\sqrt{2}}$.

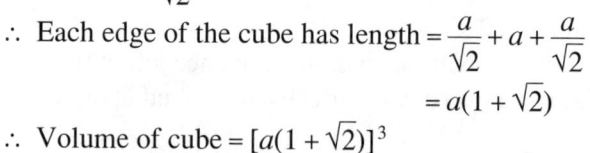

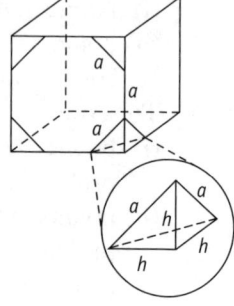

$\therefore$ Each edge of the cube has length $= \dfrac{a}{\sqrt{2}} + a + \dfrac{a}{\sqrt{2}}$

$= a(1 + \sqrt{2})$

$\therefore$ Volume of cube $= [a(1 + \sqrt{2})]^3$

88

The tetrahedron cut from each corner has base an isosceles right-angled triangle of area $\frac{a^2}{4}$, and height $h = \frac{a}{\sqrt{2}}$.

∴ Each of these tetrahedra has volume $= \frac{1}{3} \times$ (area of base) $\times$ height

$$= \frac{a^3}{12\sqrt{2}}$$

∴ Volume of remaining solid $= [a(1+\sqrt{2})]^3 - 8\frac{a^3}{12\sqrt{2}}$

$$= a^3\left(7 + 5\sqrt{2} - \frac{\sqrt{2}}{3}\right)$$

$$= a^3\left(7 + \frac{14\sqrt{2}}{3}\right)$$

$$= 7a^3\left(1 + \frac{2\sqrt{2}}{3}\right)$$

> This problem provides an opportunity to make an interesting remark. In two dimensions, unit squares (= regular 4-gons) can be used to tile the whole plane without overlaps; since four squares meet at each 'vertex', the tiling is denoted by 4^4. One can also tile the plane with equilateral triangles (regular 3-gons) – giving rise to the tiling 3^6; and with regular hexagons – giving rise to the tiling 6^3. The tilings 4^4, 3^6, 6^3 are called 'regular tilings' because each one uses a single kind of regular polygon. In two dimensions, there are exactly 13 'semi-regular tilings' – which may use more than one kind of regular polygon, but in which all vertices of the tiling must be congruent: for the 13 semi-regular tilings, see reference [52, Chapter 4] in the list of resources given in Section B.

> In much the same way as unit squares tile the plane in two dimensions, unit cubes can be used to 'tile', or fill up, the whole of three-dimensional space without overlaps, with eight cubes meeting at each vertex. This is the only possible 'regular tiling' in three dimensions. However, there are many 'semi-regular tilings'. For example, where eight cubes meet together at a vertex of the regular tiling with unit cubes, the eight corner tetrahedra (like the ones in the figure above) fit together to make a regular octahedron. Hence three-dimensional space can be tiled using a mixture of regular octahedra and shapes like the one in this problem. Some additional information may be found in the section 'Solid tesselations' in reference [29, Chapter V].

Solutions to the National Mathematics Contest problems

22 B The graph looks like the graph of a quartic (degree 4).
Since each of the five given equations is a quartic, and since '0' is not among the available options **A–E**, it is clear that the graph is meant to be interpreted as a sketch:

(a) of a quartic (i.e. a curve with equation $y = ax^4 + \ldots$) in which the coefficient a of x^4 is positive (since $y \to \infty$ as $x \to \pm\infty$);
(b) which is symmetrical about $x = 0$, so has the form $y = ax^4 + bx^2 + c$ with $a > 0$;
(c) with $c < 0$ (since c is the value of the expression when $x = 0$);
(d) which has stationary points at $x = 0$ and at two other points; these must be solutions of the equation:
$$\frac{dy}{dx} = 4ax^3 + 2bx = 2x(2ax^2 + b) = 0$$
giving $x = 0$ and $x^2 = \frac{-b}{2a}$;

(e) hence $\frac{-b}{2a} = x^2 > 0$, so $b < 0$ (since $a > 0$ from (a)).

Condition (e) rules out three of the given equations.
The other two ($y = x^4 - 2x^2 - 3$ and $y = 3x^4 - 2x^2 - 1$) are both possible, since any quartic satisfying (a)–(e) is feasible. (In a sketch, one cannot assume that there is any relation between the scale on the x-axis and that on the y-axis.)

23 B Consider two successive circles in the chain – with centres O_1 and O_2, radii O_1T_1 of length R_1 and O_2T_2 of length R_2, and with common tangent T_1T_2 meeting O_1O_2 at the point A.

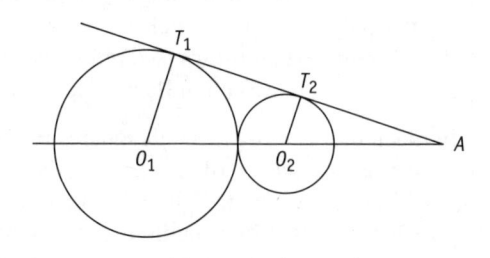

$\angle T_1AO_1 = 30°$ (given)

$\therefore O_2A = 2R_2 \quad \left(\text{since } \sin 30° = \frac{R_2}{O_2A}\right)$

90

$\triangle AO_1T_1$ and $\triangle AO_2T_2$ are similar, and $O_2O_1 = R_2 + R_1$

$$\therefore \frac{R_1}{R_2} = \frac{AO_2 + R_2 + R_1}{AO_2} = \frac{2R_2 + R_2 + R_1}{2R_2}$$

$$= \frac{2R_2 + R_2}{2R_2} + \frac{R_1}{2R_2} = \frac{3}{2} + \frac{R_1}{2R_2}$$

$$\therefore \frac{R_1}{R_2} - \frac{R_1}{2R_2} = \frac{3}{2}$$

$$\therefore \frac{R_1}{2R_2} = \frac{3}{2}$$

$$\therefore R_1 = 3R_2$$

Hence the radius of each circle in the chain is exactly one-third the radius of the next largest circle. So the total area $\mathcal{A}$ of all the circles in the chain is given by the geometric series:

$$\mathcal{A} = \pi R^2 + \pi \left(\frac{R}{3}\right)^2 + \pi \left(\frac{R}{9}\right)^2 + \ldots$$

$$= \pi R^2 (1 + (\tfrac{1}{3})^2 + (\tfrac{1}{3})^4 + (\tfrac{1}{3})^6 + \ldots)$$

$$= \pi R^2 \left(\frac{1}{1 - (\tfrac{1}{3})^2}\right) = \frac{9\pi R^2}{8}$$

Alternatively
Let $x = \angle T_1AO_1 = 30°$,
$R_1 = R$ and $R_2 = r$.

$$\therefore \frac{1}{2} = \sin x = \frac{R - r}{R + r}$$

$$\therefore R = 3r$$

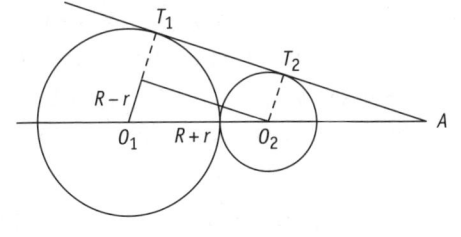

24 B A good first guess (but still a guess!) is that the largest equilateral triangle in the square *ABCD* has one corner at one vertex of the square (say *A*), and its other two vertices *X*, *Y* positioned symmetrically on the sides *BC* and *DC* respectively.

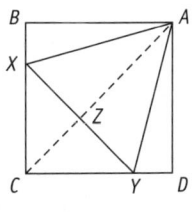

In a competition you may decide to trust this 'hunch'. But the first step in any full solution (see (a) below) is to explain why this guess is correct.

Solutions to the National Mathematics Contest problems

(a) Suppose WXY is an equilateral triangle inscribed in the square ABCD in the diagram.

If two of the three vertices W, X, Y lie on one side of the square, one can slide the triangle to position one of these three vertices at a corner of the square.

If no two of W, X, Y are on the same side of the square, then one side – say AD – contains none of W, X, Y. One can therefore slide the triangle WXY to the right *without distorting it* until either the vertex on AB arrives at A, or the vertex on CD arrives at D. Hence, in either case, we can position the same triangle so that one vertex of the triangle (say W) is at a vertex of the square (say at A).

If the triangle has a second vertex on AB or on AD, the third vertex must be in the interior of the square.

But whenever the triangle has a vertex in the interior of the square one can inscribe a slightly larger equilateral triangle in the square by rotating the given triangle slightly about A and enlarging with centre A.

Hence we can be sure that the *largest* equilateral triangle WXY inscribed in a square has one vertex (say W) at a corner of the square (say at A), and the other two vertices X and Y on BC and CD respectively.

Moreover $AB = AD$ and $AX = AY$.
$\therefore BX = DY$ (using Pythagoras in $\triangle ABX$ and in $\triangle ADY$)

(b) Once we know that triangle WXY must be positioned as shown in the above diagram (so W is at A), there are several different ways to solve the problem. We give two solutions.

(i) Let the equilateral triangle have sides of length b.

Taking XY as base, the triangle has height $\dfrac{b\sqrt{3}}{2}$.

$\therefore \text{area}(\triangle AXY) = \mathcal{A}_0 = \dfrac{b^2\sqrt{3}}{4}$

Since $\angle XAY = 60°$, we know that $\angle XAB + \angle YAD = 30°$
Fit $\triangle ABX$ and $\triangle ADY$ together along $AB = AD$ to get a triangle $X'A'Y'$ with $X'A' = Y'A' = b$ and $\angle X'A'Y' = 30°$.
$\therefore \text{area}(\triangle X'A'Y') = \mathcal{A}_1 = \tfrac{1}{2} \cdot A'X' \cdot A'Y' \cdot \sin(\angle X'A'Y')$

$= \tfrac{1}{2} \cdot b \cdot b \cdot \sin 30° = \dfrac{b^2}{4}$

$\triangle CXY$ is isosceles with $XY = b$.

$\therefore$ area$(\triangle CXY) = \mathcal{A}_2 = \frac{1}{2}\left(\frac{b}{\sqrt{2}}\right)^2 = \frac{b^2}{4}$

These three pieces fit together to make the whole square of side a:

$\therefore a^2 = \mathcal{A}_0 + \mathcal{A}_1 + \mathcal{A}_2 = b^2\left(\frac{\sqrt{3}}{4} + \frac{1}{4} + \frac{1}{4}\right) = \frac{b^2(\sqrt{3}+2)}{4}$

$\therefore$ area $\triangle AXY = \frac{b^2\sqrt{3}}{4} = \frac{a^2\sqrt{3}}{\sqrt{3}+2} = a^2\sqrt{3}(2 - \sqrt{3})$

(ii) Let AXY be an equilateral triangle with $AX = b$ and $BX = c$.
$a^2 + c^2 = AB^2 + BX^2 = AX^2 = XY^2 = 2(a - c)^2$
$\therefore c = a(2 - \sqrt{3})$ (since $c < a$)

$\therefore$ area$(\triangle AXY) = \frac{1}{2} \cdot AX \cdot AY \cdot \sin 60° = \frac{1}{2} \cdot b^2 \cdot \frac{\sqrt{3}}{2}$

$= \frac{\sqrt{3}}{4}(a^2 + c^2)$

$= \frac{\sqrt{3}}{2}(a - c)^2$

$= a^2(2\sqrt{3} - 3)$

25 A In this problem it is tempting to proceed as follows:
- let $AB = u$, $DE = v$;
- then combine Pythagoras and properties of similar triangles to set up an equation involving only u (or only v);
- solve for u and for v;
- calculate the perimeter $P = (6 + u) + (6 + v) + 20$.

Unfortunately, if you try to find u and v separately you will have to solve a quartic equation – which you don't know how to do!

The way out of this difficulty is to notice two things.

(a) Firstly, you are not asked to find u and v separately, but only their sum $u + v$.
(b) Secondly, in the given problem u and v are interchangeable: given any solution with $AB = u$, $DE = v$, you can reflect everything in the line CF to get another solution with $AB = v$, $DE = u$. Hence the equations you set up cannot distinguish between u and v.

Observations (a) and (b) suggest that u and v are the two roots of a quadratic equation $x^2 + px + q = 0$ with $p = -(u+v)$ and $q = uv$.

Now $\triangle FDE$ and $\triangle ABF$ are similar.

$$\therefore \frac{v}{6} = \frac{6}{u}$$

$\therefore uv = 36$

Hence the constant term q in the quadratic equation $x^2 + px + q = 0$ which has u and v as its two roots is very simple: namely $q = uv = 36$. Unfortunately, as you may suspect from the given options **A–E**, the coefficient $p = -(u+v)$ of x involves a nasty square root!

Thus the key lies in thinking how to calculate $u + v$ without finding u and v separately first. Here is one approach.

Let $U = AC = 6 + u$, $V = EC = 6 + v$. Then:

$$(U+V)^2 - 2UV = U^2 + V^2 = CA^2 + CE^2 = AE^2$$
$$= 20^2 \quad \text{(using Pythagoras in } \triangle FCA\text{)}$$

and:

$$U \cdot V = 36 + 6(u+v) + uv = 6(12 + (u+v)) \quad \text{(since } uv = 36\text{)}$$
$$= 6(U+V)$$

$\therefore (U+V)^2 - 12(U+V) - 400 = 0$

Solving this as a quadratic in $(U+V)$ yields:

$$U+V = \frac{12 + \sqrt{12^2 + 4 \cdot 400}}{2} = 6 + 2\sqrt{109}$$

Hence the perimeter of $\triangle ACE$ is $20 + (6 + 2\sqrt{109})$.

1995

1 E The first few prime numbers are:

2, 3, 5, 7, 11, 13, **17**, 19, ...

> Prime numbers are important because they allow one to factorise each positive integer ≥ 2 as a product of its 'simple component parts'. For example, $1995 = 3 \times 5 \times 7 \times 19$, so the prime factors of 1995 are 3, 5, 7 and 19. You could always add '$\times 1$'; but this does not tell you anything interesting about the way 1995 factorises! Hence we do not include 1 as a prime number. (If you want a strict definition: a prime number is a positive integer with exactly two factors – namely itself and 1.)

For a remarkable romp illustrating 'The primacy of primes' see reference [36, Chapter 5] in the list of resources in Section B.

2 E No net for a cube can include two squares linked to form a 3 by 3 L-shape, since when folding to try to make a cube the two end squares would have to fold on top of each other. This identifies **E**.

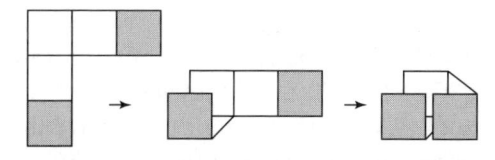

You should check that **A**, **B**, **C** and **D** all work.

3 D A $(1 \times 100)\%$ increase is the same as doubling, or multiplying by 2. A $(2 \times 100)\%$ increase is the same as trebling, or multiplying by 3. To increase from 50 000 to 5 000 000 one has to multiply by 100: i.e. a $(99 \times 100)\%$ increase.

4 B Let the houses numbered 1, 2, 3 go from left to right as shown. As you continue to the left of house number 64, there has to be one house opposite each of numbers 36, 35, ..., 3, 2, 1. So there are $64 + 36$ houses altogether.

| 1 | 2 | 3 | 4 | ... | 36 | 37 | 38 | ... |

| ? | . | . | . | ... | . | 64 | 63 | ... |

You might like to think about the (not entirely obvious) link between this problem and the 'newspaper' problem (1991, Problem 7).

5 D Calculating 'a fraction of a fraction' of a given unit involves multiplying fractions. And to calculate the fraction who *miss* grade A, it is better to multiply by $1 - \frac{1}{2}$ than to subtract.

Fraction of year group who miss a grade A $= 1 - \frac{1}{2} = \frac{1}{2}$

Fraction of these (i.e. of those who miss grade A) who also miss a grade B $= 1 - \frac{1}{3} = \frac{2}{3}$

∴ Fraction of year group who score $\leqslant$ C $= (1 - \frac{1}{2}) \times (1 - \frac{1}{3}) = \frac{1}{2} \times \frac{2}{3} = \frac{1}{3}$

Fraction of these who miss a grade C $= 1 - \frac{1}{4} = \frac{3}{4}$

∴ Fraction of year group who score $\leqslant$ D $= (1 - \frac{1}{2}) \times (1 - \frac{1}{3}) \times (1 - \frac{1}{4})$
$= \frac{1}{3} \times \frac{3}{4} = \frac{1}{4}$

Solutions to the National Mathematics Contest problems

Fraction of these who miss a grade D = $1 - \frac{1}{5} = \frac{4}{5}$
∴ Fraction of year group who score ⩽ E
$= (1 - \frac{1}{2}) \times (1 - \frac{1}{3}) \times (1 - \frac{1}{4}) \times (1 - \frac{1}{5})$
$= \frac{1}{4} \times \frac{4}{5} = \frac{1}{5}$

6 E Think of the triangles *CXA*, *XYA*, *YBA* as standing on the equal 'bases' *CX* = *XY* = *YB*. Since they have bases on the same line *BC* and the same apex *A*, the three triangles also have the same 'height' – namely the perpendicular distance from *A* to *BC*. Therefore all three triangles have the same area, so **E** is true. (Hence **A** is false.)

> This would suffice to identify the answer during an exam. However, mathematically you should want to go back later and see why **B**, **C** and **D** are false.

B If *AC* = *AB*, then *C* and *B* would lie on the same circle with centre *A*. If *AC* = *AY*, the chord *CB* would cut the circle again at *Y* – which is impossible.

C Suppose that $\angle CAX = \angle XAY = \angle YAB = \theta$.
Applying the sine rule to $\triangle ACX$ and $\triangle AXY$ in turn gives:
$$\frac{AC}{\sin AXC} = \frac{CX}{\sin \theta}$$
$$= \frac{XY}{\sin \theta} = \frac{AY}{\sin AXY}$$
∴ *AY* = *AC* (since sin *AXY* = sin *AXC*)
     = *AB* (given)
which leads to a contradiction as for **B** above.

D Suppose that perimeter($\triangle CAX$) = perimeter($\triangle AYB$)
Then *AX* = *AY* (since *AC* = *AB* and *CX* = *YB* are both given)
If also perimeter($\triangle CAX$) = perimeter($\triangle XAY$), then
AC + *AX* = *AX* + *AY*, so *AY* = *AC* (= *AB* (given)). This also leads to a contradiction as above.

Alternatively △ABC is isosceles (since AB = AC).
∴ ∠ABC = ∠ACB
∴ △ACX is congruent to △ABY
∴ AX = AY and ∠AXC = ∠AYB
∴ ∠AXY = ∠AYX
  ∠AXC = ∠XAY + ∠AYX   (exterior angle of △AXY)
∴ ∠AXC > ∠AYX
        = ∠AXY   (△AXY is isosceles)
        = ∠XAC + ∠ACX   (exterior angle of △AXC)
        > ∠ACX   (*)

B If AC = AY, then ∠ACX = ∠AYC (= ∠AYX) – contrary to (*)
C Suppose ∠CAX = ∠XAY. Then the sine rule in △ACX and △AXY gives:

$$\frac{AC}{\sin AXC} = \frac{CX}{\sin CAX} = \frac{XY}{\sin XAY} = \frac{AY}{\sin AXY}$$

∴ AC = AY   (since ∠AXY = 180° − ∠CXA)

which leads to a contradiction as in **B**.

D If perimeter(△ACX) = perimeter(△AXY), then AC = AY, which leads to a contradiction as in **B**.

7 E If you try to make a list of all the factors, and then count them, you are almost certain to miss some and not to notice. To be sure that you have counted *all* factors, you need an idea, and a method.

$1995 = 5 \times 399 = 3 \times 5 \times 133 = 3 \times 5 \times 7 \times 19$

Hence each factor of 1995 has the form $3^a \times 5^b \times 7^c \times 19^d$, with each of a, b, c, d equal to 0 or 1.

So there are 2 choices for each of a, b, c, d, and each choice corresponds to a different factor of 1995. (For example, $a = b = c = d = 0$ yields the factor $3^0 \times 5^0 \times 7^0 \times 19^0 = 1$.)

Hence 1995 has exactly $2 \times 2 \times 2 \times 2$ different factors.

For the general result, see reference [13, Part I, Section 4.4] in the list of resources in Section B.

Solutions to the National Mathematics Contest problems

8 B The 25 marks added at the end are effectively a bonus of 1 mark per question. Hence you in fact score 5 marks for each correct answer, 1 mark for each question left unanswered, and 0 marks for each wrong answer.

Imagine starting with 25 completely correct answers – with a perfect score of 125.

You then lose 4 marks each time you rub out one answer, and you lose 5 marks each time you change a correct answer to a wrong answer. Thus a mark is possible if it can be obtained by subtracting some multiples of 4 and/or 5 from the maximum possible score of 125.

Since $125 - 114 = 11$ cannot be obtained from 4s and 5s, 114 is not a possible score.

However, $113 = 125 - 3 \times 4$, $\quad 115 = 125 - 2 \times 5$,
$116 = 125 - 1 \times 4 - 1 \times 5$, and $117 = 125 - 2 \times 4$ are all possible scores.

> For the unexpected mathematics concealed behind this simple problem, see reference [51, Chapters 12–16] in the list of resources in Section B.

9 E The expression 'axis of rotational symmetry' is unfortunately vague. The cylinder has a central axis of rotational symmetry, with the remarkable extra property that the cylinder is invariant under *all* rotations about this axis.

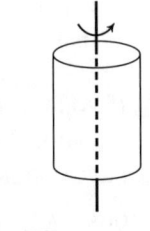

In addition, *every* horizontal line through the centre of the cylinder is an axis of 2-fold rotational symmetry.

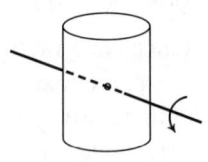

10 B Suppose Bern time is B hours ahead of London time.
Then the journey from Bern to London takes B hours + 40 minutes, and the return journey takes (2 hours 40 minutes) $- B$ hours.
Assume that the two journeys take the same time.
$\therefore B + \frac{2}{3} = 2\frac{2}{3} - B$, so $B = 1$

11 A (a) Since $x > 0$, we also have $x^{-1} > 0$.
(b) Since $x < 1$, we also have $x \cdot x < 1 \cdot x$, so $x^2 < x$.
(c) Since $x < 1$, then $x \cdot x^{-1} < 1 \cdot x^{-1}$ (since $x^{-1} > 0$), so $1 < x^{-1}$.
(d) Since $1 < x^{-1}$, then $1 \cdot x^{-1} < x^{-1} \cdot x^{-1}$, so $x^{-1} < x^{-2}$.
(e) If $x^{\frac{1}{2}} > 1$, then it would follow that:
$$x = x^{\frac{1}{2}} \cdot x^{\frac{1}{2}} > 1 \cdot x^{\frac{1}{2}} = x^{\frac{1}{2}} > 1$$
which contradicts the fact that $x < 1$.
$\therefore\ x^{\frac{1}{2}} < 1$
$\therefore\ x = x^{\frac{1}{2}} \cdot x^{\frac{1}{2}} < 1 \cdot x^{\frac{1}{2}} = x^{\frac{1}{2}}$
$\therefore\ x^2 < x < x^{\frac{1}{2}} < 1 < x^{-1} < x^{-2}$

In general, for numbers x between 0 and 1:
- $0 < x^a < x$ if $a > 1$
- $x < x^a < 1$ if $0 < a < 1$
- $x < 1 \leqslant x^a$ if $a \leqslant 0$

Alternatively It may be enough to observe that:
$x \cdot x < 1 \cdot x$ (since $x < 1$ and $x > 0$)
$x^{-1} > 1$ (since $0 < x < 1$)
$x^{\frac{1}{2}} < 1$ (since $x < 1$)
$\therefore\ x = x^{\frac{1}{2}} \cdot x^{\frac{1}{2}} < 1 \cdot x^{\frac{1}{2}} = x^{\frac{1}{2}}$

12 C When the cogwheel with 18 teeth turns once, 18 successive teeth engage on each of the four wheels: when it turns n times, $18n$ successive teeth engage. So the cogwheel with 17 teeth makes $18n/17$ complete revolutions, the cogwheel with 16 teeth makes $18n/16 = 9n/8$ complete revolutions, and the cogwheel with 15 teeth makes $18n/15 = 6n/5$ complete revolutions.

For all cogwheels to be in their original positions you require $18n/17$, $18n/16$ and $18n/15$ to be integers: that is, $n/17$, $n/8$ and $n/5$ have to be integers. The smallest such positive value of n is:
$$\text{lcm}(17, 8, 5) = 17 \times 40 = 680$$

13 B Let the number on the sixth face be n. The sum of the six probabilities has to equal 1.
$\therefore\ \frac{1}{4} + \frac{1}{8} + \frac{1}{6} + \frac{1}{12} + \frac{1}{24} + \frac{1}{n} = 1$
$\therefore\ \frac{16}{24} + \frac{1}{n} = 1$
$\therefore\ \frac{1}{n} = 1 - \frac{2}{3} = \frac{1}{3}$

Solutions to the National Mathematics Contest problems

14 C Let O be the centre of the disc. The locus of O has $2n$ separate parts:

(a) n straight line segments, each equal and parallel to one of the n edges of the polygon, having a total length p;

(b) n circular arcs centred at each of the n vertices – each arc being traced out as the disc rotates about a vertex from one edge to the next; at each vertex, if the internal angle of the n-gon is θ_i, then the 'external' angle through which the disc must rotate at the vertex is $\pi - \theta_i$, and:

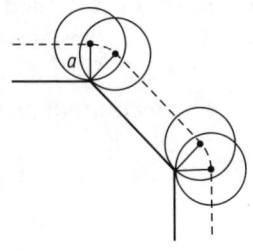

$$\sum_{i=1}^{n}(\pi - \theta_i) = n\pi - \sum_{i=1}^{n}\theta_i = n\pi - (n-2)\pi = 2\pi$$

Hence the total length of these arcs is $2\pi a$.

15 B The points P and B both lie on the perpendicular bisector of ED. Hence to calculate $\angle APB$ you first need to find $\angle EPA$.

$\angle AED = 108°$ (interior angle in a regular pentagon)
$\angle PED = 60°$ (angle in a equilateral triangle)
$\therefore \angle AEP = 108° - 60° = 48°$

$AE = ED$ (sides of regular pentagon)
$\quad = PE$ ($\triangle PED$ is equilateral)
$\therefore \triangle EAP$ is isosceles
$\therefore \angle EPA = \frac{1}{2}(180° - \angle AEP)$
$\quad = \frac{1}{2}(180° - 48°) = 66°$
$\therefore 180° = \angle MPE + \angle EPA + \angle APB$
$\quad = 30° + 66° + \angle APB$
$\therefore \angle APB = 180° - 96° = 84°$

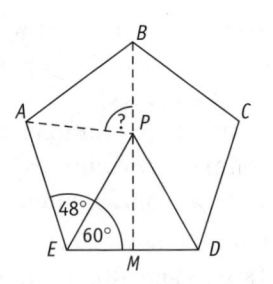

16 C There are 5 ways to choose the hundreds digit h. And for each choice of h, there are 4 ways to choose the tens digit t. And for each choice of h and t, there are 3 ways to choose the units digit u.
So you have to add up $5 \times 4 \times 3 = 60$ different three-digit numbers htu. This shows that it is no good trying to make a list! You need an idea, and a method.

How many of these three-digit numbers have '1' in the units column? Once '1' has been used as the units digit, there remain 4 ways to choose the tens digit, and then there are 3 ways to choose the hundreds digit: so '1' occurs as the units digit of $4 \times 3 = 12$ numbers in the list.

Similarly, there are 4 × 3 three-digit numbers with '2' as the units digit. And there are 4 × 3 numbers with '3' as the units digit. And so on.

So the sum of the 60 digits in the units column is equal to:
$$(4 \times 3) \times 1 + (4 \times 3) \times 2 + (4 \times 3) \times 3 + (4 \times 3) \times 4 + (4 \times 3) \times 5$$
$$= 4 \times 3 \times (1 + 2 + 3 + 4 + 5)$$
$$= 180$$

Similarly, the total of all 60 of the digits in the tens column is equal to 180, and the total of all 60 of the digits in the hundreds column is equal to 180.

∴ Sum of all 60 three-digit numbers $= 180 \times (100 + 10 + 1)$
$= 20 \times 999$
$= 20 \times (1000 - 1)$
$= 20\,000 - 20 = 19\,980$

17 D Suppose Peter has £c, and that pickled peppers cost £p per pound. Then Peter can buy $\dfrac{c}{p}$ pounds of pickled peppers.

If p is reduced to $p - \frac{1}{10}$, Peter could buy $\dfrac{c}{p - \frac{1}{10}} = \dfrac{c}{p} + 6$ (given).

∴ $c = 60p(p - \frac{1}{10})$

If p is increased to $p + \frac{1}{10}$, Peter could buy $\dfrac{c}{p + \frac{1}{10}} = \dfrac{c}{p} - 4$ (given).

∴ $c = 40p(p + \frac{1}{10})$
∴ $20p^2 = 10p$ (and $p \neq 0$)
∴ $p = \frac{1}{2}$
∴ $c = 40 \times \frac{1}{2} \times \frac{6}{10} = 12$

Alternatively Suppose Peter buys x pounds of pickled peppers at y pence per pound. Then Peter has exactly xy pence.
∴ $(y - 10)(x + 6) = xy = (y + 10)(x - 4)$
∴ $6y - 10x = 60$ and $10x - 4y = 40$
∴ $2y = 100$, $y = 50$, $x = 24$

18 C $8^2 + 15^2 = 64 + 225 = 289 = 17^2$
∴ $\triangle ABC$ is right angled (by the converse of Pythagoras' theorem)
∴ area $(\triangle ABC) = \frac{1}{2} \times 8 \times 15 = 60$

Let I be the centre of the inscribed circle, and let r be the radius of the inscribed circle.
∴ $XI = YI = ZI = r$

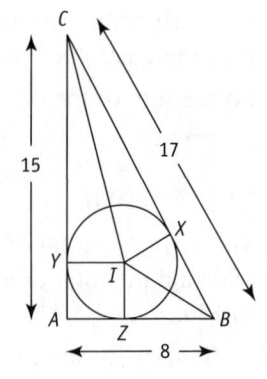

Solutions to the National Mathematics Contest problems

Now $CX = CY$ (equal tangents)
∴ area($\triangle CXI$) = area($\triangle CYI$)
Similarly, area($\triangle BXI$) = area($\triangle BZI$)
∴ area($\triangle ABC$) =
area($AYIZ$) + $2 \cdot$ area($\triangle CXI$) + $2 \cdot$ area($\triangle BXI$)
$= r^2 + 2(\frac{1}{2} \cdot r \cdot XC + \frac{1}{2} \cdot r \cdot XB)$
$= r^2 + r \cdot BC = r^2 + 17r$
∴ $60 = r^2 + 17r$
∴ $(r + 20)(r - 3) = 0$
∴ $r = 3$ (since $r > 0$)

Alternatively $60 =$ area($\triangle ABC$)
$=$ area($\triangle ABI$) + area($\triangle BCI$) + area($\triangle CAI$)
$= 4r + \frac{15}{2}r + \frac{17}{2}r = 20r$

19 A $\dfrac{a(a^3 + 2a^2 - a - 2) + (a^2 - 1)}{a(a^2 - 1)} = \dfrac{a(a^2-1)(a+2) + (a^2 - 1)}{a(a^2 - 1)}$
$= \dfrac{a(a+2) + 1}{a} = \dfrac{(a+1)^2}{a}$

20 D $\angle APB$ is a right angle precisely when P lies on the circle with diameter AB. 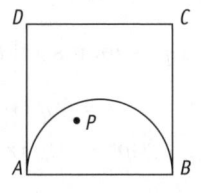
∴ $\angle APB$ is obtuse precisely when P lies inside the semicircular disc $\mathcal{S}$ on diameter AB.
∴ Probability ($\angle APB > 90°$) $= \dfrac{\text{area}(\mathcal{S})}{\text{area}(ABCD)}$
$= \dfrac{\pi r^2/2}{(2r)^2} = \dfrac{\pi}{8}$

21 D In order to calculate the total surface area, you have to 'see' the surface as consisting of three distinct parts: the first part (the bottom face) is very simple, while each of the other parts gives rise to an infinite sum which can be calculated.

(a) The bottom face of side 1 has area $= 1^2$.
(b) Each face of the nth cube has side length $\dfrac{1}{2^n}$, so has area $\left(\dfrac{1}{2^n}\right)^2$;

hence the four vertical faces of each cube have total area:
$4(1^2 + (\frac{1}{2})^2 + (\frac{1}{4})^2 + ...\ ad\ inf) = 4 \cdot \dfrac{1}{1 - (\frac{1}{2})^2} = \dfrac{16}{3}$

(c) The remaining portion of the top face of the nth cube has area $\left(\frac{1}{2^n}\right)^2 - \left(\frac{1}{2^{n-1}}\right)^2$, so these parts have total area:

$$(1^2 - (\tfrac{1}{2})^2) + ((\tfrac{1}{2})^2 - (\tfrac{1}{4})^2) + ((\tfrac{1}{4})^2 - (\tfrac{1}{8})^2) + \ldots \textit{ad inf} = 1^2$$

When an answer turns out to be simpler than you might have expected, it is worth looking for an easier explanation! In this case, it is enough to imagine looking down on the solid from above in order to see why the total area of all the top faces is equal to the area of the top face of the largest cube.

∴ Total surface area $= 1 + \frac{16}{3} + 1 = 7\frac{1}{3}$

The solid constructed in Problem 21 has finite surface area and finite volume. If you know how to calculate the surface area, and the volume, of a solid of revolution, you might like to look at reference [38, pages 84–85] listed in Section B, where a simple example is given of a very similar, but paradoxical, shape having infinite surface area, but finite volume! (The paradox lies in the fact that, if you imagine the shape as a hollowed out container – like the bell of a trumpet – then, since the surface has infinite area, it cannot be painted with a finite amount of paint. Yet, since it has finite volume, one could simply fill the hollowed out container with paint and so paint the surface!)

A simpler example still (provided you are willing to take one result on trust) is given in 'The black hole of Cal Cutter' in reference [15, problem 9].

22 C Let the light be at L and the centre of the sphere be C.
The shadow of the sphere is a circle, of radius R (say).

You have to use the equation:
πR^2 = area of circular shadow
    = surface area of sphere = $4\pi r^2$ (*)
to calculate h in terms of r: i.e. you have to find an expression for R in terms of h and r.

$\triangle TSL$ and $\triangle XCL$ are similar.

∴ $\dfrac{R}{h} = \dfrac{TS}{TL} = \dfrac{XC}{XL} = \dfrac{r}{\sqrt{(h-r)^2 - r^2}}$

∴ $R = \dfrac{rh}{\sqrt{h^2 - 2hr}}$

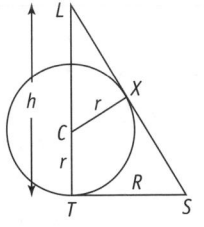

Solutions to the National Mathematics Contest problems

Now substitute for R in equation (*).

$\therefore 4\pi r^2 = \pi\left(\dfrac{r^2 h^2}{h^2 - 2hr}\right)$

$\therefore 4h^2 - 8hr = h^2$

$\therefore h(3h - 8r) = 0$

$\therefore h = \dfrac{8r}{3}$ (since $h \neq 0$)

23 D Each hour, there are four number 17s and five number 29s; so the pattern of buses repeats every 60 minutes.

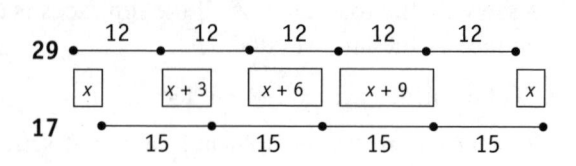

During the first (and each successive) interval of 60 minutes, there are four intervals (of lengths x, $x + 3$, $x + 6$, $x + 9$ minutes respectively) during which the *next* bus is a number 17.

I arrive at the bus stop at random.

$\therefore$ Probability (next bus is a number 17) $= \dfrac{x + (x + 3) + (x + 6) + (x + 9)}{60}$

$= \dfrac{4x + 18}{60} = \dfrac{2x + 9}{30}$

24 A Let A be a vertex of the cube and AB a diagonal of the cube. Then $AB = 10\sqrt{3}$.

Let X, Y, Z be the centres of the three spheres on the diagonal AB; then $XY = 2r = YZ$, and Y is the centre of the cube, so $AY = YB$.

The sphere with centre X 'fits tightly' in the upper corner of the cube, so X is at distance r from each of the three faces which meet at A. Hence AX is the diagonal of a small cube of side r, so $AX = r\sqrt{3}$. Similarly, $ZB = r\sqrt{3}$.

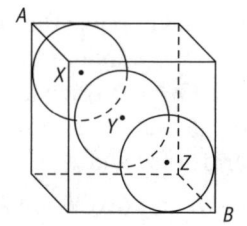

$\therefore AB = (AX + XY) + (YZ + ZB)$
$= 2 \cdot AY = 2(r\sqrt{3} + 2r) = 2r(\sqrt{3} + 2)$
$= 10\sqrt{3}$

$\therefore r = \dfrac{10\sqrt{3}}{2(\sqrt{3} + 2)} = 5\sqrt{3}(2 - \sqrt{3}) = 5(2\sqrt{3} - 3)$

Alternatively Since the sphere with centre X touches the sphere with centre Y and the sphere with centre Y touches the sphere with centre Z, $XZ = 4r$.
Let A be the origin of coordinates, with axes along the edges of the cube at A. Then X has coordinates (r, r, r) and Z has coordinates $(10 - r, 10 - r, 10 - r)$.
$$\therefore 4r = XZ = \sqrt{((10-r)-r)^2 + ((10-r)-r)^2 + ((10-r)-r)^2}$$
$$= (10 - 2r) \cdot \sqrt{3}$$

25 C You are told that $5 \cos x + 12 \cos y = 13$.
$$\therefore (5 \cos x + 12 \cos y)^2 + (5 \sin x + 12 \sin y)^2$$
$$= 13^2 + (5 \sin x + 12 \sin y)^2$$
LHS $= 25(\cos^2 x + \sin^2 x) + 144(\cos^2 y + \sin^2 y)$
$\qquad + 120(\cos x \cos y + \sin x \sin y)$
$= 169 + 120 \cos (x - y)$
$\therefore (5 \sin x + 12 \sin y)^2 = 120 \cos (x - y)$
$\therefore$ LHS is a maximum when $x = y$ (i.e. when $\cos x = \tfrac{13}{17}$) and then $5 \sin x + 12 \sin y = 17 \sin x = \sqrt{120}$.

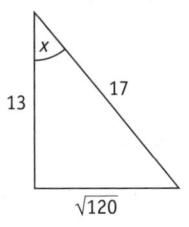

1994

1 C The average of x and $8x = \tfrac{1}{2}(x + 8x) = 18$
$\therefore 9x = 36$
$\therefore x = 4$

2 E **A**, **B**, **C** and **D** are all based on a regular hexagon, so have six lines of reflection symmetry.

E has a central equilateral triangle, which eliminates three of these lines of reflection symmetry.

3 D This is entirely elementary (as befits an early question). However, it encourages efficient ways of counting, and at the same time manages to conceal a surprise or two.

None of the names for counting numbers uses the letter 'c', and the numbers below a million do not use the letter 'm'! Hence $M = C = 0$, so $N + M + C = N$.

To calculate N, you have to run through the number words:
$\qquad$ o**n**e, two, three, four, five, six, seve**n**, eight, **n**i**n**e, te**n**, eleve**n**, etc.

Solutions to the National Mathematics Contest problems

Those numbers that contribute to the total are:
1, 7, 9(×2), 10, 11, 13, 14, 15, 16, 17(×2), 18, 19(×3), 20, 21(×2), 22, 23, 24, 25, 26, 27(×2), 28, 29(×3)
∴ $N = 30$

4 D $91 = 7 \times 13$, $\quad 52 = 2^2 \times 13$, $\quad 39 = 3 \times 13$, $\quad 35 = 5 \times 7$, $\quad 24 = 2^3 \times 3$

5 E $ABCD$ is a kite with $AB = AD$ and $CB = CD$.
∴ $AC \perp BD$ and AC bisects BD.
Let AC and BD meet at M. Then $AB = 25$, $BM = 20$.
∴ $AM = \sqrt{25^2 - 20^2} = \sqrt{625 - 400} = \sqrt{225} = 15$
Also $BC = 52$, $BM = 20$
∴ $CM = \sqrt{52^2 - 20^2} = \sqrt{2704 - 400} = \sqrt{2304} = 48$
∴ $AC = AM + MC = 15 + 48 = 63$

6 B Suppose pickled peppers cost £p per pound.
∴ Number of pounds of pickled peppers purchased for £59 = $\dfrac{59}{p}$
∴ $\dfrac{59}{p} = 236p$ (given)
∴ $p^2 = \dfrac{59}{236} = \dfrac{1}{4}$
∴ $p = \dfrac{1}{2}$
∴ 20 pounds of pickled peppers would cost £$(20 \times \tfrac{1}{2})$.

7 A $2^{\frac{1}{x}} = 2^{-2} = \tfrac{1}{4}$; $\quad -\dfrac{1}{x} = 2$; $\quad \dfrac{1}{x^2} = \dfrac{1}{\frac{1}{4}} = 4$; $\quad 2^x = \dfrac{1}{\sqrt{2}}$; $\quad \dfrac{1}{\sqrt{-x}} = \dfrac{1}{\sqrt{\frac{1}{2}}} = \sqrt{2}$

8 D A heart beats roughly 70 times a minute, and an average lifetime is a bit more than 75 years.
Number of heartbeats in 75 years ≈ 70 × (number of minutes in 75 years)
$\approx 70 \times (75 \times 365 \times 24 \times 60)$
$= 70 \times 25 \times 3 \times 365 \times 24 \times 15 \times 4$
$= 70 \times (365 \times 3) \times (25 \times 4) \times (24 \times 15)$
$\approx 70 \times (1.1 \times 10^3) \times 10^2 \times (3.6 \times 10^2)$
$\approx 3 \times 10^9$

9 B The nth triangular number $T_n = 1 + 2 + 3 + \ldots + n$, so the first six triangular numbers are 1, 3, 6, 10, 15, 21.

$$\tfrac{1}{1} + (\tfrac{1}{3} + \tfrac{1}{6}) + (\tfrac{1}{10} + \tfrac{1}{15}) + \tfrac{1}{21} = 1 + \tfrac{1}{2} + \tfrac{1}{6} + \tfrac{1}{21}$$

$$= \tfrac{5}{3} + \tfrac{1}{21} = \tfrac{35+1}{21} = \tfrac{12}{7}$$

Alternatively In general, the nth triangular number can be expressed more compactly in the 'closed form' $T_n = \tfrac{1}{2} n(n+1)$. Hence the sum of the reciprocals of the first N triangular numbers is given by:

$$T_1^{-1} + T_2^{-1} + T_3^{-1} + \ldots + T_N^{-1} = \sum_{n=1}^{N} \frac{2}{n(n+1)} = 2 \sum_{n=1}^{N} \left(\frac{1}{n} - \frac{1}{n+1} \right)$$

$$= 2\left(1 - \frac{1}{N+1} \right)$$

For more on triangular numbers, see references [31, page 72], [32, pages 34–36], [36, page 33], and [14, Chapter 17] in the list of resources in Section B.

10 B Horizontal cross-sectional area of bird's eye view of 1500 cm of rope with diameter 5 cm when stretched straight $\Big\} = 1500 \times 5 = 7500 \text{ cm}^2$

Area of bird's eye view of same amount of rope when coiled to fill a circle of diameter d cm $\Big\} = \pi \left(\dfrac{d}{2}\right)^2 \text{ cm}^2$

$$\therefore d = \sqrt{\frac{30\,000}{\pi}} = 100 \sqrt{\frac{3}{\pi}} \quad \text{(which is just less than 100)}$$

11 B $(ab + a + b + 1) = (a+1)(b+1)$

$$\therefore a \otimes b = \frac{(a+1)(b+1)}{a}$$

$$\therefore 19 \otimes 94 = \frac{20 \times 95}{19} = 20 \times 5 = 100$$

12 E $AC^2 + BC^2 = AB^2 = (AO + OB)^2 = AO^2 + OB^2 + 2 \cdot AO \cdot OB \neq AO^2 + OB^2$

A The angle in a semicircle is always a right angle.
B AO and OC are both radii, so $AO = OC$; hence $\triangle AOC$ is isosceles.
C $\triangle ABC$ has base AB of length 2, and height $\leq OC = 1$.
D $\triangle AOC$ and $\triangle OBC$ have equal bases $AO = OB$, and the same height.

Solutions to the National Mathematics Contest problems

13 E Initially the marrow is 98% water and 2% matter.
∴ Weight of matter = $\frac{2}{100} \times 50$ pounds = 1 pound
∴ Weight of water = $50 - 1 = 49$ pounds

The marrow absorbs water to become 99% water, so still contains only 1 pound of matter; hence 1 pound is now 1%.
∴ The '99% water' weighs 99 pounds
∴ Total weight after rain = $1 + 99 = 100$ pounds

14 A The cuboid has two a by b faces, two b by c faces and two c by a faces.
∴ Surface area = $2(ab + bc + ca) = (a + b + c)^2 - (a^2 + b^2 + c^2)$

15 A The question is concerned with the ratio of the two areas. Ratios are not affected by a change of scale, so you are free to choose $AB = 2$ (say).

$\triangle FAE$ and $\triangle FBE$ are isosceles right-angled triangles.
∴ $AF = FE = FB$
$AF + FB = AB = 2$
∴ $BF = 1$
∴ area($BDEF$) = 1
Let $BS = x$
∴ $PS = x\sqrt{2} = RS$ (since $PQRS$ is a square)
∴ $AS = RS \cdot \sqrt{2} = 2x$ (since $\triangle RSA$ is an isosceles right-angled triangle)
∴ $2 = AB = AS + BS = 3x$, so $x = \frac{2}{3}$
∴ area($PSRQ$) = $RS^2 = (\frac{2}{3}\sqrt{2})^2 = \frac{8}{9}$

Alternatively Let $\triangle AFE$ have area a. Then $\triangle AFE$, $\triangle BFE$, $\triangle BDE$, $\triangle CDE$ are all congruent, so area($BDEF$)/area ($\triangle ABC$) = $2a/4a = \frac{1}{2}$.
$\triangle ASQ$ is an isosceles right-angled triangle; so $\triangle ARS \equiv \triangle QRS$.
Similarly, $\triangle CQP \equiv \triangle RQP$.
Let RP and QS meet at X, and let $\triangle XSP$ have area b.
Then area($PQRS$) = $4b$, $\triangle BPS \equiv \triangle XSP$, and area($\triangle ARS$) = $2b$ = area($\triangle CQP$);
so area($PQRS$)/area($\triangle ABC$) = $4b/9b = \frac{4}{9}$.

16 C The units digit of 1994^n is the same as the units digit of 4^n. 4×4 ends in 6, and 6×4 ends in 4.
$\therefore$ For each positive integer m:
(a) 4^{2m} has units digit 6;   (b) 4^{2m+1} has units digit 4.

In the question the exponent $n = 1995 + 1996 + 1997 + 1998 + 1999 + 2000$, which is *odd*, so 4^n has units digit 4.

> To learn how to calculate with congruences (which is what lies behind Problem 16) see references [13, Part I, Section 4.5], [28, Section 2 of the Supplement to Chapter I], and [49] in the resources listed in Section B.

17 E In the absence of any indication to the contrary, dice, coins, etc. are assumed (by convention) to be 'fair'.

When two dice are thrown there are 6×6 possible outcomes $i + j$, each of which occurs with probability $\frac{1}{36}$.

1 + 6	2 + 6	3 + 6	4 + 6	5 + 6	6 + 6
1 + 5	2 + 5	3 + 5	4 + 5	5 + 5	6 + 5
1 + 4	2 + 4	3 + 4	4 + 4	5 + 4	6 + 4
1 + 3	2 + 3	3 + 3	4 + 3	5 + 3	6 + 3
1 + 2	2 + 2	3 + 2	4 + 2	5 + 2	6 + 2
1 + 1	2 + 1	3 + 1	4 + 1	5 + 1	6 + 1

For each value of n, count the number of outcomes k_n for which the score is a multiple of n to see whether the probability $\frac{k_n}{36} = \frac{1}{n}$ (i.e. $k_n = \frac{36}{n}$):

✓ $n = 1$: $k_1 = 36 = 36/1$
(✓) $n = 2$: $k_2 = 18 = 36/2$ (given)
✓ $n = 3$: $k_3 = 12 = 36/3$
✓ $n = 4$: $k_4 = 9 = 36/4$
✗ $n = 5$: impossible   (36/5 is not an integer)
✓ $n = 6$: $k_6 = 6 = 36/6$
✗ $n = 7, n = 8$: impossible   (36/7 and 36/8 are not integers)
✓ $n = 9$: $k_9 = 4 = 36/9$
✗ $n = 10, n = 11$: impossible   (36/10 and 36/11 are not integers)
✗ $n = 12$: there is only one way to score a multiple of 12 – namely $6 + 6$; so $k_{12} = 1 \neq 36/12$
✗ $n \geqslant 13$: impossible   (since $k_n = 0$)

Solutions to the National Mathematics Contest problems

18 C An integer is divisible by 99 = 9 × 11 precisely when it is divisible both by 9 and by 11 (since hcf(9, 11) = 1).

If the integer N is written in base 10 and consists entirely of 5s, then:
(a) N is divisible by 11 precisely when the number of digits is *even* (since 11 goes exactly in to 55, and hence into 5555, 555 555, etc., whereas dividing 11 into any integer 55 ... 5 with an odd number of 5s leaves remainder 5);
(b) N is divisible by 9 precisely when the sum of its digits is divisible by 9, so the number of 5s must be a *multiple of 9*.

The smallest 'even multiple of 9' is 18, so the smallest positive integer N has eighteen 5s.

> To learn more about testing for 'divisibility by 9' see reference [33, Chapter 1] and [14, Chapter 12] in the resource list in Section B.

19 B Let the price be £abcd.
$\therefore 100b + 10c + d = \frac{1}{49}(1000a + 100b + 10c + d)$
$\therefore 1000a = 48(100b + 10c + d)$ (*)

3 is a factor of 48, so 3 is a factor of the RHS of (*).
$\therefore$ 3 must be a factor of the LHS – and hence of the thousands digit a
$\therefore a = 3$ or $a = 6$ or $a = 9$

$16 = 2^4$ is a factor of the RHS of (*).
$\therefore 2^4$ must be a factor of the LHS = $1000a = 10^3 a = (2^3 \times 5^3)a$
$\therefore a$ must be even, so $a = 6$

20 D The same scale is used on both x- and y-axes.
$\therefore y - x = k(y + x)$ for some value of $k \approx 2$
$\therefore y = \left(\frac{k+1}{1-k}\right)x$

Hence the graph of y against x is a straight line with gradient ≈ -3.

21 C You should calculate exactly – without using a calculator. This is fairly easy to do in rough, but rather hard to write out in a strictly deductive way.

$A - C = \sqrt{7} - 1 > 0$; hence $A > C$
$5 \times 7^2 = 245 > 175 = 7 \times 5^2$, so $7\sqrt{5} > 5\sqrt{7}$, so $E > C$
$5 \times 6^2 = 180 > 150 = 6 \times 5^2$, so $6\sqrt{5} > 5\sqrt{6}$, so $B > D$
Hence the smallest is either **C** or **D**.

Clearly $36 < 42$
$\therefore 6 < \sqrt{7} \cdot \sqrt{6}$
$\therefore 5^2 < (\sqrt{7} + \sqrt{6})^2$
$\therefore 5 < \sqrt{7} + \sqrt{6}$
$\therefore (\sqrt{7} - \sqrt{6})(\sqrt{7} + \sqrt{6}) = 1 < \dfrac{\sqrt{7}+\sqrt{6}}{5}$
$\therefore \sqrt{7} - \sqrt{6} < \tfrac{1}{5}$
$D - C = 1 - 5(\sqrt{7} - \sqrt{6}) > 0$

22 B *OA* is the straight-line graph of the distance of the first train from London as a function of time. *BC* is the corresponding graph for the second train.
Let $d = AC = BD$ denote the distance from London to Newcastle, let X be the point where the two graphs cross and suppose that this is x hours after 06:00. 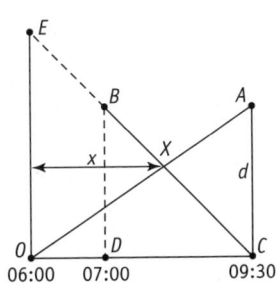
Let the line *CB* meet the y-axis at E.
$\triangle CBD$ and $\triangle CEO$ are similar.
$\therefore \dfrac{7/2}{5/2} = \dfrac{EO}{BD}$, so $EO = \tfrac{7}{5}d$.
$\triangle XEO$ and $\triangle XCA$ are similar.
$\therefore \tfrac{7}{5}d : d = x : (\tfrac{7}{2} - x)$
$\therefore \tfrac{49}{10} = \tfrac{12}{5}x$, So $x = \tfrac{49}{24}$, and the trains meet $2\tfrac{1}{24}$ hours after 06:00.

Alternatively Let $XF = y$
$\therefore \dfrac{y}{x} = \dfrac{d}{7/2}$ ($\triangle XFO$ and $\triangle ACO$ are similar)
$\therefore d = \dfrac{7y}{2x}$

$\dfrac{d}{5/2} = \dfrac{y}{7/2 - x}$ ($\triangle BDC$ and $\triangle XFC$ are similar)
$\therefore d = \dfrac{5y}{7 - 2x}$
$\therefore \dfrac{7y}{2x} = \dfrac{5y}{7 - 2x}$
$\therefore 49 - 14x = 10x$, so $x = \tfrac{49}{24}$

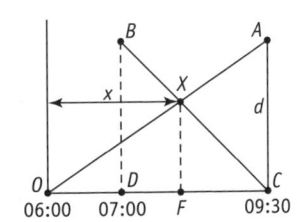

Solutions to the National Mathematics Contest problems

23 E Apply the cosine rule to $\triangle ABM$ and to $\triangle ANM$ to get:

$$c^2 = \left(\frac{a}{3}\right)^2 + x^2 - 2 \cdot x \cdot \cos AMB$$

$$y^2 = \left(\frac{a}{3}\right)^2 + x^2 - 2 \cdot \left(\frac{a}{3}\right) \cdot x \cdot \cos AMN$$

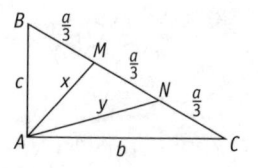

$$\therefore c^2 + y^2 = \frac{2a^2}{9} + 2x^2 \quad \text{(since } \angle AMB = 180° - \angle AMN\text{)}$$

Similarly, the cosine rule in $\triangle ACN$ and $\triangle AMN$ gives:

$$b^2 + x^2 + \frac{2a^2}{9} + 2y^2$$

$$\therefore b^2 + c^2 + x^2 + y^2 = \frac{4a^2}{9} + 2(x^2 + y^2)$$

$$\therefore \frac{5a^2}{9} = x^2 + y^2 \quad \text{(since } b^2 + c^2 = a^2\text{)}$$

$$\therefore \frac{a}{3} = \sqrt{\frac{x^2 + y^2}{5}}$$

Alternatively Since $\cos \angle ABC = \frac{c}{a}$, the cosine rule in $\triangle BAM$ gives:
$$x^2 = (a/3)^2 + c^2 - 2(a/3)c(c/a) = a^2/9 + c^2/3$$
The cosine rule in $\triangle BAN$ gives:
$$y^2 = (2a/3)^2 + c^2 - 2(2a/3)c(c/a) = 4a^2/9 - c^2/3$$
$$\therefore x^2 + y^2 = 5a^2/9$$

24 A Let the distance to be travelled be d miles, and let the time available be t hours.

If Susan is 1 minute late, she uses $t + \frac{1}{60}$ hours.
$$\therefore d = x(t + \tfrac{1}{60})$$

If Susan is 1 minute early, she uses $t - \frac{1}{60}$ hours.
$$\therefore d = y(t - \tfrac{1}{60})$$

$$\therefore \frac{d}{x} - \frac{d}{y} = \frac{1}{30}$$

$$\therefore d = \frac{xy}{30(y - x)}$$

Alternatively You may prefer to observe directly that the two journeys differ by exactly 2 minutes, i.e. by $\frac{1}{30}$ hour. Hence $\frac{d}{x} - \frac{d}{y} = \frac{1}{30}$.

25 E Let *ABB'A'* be one of the isosceles trapezia and let $A'B' = x$. The lines $A'A$ and $B'B$ meet at O, the centre of the figure. Let $OB = OA = r$.

The outer and inner octagons are regular octagons.
The internal angle in a regular octagon is 135°.
∴ $\angle B'A'A = \frac{1}{2} \times 135° = 67\frac{1}{2}°$
The angles of $\triangle OA'B'$ sum to 180°,
∴ $\angle AOB = 45°$
Apply the cosine rule to $\triangle OAB$ to get:
$$1^2 = 2r^2 - 2r^2 \cos 45°$$
∴ $r^2 = \dfrac{1}{2 - \sqrt{2}}$

$\triangle OA'B'$ and $\triangle OAB$ are similar.
∴ $\dfrac{r+1}{r} = \dfrac{OA'}{OA} = \dfrac{A'B'}{AB} = \dfrac{x}{1}$
∴ $x = 1 + \dfrac{1}{r} = 1 + \sqrt{2 - \sqrt{2}}$

Alternatively Let the line through *A* and parallel to *BB'* meet *AB'* at *P*.
∴ $AP = BB' = 1$, $PB' = AB = 1$ and $\angle A'AP = 45°$
∴ $A'P^2 = 1^2 + 1^2 - 2 \cdot 1 \cdot 1 \cdot \cos 45°$
$= 2 - \sqrt{2}$
∴ $A'B' = A'P + PB' = \sqrt{2 - \sqrt{2}} + 1$

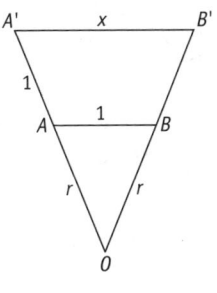

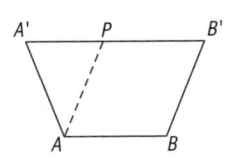

1993

1 D We each have 2 parents, $2 \times 2 = 2^2$ grandparents, $2 \times 2^2 = 2^3$ great-grandparents and $2 \times 2^3 = 2^4$ great-great-grandparents.

2 B Green was born in July 1793. Hence July 1841 would have marked his 48th birthday – but he died in May.

Solutions to the National Mathematics Contest problems

3 A Each item costs 1p less than a whole number of pounds.
The final bill is:
> 28p less than a whole number of pounds, and
> 128p less than a whole number of pounds, and
> 228p less than a whole number of pounds, etc.

Since each item costs at least 99p, the only option is **A**.

> Note that if the final bill had been as large as £126.72, then the shopper might have bought 128 items (at 99p each), rather than just 28.

4 C Simplify each bracket as a single fraction, and then cancel:
$(1 + \frac{1}{2})(1 + \frac{1}{3})(1 + \frac{1}{4})(1 + \frac{1}{5}) = \frac{3}{2} \times \frac{4}{3} \times \frac{5}{4} \times \frac{6}{5} = \frac{6}{2} = 3$

5 B Let the cuboid be a cm by b cm by c cm, with $a \leq b \leq c$
$\therefore bc = 72$, $ac = 54$, $ab = 48$
$\therefore c^2 = \dfrac{(ac \times bc)}{ab} = \dfrac{(72 \times 54)}{48} = \dfrac{(9 \times 8) \times (6 \times 9)}{48}$

6 A $3 \otimes 48 = \sqrt{3 \times 48} = \sqrt{3 \times (3 \times 16)} = 3 \times 4$
$\therefore (3 \otimes 48) \otimes 9 = 12 \otimes 9 = \sqrt{12 \times 9} = 6\sqrt{3}$

7 C 64 stubs → *16 candles*
$\quad\quad\quad$ → 16 stubs → *4 candles*
$\quad\quad\quad\quad\quad\quad$ → 4 stubs → *1 candle*

8 D In each of the solids **A**, **B**, **C** and **E**, exactly three edges meet at each vertex.
Cutting off a corner in such a solid produces a triangular cross-section. By tilting the cutting plane, one can always make the cross section into an equilateral triangle. (Imagine a piece of wire bent in the shape of an equilateral triangle. Slip the wire frame onto the corner P, with one vertex touching each of the three edges at P. The three points in contact with the wire on these three edges define the cutting plane.)

The regular octahedron only has cross-sections with four, five and six edges.

9 A w wabbits dig 1 warren in w weeks

∴ w wabbits dig $\dfrac{1}{w}$ warrens in 1 week.

∴ 1 wabbit digs $\dfrac{1}{w^2}$ warrens in 1 week.

∴ $w + 3$ wabbits dig $\dfrac{w+3}{w^2}$ warrens in 1 week.

∴ $w + 3$ wabbits dig 1 warren in $\dfrac{w^2}{w+3}$ weeks.

Alternatively

(a) w wabbits dig 1 warren in w weeks.

∴ $\dfrac{w+3}{w} \times w$ wabbits dig $\dfrac{w+3}{w}$ warrens in w weeks.

∴ $\dfrac{w+3}{w} \times w$ wabbits dig 1 warren in $w \times \dfrac{w}{w+3}$ weeks.

(b) w wabbits dig 1 warren in w weeks.

∴ 1 wabbit digs 1 warren in w^2 weeks.

∴ $w + 3$ wabbits dig 1 warren in $\dfrac{w^2}{w+3}$ weeks.

10 D The first occurrence after midday is just after 12:30 (and before 12:35).
Then soon after 1:35 (and before 1:40).
Then soon after 2:40 (and before 2:45).
Then soon after 3:45 (and before 3:50).
Then soon after 4:50 (and before 4:55).
Then next occurrence is at 6:00 exactly.
Then soon after 7:05 (and before 7:10).
And so on, until the last time soon after 11:25
(and before 11:30).

Alternatively

(a) Imagine a perfectly circular clock face with all the numbers removed, but with the two hands working as normal. If the two hands start off pointing in opposite directions, then the minute hand must make one and a bit complete revolutions before the second occasion when the hands point in opposite directions. The clock face then looks exactly as it did at the start! So exactly the same time must elapse before the third occasion when the hands point in opposite directions. Hence the times when the hands point in opposite directions are equally spaced.

Solutions to the National Mathematics Contest problems

(b) In fact, the times are exactly $\frac{12}{11}$ hours apart. T hours after midday the hour hand has moved through $30T°$ and the minute hand has moved through $360T°$. So you need to find all values of T with $0 \leqslant T \leqslant 12$ which satisfy the equation:
$$360T - 30T = (2k + 1)180 \text{ for some integer } k$$
$$\therefore T = \frac{6(2k+1)}{11}, \text{ with } 0 \leqslant k \leqslant 10$$

If you can find a copy, there is further discussion of this and related puzzles in Y. I. Perelman's book *Algebra can be fun* (Mir Publishers, 1979, pages 55–58).

11 C You are clearly meant to decide which of the options could equal 'the number of elves in Bri-tain'. **E** has only five digits, so is impossible. To decide between the other options requires some simple reasoning.

If an integer N is a cube and a square, it must be a sixth power:
$\therefore N = m^6$ for some integer m

If $N - 6$ is a prime, then N (and hence m) must be odd (since the only way N could be even is if $N - 6 = 2$, so $N = 8$ – contrary to the given fact that N has six digits).
Now $5^6 = 125^2 < 130^2 = 16\,900$ and $10^6 = 1\,000\,000$; hence, if N has six digits, then $6 \leqslant m \leqslant 9$.
$\therefore m = 7$ or $m = 9$ (since m is odd)
$\therefore m = 7$ (since $9^6 - 6$ is clearly divisible by 3)
So $N = 7^6$ has units digit 9.

Alternatively Options **A** and **B** are impossible (since squares end in 0, 1, 4, 5, 6 or 9. **E** contains only five digits. And **D** is even, so **D** – 6 is a multiple of 2.

12 E $\angle PBA = 30°$ (since $\angle ABC = 90°$ and $\angle PBC = 60°$)
$\triangle BAP$ is isosceles (since $PB = BC = BA$)
$\therefore \angle BPA = \frac{1}{2}(180° - 30°) = 75° = \angle DPC$
$\therefore \angle APD = 360° - (60° + 75° + 75°) = 150°$

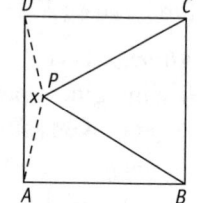

13 B Suppose I pass the first bus exactly as I begin my walk.
The second bus would be 15 minutes behind – i.e. the second bus would be just leaving town as I started walking.
During the next $1\frac{1}{4}$ hours of my walk five further buses would leave town: one (the third) after 15 minutes, one after 30 minutes, one after

45 minutes, one after 60 minutes and one (the seventh) after 75 minutes – just as I arrive in town.

Hence, though it is just possible to meet seven buses, the probability of this is zero (since I would have to set out at *exactly* the same time as a bus passes my home).

In general, I will meet my first bus t minutes (for some positive value of t, $0 < t < 15$) after beginning my walk, and will arrive in town t minutes before the seventh bus leaves. In fact, because I am walking at $\frac{1}{5}$ the speed of the bus, I pass a bus every $12\frac{1}{2}$ minutes.

Alternatively Choose a new unit of distance equal to the distance from my home to town, and a new unit of time equal to $1\frac{1}{4}$ hours – the time it takes for me to walk into town (instead of the usual 1 hour). Then buses travel 5 units of distance in 1 unit of time, whereas I walk 1 unit of distance in 1 unit of time – in the opposite direction. Hence our relative speed is **6** units of distance per unit of time, with buses separated by 1 unit of distance

∴ I will almost always pass 6 buses during 1 unit of time (the only exception being if I meet my first bus exactly as I start walking).

> Part of Problem 13 is the perennial subtlety of distinguishing between 'posts' (or buses) and 'gaps' (or intervals between buses). The need to make this distinction arises in many settings but is rarely taught explicitly. An activity designed to confront the issue head-on may be found in Chapter 12 of *Developing mathematical imagery: activities in the classroom* (Cambridge University Press 1994).

14 D In the given net, the square face that is shaded, and the face that is divided into exactly two triangles have to land up as opposite faces of the cube. So option **D** is impossible. (You should check that all the other views are in fact possible.)

15 B A diagonal of an n-gon is obtained by joining a vertex A of the n-gon to some vertex B, where $B \neq A$ and B is not one of the two vertices adjacent to A. So for each choice of A there are $n - 3$ choices for B.

∴ Number of diagonals $= \dfrac{n(n-3)}{2} = 119$

∴ $n^2 - 3n - 2 \times 119 = 0$
∴ $(n + 14)(n - 17) = 0$
∴ $n = 17$ (since $n > 0$)

Alternatively $\dfrac{n(n-3)}{2} = 119 = 7 \times 17 = \dfrac{17 \times 14}{2}$, so $n = 17$.

Solutions to the National Mathematics Contest problems

16 E Let $f(n) = \dfrac{n+13}{n-4}$. If $f(n)$ is an integer, then $n-4$ must be a factor of $n+13$; in particular, $n-4 = \pm \text{hcf}(n-4, n+13)$.

If d divides both of the integers k and m, then d divides their difference $m-k$.

$\therefore$ hcf$(n-4, n+13)$ divides $(n+13) - (n-4) = 17$

$\therefore n-4 = \pm 1$, or ± 17

If $n-4 = -17$, then $n = -13$, $f(n) = 0$
if $n-4 = -1$, then $n = 3$, $f(n) = -16$
if $n-4 = 1$, then $n = 5$, $f(n) = 18$
if $n-4 = 17$, then $n = 21$, $f(n) = 2$

17 E Time to print all 26! arrangements $= \dfrac{26 \times 25 \times \ldots \times 2 \times 1}{1000}$ seconds

$= \dfrac{26 \times 25 \times \ldots \times 2 \times 1}{1000 \times 60 \times 60 \times 24 \times 365}$ years

Now

$\dfrac{26 \times 25 \times \ldots \times 2 \times 1}{1000 \times 60 \times 60 \times 24 \times 365}$

$= \dfrac{26 \times 25 \times \ldots \times 2 \times 1}{10^5 \times 24 \times 6^2 \times 5 \times 73}$

$= \left(\dfrac{(25 \times 4) \times (20 \times 5) \times 10 \times 24 \times 6 \times 3 \times 2 \times 5}{10^2 \times 10^2 \times 10 \times 24 \times 6^2 \times 5} \right) \times$

$\left(\dfrac{26 \times 23 \times 22 \times 21 \times 19 \times 18 \times 17 \times 16 \times 3 \times 14 \times 13 \times 12 \times 11 \times 9 \times 8 \times 7}{73} \right)$

$= \dfrac{26 \times 23 \times 22 \times 21 \times 19 \times 18 \times 17 \times 16 \times 3 \times 14 \times 13 \times 12 \times 11 \times 9 \times 8 \times 7}{73}$

$= \dfrac{26 \times 3}{73} \times (23 \times 22 \times 7 \times 19 \times 18 \times 17 \times 16 \times 3 \times 14 \times 13 \times 12 \times 11 \times 9 \times 8 \times 7)$

which is much, much larger than 10^{10}.

18 E You have to choose the four family birthdays from the 12 available months – with repetitions allowed.

Total number of possible ways to choose $= 12 \times 12 \times 12 \times 12$

Total number of unfavourable choices

(all different months) $= 12 \times 11 \times 10 \times 9$

∴ Probability (at least two birthdays in the same month)

$$= \frac{12^4 - (12 \times 11 \times 10 \times 9)}{12^4} = 1 - \frac{11 \times 10 \times 9}{12^3}$$

$$= 1 - \frac{11 \times 5}{12 \times 8}$$

$$= 1 - \frac{55}{96} = \frac{41}{96}$$

19 A Suppose $\dfrac{a}{b} + \dfrac{c}{d} = \dfrac{a+c}{b+d}$

∴ $\dfrac{ad + bc}{bd} = \dfrac{a+c}{b+d}$

∴ $(ad + bc)(b + d) = bd(a + c)$

∴ $ad^2 = -cb^2$

∴ $a = -c \cdot \left(\dfrac{b}{d}\right)^2$

Since a and c are non-zero and $\left(\dfrac{b}{d}\right)^2 > 0$, a and c must have opposite sign.

Note that **B** and **E** are both false, since $\dfrac{-1}{1} + \dfrac{1}{1} = \dfrac{0}{2}$;

and **C** and **D** are both false, since $\dfrac{-1}{1} + \dfrac{4}{2} = \dfrac{3}{3}$.

In general, if $a, b, c, d > 0$ and $\dfrac{a}{b} < \dfrac{c}{d}$, then $\dfrac{a}{b} < \dfrac{a+c}{b+d} < \dfrac{c}{d}$.

For an interesting glimpse of the fascinating properties of Farey series (in which the fraction between a/b and c/d is precisely $(a + c)/(b + d)$), see reference [36, pages 152–54] in the list of resources in Section B.

Solutions to the National Mathematics Contest problems

20 C Let O be the centre of the circle, let M be the mid-point of BC, and let N be the mid-point of the chord AM.

$\therefore AM = \sqrt{5}$ (by Pythagoras in $\triangle ABM$)

$\angle AMO = \angle MAB$ (since OM, AB are parallel)

$\therefore \cos AMO = \dfrac{2}{\sqrt{5}}$

$= \dfrac{MN}{MO} = \dfrac{\sqrt{5}/2}{r}$

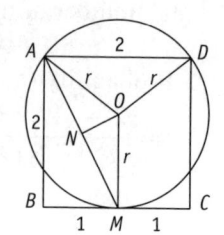

$\therefore r = \tfrac{5}{4}$

Alternatively Let the line through O parallel to AD meet AB at X. Then $OX = 1$, so $1 + AX^2 = r^2$; and $XB = r$, so $1 + (2-r)^2 = r^2$.

21 D Suppose K integers are excluded, with mean k.

Then the sum of these K integers is $K \times k$.

The remaining $1993 - K$ integers also have mean k (given), and hence have sum $(1993 - K) \times k$.

Adding the two sets of integers together, the total sum is:

- $K \times k + (1993 - K) \times k = 1993 \times k$

and

- $1 + 2 + 3 + \ldots + 1993 = \dfrac{1993 \times 1994}{2} = 1993 \times 997$

$\therefore k = 997$

22 C Let $\angle A = 3x°$, $\angle B = 4x°$, $\angle C = 5x°$

$\therefore 3x + 4x + 5x = 180$

$\therefore x = 15$, $\angle A = 45°$, $\angle B = 60°$, $\angle C = 75°$.

$\therefore \sin A = \dfrac{1}{\sqrt{2}}$, $\sin B = \dfrac{\sqrt{3}}{2}$,

$\sin C = \sin(30° + 45°) = \dfrac{1}{2} \cdot \dfrac{1}{\sqrt{2}} + \dfrac{\sqrt{3}}{2} \cdot \dfrac{1}{\sqrt{2}} = \dfrac{1 + \sqrt{3}}{2\sqrt{2}}$

$\therefore \dfrac{1/\sqrt{2}}{BC} = \dfrac{\sqrt{3}/2}{CA} = \dfrac{(1+\sqrt{3})/2\sqrt{2}}{AB}$ (by the sine rule)

$\therefore BC : CA : AB = \dfrac{\sqrt{2}}{2} : \dfrac{\sqrt{3}}{2} : \dfrac{1 + \sqrt{3}}{2\sqrt{2}}$

$= \sqrt{2} : \sqrt{3} : \dfrac{1 + \sqrt{3}}{\sqrt{2}}$

$= 2 : \sqrt{6} : (1 + \sqrt{3})$

23 B You have to locate the point P on CD such that $\angle APB$ is as large as possible.

If P is any point on CD, and O is the centre of the circle through A, B and P, then the angle $\angle APB$ is equal to half of the angle subtended by AB at O (by the circle theorems).

If the circle is to pass through A and B, then the centre O must lie on the perpendicular bisector of AB.

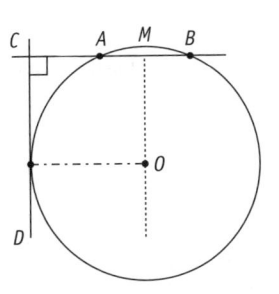

Hence you want to find a point O on the perpendicular bisector of AB such that:

(a) $\angle AOB$ is as large as possible (so O should be as close to M as possible):
(b) the circle which has centre O, and which passes through A, cuts or touches the line CD.

If $O = M$ lies on AB, then the circle centre O through A and B does not touch the line CD.

As O moves down the perpendicular bisector of AB, the circle with centre O which passes through A (and B) grows in size until it just touches the line CD – at P, say.

The line CD is tangent to the circle, so OP is perpendicular to CD.
∴ Radius of circle $= OP = MC$
$= MA + AC = \frac{5}{2} + 4 = \frac{13}{2}$
$= OA$

∴ $CP = MO = \sqrt{OA^2 - AM^2} = \sqrt{(\frac{13}{2})^2 - (\frac{5}{2})^2} = \sqrt{\frac{169}{4} - \frac{25}{4}} = 6$

Alternatively If P lies on CD with $CP = d$, then:

$\tan APB = \tan(CPB - CPA)$
$= \dfrac{\tan CPB - \tan CPA}{1 + \tan CPB \cdot \tan CPA}$
$= \dfrac{9/d - 4/d}{1 + (9/d)(4/d)}$
$= \dfrac{5d}{d^2 + 36}$ (*)

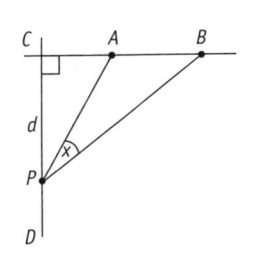

Each value of d determines the corresponding value of $\tan APB$. Since $\tan x$ is an increasing function of x, $x = \angle APB$ is a maximum when $\tan x$ is a maximum. Differentiating (*) with respect to d and setting equal to 0 gives $d^2 = 36$, so $d = 6$ (since $d > 0$).

Solutions to the National Mathematics Contest problems

This question is 'isomorphic to' the question of deciding where to place the ball when taking the conversion kick after a try in rugby. If the try is scored at C, which point P on the line CD gives the largest angle $\angle APB$ to aim at. See reference [32, pages 202–5] in the list of resources in Section B.

24 A You are told that if $\dfrac{1}{a\sqrt{2}+b}$ and $\dfrac{1}{c\sqrt{2}+d}$ are successive terms in the infinite sum, then $c = a + b$ and $d = c + a$

$\therefore c\sqrt{2} + d = (a\sqrt{2} + b)(\sqrt{2} + 1)$

Hence you have to sum the geometric series:

$$a + ar + ar^2 + \ldots = \sum_{n=2}^{\infty} \frac{1}{(\sqrt{2}+1)^n}$$

with first term $a = \dfrac{1}{(\sqrt{2}+1)^2}$ and with common ratio $r = \dfrac{1}{\sqrt{2}+1}$.

$\therefore \text{Sum} = \dfrac{a}{1-r} = \dfrac{1/(\sqrt{2}+1)^2}{1 - 1/(\sqrt{2}+1)} = \dfrac{1}{\sqrt{2}(\sqrt{2}+1)} = \dfrac{1}{2+\sqrt{2}} = \dfrac{2-\sqrt{2}}{2} = 1 - \dfrac{1}{\sqrt{2}}$

25 E You have to find how many positive values of x (with $[x] \neq 0 \neq [3x]$) satisfy:

$$\frac{1}{[x]} + \frac{1}{[3x]} = x - [x] \quad (*)$$

The LHS of (*) is never 0. Hence x is not an integer (or else the RHS of (*) would equal 0).

So you may write $x = n + \varepsilon$ with $0 < \varepsilon < 1$.

Case 1 $\varepsilon < \tfrac{1}{3}$
$\therefore 3x = 3n + 3\varepsilon$ with $0 < 3\varepsilon < 1$
$\therefore [3x] = 3n$ and (*) simplifies to:

$$\frac{4}{3n} = \frac{1}{n} + \frac{1}{3n} = \varepsilon$$

$\therefore \dfrac{4}{3n} = \varepsilon < \tfrac{1}{3}$

$\therefore n > 4$

Moreover for each value of $n > 4$, $0 < \varepsilon = \dfrac{4}{3n} < \tfrac{1}{3}$, and $x = n + \varepsilon$ satisfies (*). Hence there are infinitely many solutions in Case 1.

Case 2 $\frac{1}{3} \leq \varepsilon < \frac{2}{3}$
∴ $3x = 3n + 1 + (3\varepsilon - 1)$ with $0 \leq 3\varepsilon - 1 < 1$
∴ $[3x] = 3n + 1$ and (*) simplifies to:
$$\frac{1}{n} + \frac{1}{3n+1} = \varepsilon$$
∴ $\frac{4n+1}{n(3n+1)} = \varepsilon$
∴ $\frac{1}{3} \leq \frac{4n+1}{n(3n+1)} < \frac{2}{3}$
∴ $3n^2 - 11n - 3 \leq 0$ and $6n^2 - 10n - 3 > 0$
∴ $0 \leq n \leq 3$ and ($n \leq -1$ or $2 \leq n$)
∴ $n = 2$ or $n = 3$, so there are two solutions in Case 2.

Case 3 $\frac{2}{3} \leq \varepsilon < 1$
∴ $3x = 3n + 2 + (3\varepsilon - 2)$ with $0 \leq 3\varepsilon - 2 < 1$
∴ $[3x] = 3n + 2$ and (*) simplifies to:
$$\frac{1}{n} + \frac{1}{3n+2} = \varepsilon$$
∴ $\frac{4n+2}{n(3n+2)} = \varepsilon$
∴ $\frac{2}{3} \leq \frac{4n+2}{n(3n+2)} < 1$
∴ $6n^2 - 8n - 6 \leq 0$ and $3n^2 - 2n - 2 > 0$
∴ $0 \leq n \leq 1$ and ($n \leq -1$ or $2 \leq n$) – so no solutions.

1992

1 D $11^2 - 2 = 119 = 7 \times 17$

Alternatively If you prefer a more systematic approach, you could identify possible prime factors as follows.

(a) All five options $3^2 - 2, 5^2 - 2, 7^2 - 2, 11^2 - 2, 13^2 - 2$ are odd.
∴ None is divisible by 2.
(b) $3^2 - 2$ is not divisible by 3.
And if x is not divisible by 3, then x^2 is 1 more than a multiple of 3.
∴ $x^2 - 2$ is not divisible by 3.
∴ $5^2 - 2, 7^2 - 2, 11^2 - 2, 13^2 - 2$ are not divisible by 3.

Solutions to the National Mathematics Contest problems

    (c) $5^2 - 2$ is not divisible by 5.
    And if x is not divisible by 5, the x^2 is 1 or 4 more than a multiple of 5.
    $\therefore$ $x^2 - 2$ is not divisible by 5 (so $5^2 - 2$, $7^2 - 2$, $11^2 - 2$, $13^2 - 2$ aren't).

    (d) Hence none of the given integers is divisible by 2, 3, or 5; so the first possible prime factor you need to check is 7.
    The value of x^2 is '2 more than a multiple of 7' roughly one-third of the time: e.g. $3^2 - 2$, $4^2 - 2$, $10^2 - 2$, $11^2 - 2$, ... are all divisible by 7.

2 B The 'standard form' notation focuses on the most significant digits:
$$1 \times 10^{78} + 2 \times 10^{77} + 3 \times 10^{76} + 4 \times 10^{75} + 5 \times 10^{74} + 6 \times 10^{73}$$
so ignores the relatively insignificant smaller powers of 10.

3 B The edge lengths a, b, c of a triangle, where $a \leq b \leq c$ say, have to satisfy the *triangle inequality*: $a + b > c$.
Hence the only possible triples are:
2, 3, 4;   2, 4, 5;   2, 5, 6;   3, 4, 5;   3, 4, 6;   3, 5, 6;   4, 5, 6

4 C '$htu1$' = $1000h + 100t + 10u + 1$

5 D No one has >2 arms; almost everyone has exactly 2 arms; some people have <2 arms.
$\therefore$ Average (= mean) number of arms is slightly less than 2.
$\therefore$ Probability (next person you meet has above average number of arms) = $1 - \varepsilon$, where ε is very small, but positive.

Alternatively In any representative large sample of N people:
(a) a very small number $k > 0$ will have less than 2 arms;
(b) the remaining $N - k$ will have 2 arms.
$\therefore$ Probability (random person has above average number of arms)
$$= \frac{N-k}{N} = 1 - \frac{k}{N}$$

6 D UN has two letters ($\therefore$ UN $\to$ DEUX).
DEUX has four letters ($\therefore$ DEUX $\to$ QUATRE).
QUATRE has six letters ($\therefore$ QUATRE $\to$ SIX).
SIX has three letters ($\therefore$ SIX $\to$ TROIS).
TROIS has five letters ($\therefore$ TROIS $\to$ CINQ).
CINQ has four letters.

7 D An average lifetime is a bit more than 70 years.

∴ Each year around $\dfrac{50\,000\,000}{70}$ people die and the same number are born.

8 A $\mathcal{M}^2(\text{Alan}) = \mathcal{M}(\text{Betty})$ states that 'the mother of Alan's mother' (Alan's grandmother) is the same person as 'Betty's mother'.
$\mathcal{M}(\text{Alan}) \neq \text{Betty}$ states that Betty is not Alan's mother.
∴ Betty's and Alan's mothers must have been sisters.

9 D Let the edge length of each cube be x cm.
∴ The solid has volume $4x^3$ cm^3.

Each face of one of the cubes has area x^2 cm^2.
The four cubes have 4×6 faces altogether, but six of these are internal to the given solid.
∴ Surface area of solid $= (24 - 6)x^2$ cm^2
∴ $4x^3 = 18x^2$
∴ $2x = 9$ (since $x \neq 0$)

10 E $\dfrac{\text{Lill's height}}{\text{Gill's height}} = \dfrac{5}{4}$ (given)

You are told that 'Lill and Gill are similar'.
∴ Their volumes (and hence their weights) are in the ratio $(\tfrac{5}{4})^3$.
∴ $\dfrac{\text{Lill's weight}}{\text{Gill's weight}} = \dfrac{\text{Lill's volume}}{\text{Gill's volume}} = (\tfrac{5}{4})^3$
∴ Lill's weight $= (\text{Gill's weight}) \times (\tfrac{125}{64}) = \tfrac{125}{4}$ kg

11 C n square sheets of paper are arranged in a square.
∴ There are $\sqrt{n}$ sheets along the top, and $\sqrt{n}$ sheets down the side.
∴ There are $1 + \sqrt{n}$ pins along the top and $1 + \sqrt{n}$ pins down the side.
∴ Total number of pins used $= (1 + \sqrt{n})^2$

12 E Their initial salaries are the same, and 10% > 8%, so M clearly earns more than N in 1990.

Suppose both earned £S in 1989.
∴ On 1 January 1990, M's salary rose to £$(\tfrac{110}{100} \times S)$
and N's salary rose to £$(\tfrac{108}{100} \times S)$.
∴ On 1 January 1991, M's salary rose to £$\tfrac{108}{100} \times (\tfrac{110}{100} \times S)$
and N's salary rose to £$\tfrac{110}{100} \times (\tfrac{108}{100} \times S)$.

Solutions to the National Mathematics Contest problems

13 E The clock loses 12 minutes every hour, i.e.
  4 clock minutes = 5 real minutes
  ∴ Clock reaches 1 am after 60 (= 15 × 4) clock minutes
  which is the same as 15 × 5 = 75 real minutes (i.e. at 1:15 am).

14 D Let $\mathcal{P}$ be a plane of symmetry of the regular octahedron.
  No plane $\mathcal{P}$ can pass through all six vertices.
  ∴ Given any plane $\mathcal{P}$, there is some vertex P of the octahedron which does not lie on the plane $\mathcal{P}$.
  ∴ The reflection P' of P in the plane $\mathcal{P}$ must also be a vertex of the octahedron.
  ∴ Either P' is diametrically opposite P (corresponding to one possible plane $\mathcal{P}$ for each of the three pairs of opposite vertices); or P' is adjacent to P, so $\mathcal{P}$ is the plane which is the perpendicular bisector of the edge PP' (corresponding to one possible plane $\mathcal{P}$ for each of the six pairs of opposite edges).

15 C Number the days of the week 0 (= Saturday), 1 (= Sunday), 2 (= Monday), etc.

There are 365 = 7 × 52 + 1 days in an ordinary year.
  ∴ If in year N a wedding or anniversary occurs on day number k, then you expect that in year $N + 1$ the anniversary will occur on day $k + 1$.

This simple rule is complicated by the fact that a leap year contains 366 = 7 × 52 + 2 days; so if 29 February in a leap year occurs between the two anniversaries, then the anniversary day jumps two days, from day k to day $k + 2$.

In 25 years there are either six or seven leap years.
  ∴ If a wedding takes place on day 0, its silver wedding anniversary will take place on day 25 + 6 ≡ 3 (mod 7) or 25 + 7 ≡ 4 (mod 7).
  ∴ None of the silver wedding anniversaries occur at weekends (i.e. on Saturday or Sunday).

In 40 years there are usually ten leap years.
  ∴ If a wedding takes place on day 0, its ruby wedding anniversary will take place on day 40 + 10 ≡ 1 (mod 7).
  ∴ All ruby wedding anniversaries occur at weekends.

(In 40 years there could exceptionally be 11 leap years. But then the first and last years are both leap years. so there are still exactly ten 29 Februarys between the wedding and the ruby anniversary, so the same conclusion holds.

This leaves the possibility that one or more of the weddings could have taken place on 29 February! If, that is, 29 February was ever a Saturday during the 1940s – in which case it is unclear when the 'anniversary' should be celebrated. (In fact, 29 February did not fall on a Saturday in 1940, 1944 or 1948.)

In 50 years there are either 12 or 13 leap years.
∴ If a wedding takes place on day 0, its golden wedding anniversary will take place on day $50 + 12 \equiv 6 \pmod 7$ or $50 + 13 \equiv 0 \pmod 7$.
∴ The golden wedding anniversaries may occur at weekends, but may not.

16 B $\angle A + \angle B = 180°$
∴ $\angle CAB + \angle CBA = \frac{1}{3} \times 180° = 60°$
∴ $\angle MCN = \angle ACB$ (vertically opposite angles)
$= 180° - (\angle CAB + \angle CBA)$
$= 180° - 60° = 120°$

17 A Distance travelled during the first d days $= dk$ miles
Distance travelled during the next b days $= bm$ miles
∴ Total distance travelled during the $d + b$ days $= dk + bm$ miles
$$= \frac{dk + bm}{100} \times 100 \text{ miles}$$
The car uses x litres of fuel per 100 miles.
∴ In travelling $\frac{dk + bm}{100} \times 100$ miles, the car uses $\frac{dk + bm}{100} \times x$ litres.

18 E 1 mile ≈ 1600 metres
∴ In travelling 1 mile, there are roughly 160 audible clicks.
If the train travels at x mph, the number of clicks per hour $\approx 160x$;
i.e. x clicks in each $\frac{1}{160}$ hour $(= \frac{3}{8}$ minute).

19 E Addition is easier than subtraction, so rewrite the given subtraction as an addition.

In the tens column 'M + 9' cannot end in 'M'; hence there must be a carry of 1 from the units column.
∴ E = 8 or 9

```
  4 M E
+   9 2
-------
  N M C
```

For more 'word sums' see reference [14, Chapter 8] in the list of resources in Section B.

Solutions to the National Mathematics Contest problems

20 C Remove the modulus signs in $|x|+|y|=1$ for each quadrant separately, and so sketch the graph in four stages.

(a) For $x \geq 0$ and $y \geq 0$, $|x|+|y|=x+y$,
so the equation simplifies to $x+y=1$.
(b) For $x \geq 0$ and $y \leq 0$, $|x|+|y|=x-y$,
so the equation simplifies to $x-y=1$.
(c) For $x \leq 0$ and $y \geq 0$, $|x|+|y|=-x+y$,
so the equation simplifies to $-x+y=1$.
(d) For $x \leq 0$ and $y \leq 0$, $|x|+|y|=-x-y$,
so the equation simplifies to $-x-y=1$.

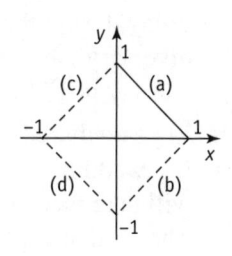

21 D $20° = \angle ABE$ (given)
$= \angle ACE$ (angles in the same segment)
$= \angle DEC$ (since AC is parallel to ED)
$= \angle DAC$ (angles in the same segment)
$\therefore \angle AXC = 180° - (\angle XAC + \angle XCA) = 140°$

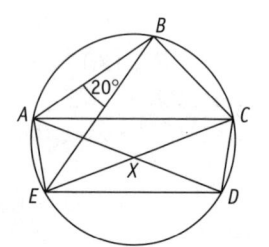

22 C The cyclometer calibrated for the 28-inch wheel clicks once each time the bicycle travels forward 28π inches.
If this cyclometer is attached to the 26-inch wheel, it clicks once each time the bicycle moves 26π inches.
$\therefore$ Distance actually travelled = $\frac{13}{14}$ of distance measured.

Similarly, for the other cyclometer:
Distance actually travelled = $\frac{14}{13}$ of distance measured.

Let the true distance travelled be d miles.
$\therefore \frac{14}{13}d - \frac{13}{14}d = 27$
$\therefore d = 13 \times 14 = 182$

23 A First, suppose the *centre* of the coin lands inside a particular square, and calculate the probability that the *whole* coin lands completely inside that square.

This happens precisely when the centre of the coin lands inside the central $(x-2r) \times (x-2r)$ square.

$\therefore$ Probability $= \dfrac{(x-2r)^2}{x^2}$

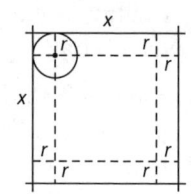

128

If the board is large, then this probability for a single square is roughly equal to the probability for the whole board.

$$\therefore \left(\frac{x-2r}{x}\right)^2 = 0.64 = 0.8^2.$$

Now $\frac{x-2r}{x} \geq 0$ (since $x - 2r \geq 0$ and $x > 0$)

$$\therefore \frac{x-2r}{x} = 1 - \frac{2r}{x} = 0.8$$

$$\therefore \frac{2r}{x} = 0.2$$

24 A Let A, B, C be the centres of the first three balls. Then A, B, C are exactly 1 unit above the table, and, since the three balls touch, $AB = BC = CA = 2$.

∴ ABC is an equilateral triangle of side 2.

Let D be the centre of the fourth sphere.
The fourth sphere touches each of the first three spheres.
∴ $DA = DB = DC = 2$
∴ $ABCD$ is a regular tetrahedron of side 2.

Let E be the point where the perpendicular from D hits the plane of $\triangle ABC$, and let M be the mid-point of BC.
∴ $DB = 2$, $BM = 1$ and $\angle DMB = 90°$
∴ $DM = \sqrt{3}$ (by Pythagoras in $\triangle DMB$)
Similarly, $AM = \sqrt{3}$

The cosine rule in $\triangle DMA$ gives $\cos DMA = \frac{1}{3}$

$$= \frac{ME}{DM} = \frac{ME}{\sqrt{3}}$$

$$\therefore ME = \frac{\sqrt{3}}{3}$$

$$\therefore DE = \sqrt{MD^2 - ME^2} = \sqrt{3 - \tfrac{1}{3}} = \frac{2\sqrt{2}}{\sqrt{3}}$$

∴ Height of D above the table $= 1 + \dfrac{2\sqrt{2}}{\sqrt{3}}$

Solutions to the National Mathematics Contest problems

25 B It is often more enlightening, and more suggestive, to think and to calculate *algebraically*, rather than numerically. This is partly because it is much easier to calculate with letters than with very large numbers; but it is also the only way to keep track of how the input ingredients relate to the output after a messy calculation.

So replace 1992 by n and 1993 by $n + 1$ and let:

$$f(n) = \sqrt{1 + n^2 + \left(\frac{n}{n+1}\right)^2} + \frac{n}{n+1}$$

Notice that $f(0) = 1, f(1) = 2, f(2) = \underline{}, f(3) = \underline{}$
This suggests that $f(n)$ can be simplified.

$$1 + n^2 + \left(\frac{n}{n+1}\right)^2 = \frac{(n+1)^2 + n^2(n+1)^2 + n^2}{(n+1)^2}$$

$$= \frac{n^2(n+1)^2 + 2n^2 + 2n + 1}{(n+1)^2}$$

$$= \frac{n^2(n+1)^2 + 2n(n+1) + 1}{(n+1)^2} = \frac{(n(n+1) + 1)^2}{(n+1)^2}$$

$$\therefore \sqrt{1 + n^2 + \left(\frac{n}{n+1}\right)^2} = \sqrt{\frac{(n(n+1)+1)^2}{(n+1)^2}} = \frac{n(n+1)+1}{n+1}$$

$$\therefore f(n) = \frac{n(n+1)+1}{n+1} + \frac{n}{n+1} = \frac{n^2 + 2n + 1}{n+1} = n + 1$$

1991

1 D Once you know that $A = 2^2 - 2 + 1 = 3$, it is easy to calculate:
$B = 2^3 - A = 5$, $C = 2^4 - B = 11$, $D = 2^5 - C = 21$, $E = 2^6 - D = 43$

Alternatively
$$(x^n - x^{n-1} + x^{n-2} - \cdots \pm 1)(x + 1) = x^{n+1} \pm 1$$

$$\therefore 2^5 - 2^4 + 2^3 - 2^2 + 2 - 1 = \frac{2^6 - 1}{2 + 1} = (2^3 - 1) \times \frac{(2^3 + 1)}{2 + 1}$$
$$= (2^3 - 1) \times (2^2 - 2 + 1) \text{ (not prime)}$$

A related, and important, question is: 'When can an integer of the form $n^m + 1$ or $n^m - 1$ be a prime number?' The answer leads naturally to Mersenne and Fermat primes: see references [14, Chapter 6], [32, page 236], [29, pages 64–66 and 67–69] and [36, pages 135–41] in the list of resources in Section B.

In connection with the alternative solution, there is an interesting discussion of the need for fluency in handling algebraic factorisations in reference [32, Chapter 4, pages 82–102].

2 D $1991^2 - 1991 = 1991(1991 - 1) = 1991 \times 1990$
$= (1900 + 91) \times (1900 + 90)$
$= [1900^2 + (90 + 91) \times 1900] + 91 \times 90$

The terms in the square bracket do not affect the tens and units digits of the answer.

∴ 1991×1990 has the same tens and units digits as:
$91 \times 90 = (90 + 1) \times 90 = 8100 + \underline{90}$

> Problem 2 is really about calculating modulo 100. For information on how to calculate mod n, see references [13, Part I, Section 4.5], [28, Section 2 of the Supplement to Chapter I] and [49] in the list of resources in Section B.

3 C

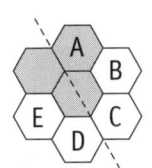

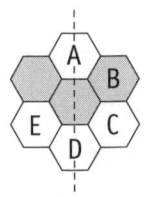

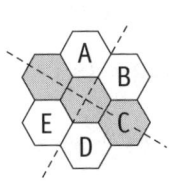

4 D Three days ago 'yesterday was the day before Sunday'.
∴ Three days ago was Sunday.
∴ Today is Wednesday.

> For more similar puzzles of this kind, see reference [14, Chapter 25] in the list of resources in Section B.

5 B Since in the units column O = 7 (given), it follows that R = 4 with a carry of 1 to the tens column.
∴ U is odd.
∴ W ≠ 9 (or else U = W = 9)

The maximum carry to the thousands column is 1, so F = 1.
∴ U = 3, 5, or 9

In the hundreds column, O = 7 (given), which is odd, so there must have been a carry of 1 from the tens column.
∴ W ⩾ 5 and W ≠ 9

Now W ≠ 5 (or U = 1 = F), W ≠ 7 (since O = 7) and W ≠ 8 (or U = O = 7)
∴ W = 6, so U = 3

> For more 'word sums', see reference [14, Chapter 8] in the list of resources in Section B.

6 E Probability of **A** = $(\frac{1}{2})^4 + (\frac{1}{2})^4 = \frac{1}{8}$
Probability of **B** = $\frac{1}{6}$
Probability of **C** = $\frac{1}{7}$
Probability of **D** = $\frac{4}{36} = \frac{1}{9}$ (possible sums = 3 + 6, 4 + 5, 5 + 4, 6 + 3)
Probability of **E** = $\frac{1}{5}$

7 A On each single sheet (= half of a double sheet) the *odd* numbered page comes first (1 or 3 or 5 or …) and the *even* numbered sheet comes second.
∴ Page 6 is the second side of the left-hand sheet (with page 5 coming before it), and page 20 is the second side of the right-hand sheet (with page 19 before it).

You might like to think about the (not entirely obvious) connection between this problem and 1995, Problem 4.

8 E 2 × (1s 6d) + 3 × (1s 3d) = 2s 12d + 3s 9d
 = 3s 0d + 3s 9d = 6s 9d
∴ £1 − (6s 9d) = 20s − (6s 9d) = 13s 3d

9 D The words 'percentage increase' regularly mislead beginners into thinking that they should first calculate the increase, then add this to (or subtract this from) the given quantity. While that should always give the right answer, it leaves students with a mistaken impression about the nature of percentages.
A percentage is always a percentage *of something*, i.e. a percentage is an *operator*, or *scale factor*. Hence percentages are essentially *multiplicative*.

Let N be the number of items in the syllabus in 1981.
∴ The number of items in 1991 (100% increase) was $2N$
and the number of items in 1986 (40% increase) was $\frac{140}{100} N$.
Now $2N = \frac{200}{140} \times \frac{140}{100} N$
∴ If $2N = \frac{p}{100} \times (\frac{140}{100} N)$, then $p = \frac{2000}{14} \approx 142.9$

10 D Each soldier would measure roughly 1 yard (= 3 feet) across the shoulders.
1 mile = 1760 yards
∴ Around 2000 soldiers would be needed per mile
∴ Around 80 × 2000 = 160 000 soldiers for the length of the wall

11 E Let area(*BEA*) = 1 unit 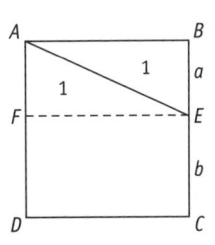
∴ area(*CDAE*) = 4 units
area(*BEA*) = area(*FAE*)
∴ area(*CDFE*) = area(*CDAE*) − area(*FAE*)
      = 3 units
∴ *a* : *b* = area(*EFAB*) : area(*CDFE*) = 2 : 3

Alternatively Let the rectangle have width *w*. Then the triangle has area $(a \times w)/2$, while the trapezium *ADCE* has parallel sides *AD*, *EC* of lengths $a + b$ and b respectively, and so has area $[(2b + a) \times w]/2$.
∴ $aw/2 : (2b + a)w/2 = 1 : 4$
∴ $4a = (2b + a)$
∴ $4a/b = 2 + a/b$

12 B 76.482 rounds *down* to 76.48 (4 s.f.), and rounds *up* to 76.5 (3 s.f.). Hence the actual reading must have been *less than* 76.5; so 76.482 and 76.48 should round down to 76 (2 s.f.).

13 E 170° is 10° less than 180°.
In one hour, the hour hand moves through $\frac{360}{12} = 30° = 3 \times 10°$.
∴ 10° corresponds to the movement of the hour hand in $\frac{1}{3}$ hour.
∴ At 10:20 the minute hand points exactly at '4', but the hour hand has moved exactly 10° beyond the '10'.

14 D The list 21 32 33 24 15 contains two 1s, three 2s, three 3s and one 5 – but only one 4!

> For a variation on 'self-descriptive lists' see reference [51, Chapter 3] and the puzzles in reference [23] in the list of resources in Section B.

15 A *OA* = radius of circle 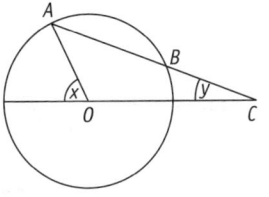
      = *OB*
      = *BC*   (given)
∴ △*OAB* and △*BOC* are isosceles triangles.
∴ ∠*BOC* = *y*
∴ ∠*OBA* = 2*y*   (exterior angle of △*BOC*)
      = ∠*OAB*
∴ *x* = ∠*OAC* + ∠*OCA*   (exterior angle of △*OAC*)
   = 2*y* + *y* = 3*y*

Solutions to the National Mathematics Contest problems

16 B $(a^b)^c = a^{bc}$
$\therefore ((\sqrt{50})^{\sqrt{50}})^{\sqrt{50}} = (\sqrt{50})^{\sqrt{50} \times \sqrt{50}} = (\sqrt{50})^{50}$
$= (\sqrt{50})^{2 \times 25} = ((\sqrt{50})^2)^{25}$
$= 50^{5 \times 5} = (50^5)^5$

so **B** is true.

50^{25} is an integer, so **A** is false; 25 is odd and 50 is not a perfect square, so **C** is false; 25 is not divisible by 3 and 50 is not a perfect cube, so **E** is false.

It is a bit harder to see why **D** is false.

The nth triangular number $T_n = \dfrac{n(n+1)}{2}$ factorises as a product of two integers with no common factor:

$T_n = \dfrac{n}{2} \times (n+1)$ if n is even, and $T_n = n \times \dfrac{n+1}{2}$ if n is odd.

Since $50^{25} = (2 \times 5^2)^{25} = 2^{25} \times 5^{50}$, there is only one way to factorise 50^{25} as a product of two integers with no common factors, neither of which are of the required form:

- if $2^{25} = \dfrac{n}{2}$, then $n = 2^{26}$ and $5^{50} \neq n+1$
- if $50^{50} = n$, then $2^{25} \neq \dfrac{(n+1)}{2}$

17 A The car travels at a speed of k km/h $= \dfrac{k}{100} \times 100$ km per hour.
The car uses l litres of petrol per 100 km.
$\therefore$ The car uses $\dfrac{k}{100} \times l$ litres of petrol per hour.
$\therefore$ The car uses $\dfrac{kl}{100 \times 60}$ litres of petrol per minute.
$\therefore$ The car uses $\dfrac{kl}{100 \times 60} \times m$ litres of petrol in m minutes.

18 D The first two shaded squares have area $\frac{2}{4} \times 1$;
the second two shaded squares have area $\frac{2}{4} \times \frac{1}{4}$;
the third two shaded squares have area $\frac{2}{4} \times (\frac{1}{4})^2$; and so on.
$\therefore$ Total shaded area $= \frac{1}{2} + \frac{1}{2} \times \frac{1}{4} + \frac{1}{2} \times (\frac{1}{4})^2 + \ldots$ *ad inf*
This is a geometric series with first term $a = \frac{1}{2}$ and common ratio $r = \frac{1}{4}$.
$\therefore$ Sum $= \dfrac{a}{1-r} = \dfrac{\frac{1}{2}}{1-\frac{1}{4}} = \dfrac{2}{3}$

19 C Suppose that on the journey from B to C d km are downhill, l km are on the level and u km are uphill.

Then on the return journey from C to B, u km are downhill, l km are on the level and d km are uphill.

∴ Aileen walks:

$(u + d)$ km $= \left(\dfrac{u+d}{3}\right) \times 3$ km uphill at 3 km/h, taking $\dfrac{u+d}{3}$ hours

$(d + u)$ km $= \left(\dfrac{d+u}{6}\right) \times 6$ km downhill at 6 km/h, taking $\dfrac{d+u}{6}$ hours

$2l$ km $= \left(\dfrac{2l}{4}\right) \times 4$ km on the level at 4 km/h, taking $\dfrac{2l}{4}$ hours

∴ Number of hours for whole journey $= 6$
$$= \dfrac{u+d}{3} + \dfrac{d+u}{6} + \dfrac{2l}{4}$$
$$= \dfrac{d+u}{2} + \dfrac{l}{2} = \dfrac{d+u+l}{2}$$

∴ Total distance walked $= 2(d + l + u) = 24$

20 A You are told that the infinitely long expression has a finite value. So you can give this value a name and calculate with it.

Let $x = \sqrt{6 + \sqrt{6 + \sqrt{6 + \sqrt{6 + \ldots}}}}$ *ad inf*

∴ $x^2 = 6 + \sqrt{6 + \sqrt{6 + \sqrt{6 + \ldots}}}$ *ad inf*

$ = 6 + x$

∴ $x^2 - x - 6 = 0$

∴ $(x - 3)(x + 2) = 0$

∴ $x = 3$ (since $\sqrt{y}$ denotes the *positive* square root)

> In general, one has to be very careful with infinitely long expressions. Suppose you replace the repeated square root by some other function, such as 'tan', and simply write:
>
> $\tan(6 + \tan(6 + \tan(6 + \tan(6 + \ldots \textit{ad inf}))))$ (*)
>
> On the one hand, experimental evaluation of successive terms of the sequence:
>
> $\tan 6, \tan(6 + \tan 6), \tan(6 + \tan(6 + \tan 6)), \ldots$
>
> seems to suggest that *whether the expression (*) has a value or not appears to depend on whether the variable is interpreted as being in degrees or in radians!*

On the other hand, if you blithely assume that the expression has a well-defined value, write:

$$x = \tan(6 + \tan(6 + \tan(6 + \tan(6 + \ldots \text{ ad inf}))))$$

and try to calculate x more or less as in the solution of Problem 20, then you have to solve the equation:

$$x = \tan(6 + x)$$

which has *infinitely many different solutions* (since the graph of $y = x$ cuts the graph of $y = \tan x$ once in each of the intervals $(k\pi - \pi/2, \; k\pi + \pi/2)$.

You might also like to consider the significance of the apparently spurious solution $x = -2$ in the solution to Problem 20. Suppose we define $\text{NEGRT}(y) = -\sqrt{y}$. We could then consider the infinite expression $\text{NEGRT}(6 + \text{NEGRT}(6 + \text{NEGRT}(6 + \ldots))))$. If this has a finite value, and we denote it by x, then squaring shows that x satisfies the same equation $x^2 = 6 + x$.

$$\therefore \; -2 = \text{NEGRT}(6 + \text{NEGRT}(6 + \text{NEGRT}(6 + \text{NEGRT}(6 + \ldots \text{ ad inf}))))$$

For more on the need for care when dealing with infinite expressions see references [32, pages 322–24], [37] and [38, Chapter 8 and Appendix pages 237–41] in the list of resources in Section B. I would also encourage you to read [39], which includes some interesting mathematics alongside biographies of Srinivasa Ramanujan and G. H. Hardy.

21 C To shade one-quarter of the rectangle, two small squares must be shaded.

If one of these is the top left square, there are just two squares which have a common side with it; so there are $8 - (1 + 2) = 5$ choices for the second square.

The same is true for the other three corner squares.

If you shade one of the four central squares, three squares have a common side with it; so there are $8 - (1 + 3) = 4$, choices for the second square.

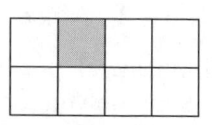

Now add up all the possibilities $(4 \times 5 + 4 \times 4) = 36$, and remember that each possible shading has been *counted twice*.

5	4	4	5
5	4	4	5

Alternatively The total number of ways of choosing two squares from eight is $\binom{8}{2} = 28$. There are $(2 \times 3) + 4 = 10$ lines separating adjacent squares and hence 10 pairs of squares with a common side. Hence there are $28 - 10 = 18$ pairs of squares without a common side.

22 D The volume of the remaining solid is equal to the volume of the cube minus the total volume of the eight identical pieces removed.

The volume of the cube $= (2a)^3 = 8a^3$

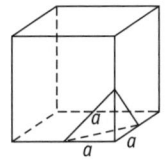

Each of the eight corners that are cut off is a tetrahedron – with base an isosceles right angled triangle having sides of lengths a, a, $a\sqrt{2}$, and with height a.

∴ Volume of each corner tetrahedron $= \frac{1}{3} \times$ (area of base) $\times$ height
$= \frac{1}{3} \times \frac{1}{2}(a \times a) \times a = \frac{1}{6}a^3$

∴ Volume of remaining solid
$= 8a^3 - 8 \times \frac{1}{6}a^3$
$= 8a^3(1 - \frac{1}{6}) = \frac{40}{6}a^3 = \frac{20}{3}a^3$

> You might like to compare this problem with 1996, Problem 21. In this problem, the polyhedron which remains after the eight corners have been removed has six square faces and eight triangular faces, with two squares and two triangles alternating at each vertex; so it is denoted by 4.3.4.3 and is called a cuboctahedron (see reference [52, page 203 and Figure 259 on page 205] from the resource list in Section B). The same approach as in 1996, Problem 21 shows that the truncated cube in the problem above gives rise to a 'semi-regular tiling' of three-dimensional space by cuboctahedra and regular octahedra, with four cuboctahedra and two octahedra (apex-to-apex) at each vertex.

23 E The only actual values of the function $f(x, y)$ which are given are those when $x = y$: namely $f(x, x) = x$. So you have to use the other rules to evaluate $f(19, 91)$ in terms of some $f(x, x)$: i.e. you have to work to reduce the difference between $x = 19$ and $y = 91$.

Solutions to the National Mathematics Contest problems

The key relation is:
$$f(x, x+y) = \frac{x+y}{2x+y} \cdot f(x,y) \quad (*)$$

$\therefore f(19, 91) = \frac{91}{110} \cdot f(19, 72)$ (by (*) with $x = 19, y = 72$)
$= \frac{91}{110} \times \frac{72}{91} \cdot f(19, 53)$
$= \frac{91}{110} \times \frac{72}{91} \times \frac{53}{72} \cdot f(19, 34)$
$= \frac{91}{110} \times \frac{72}{91} \times \frac{53}{72} \times \frac{34}{53} \cdot f(19, 15)$
$= \frac{91}{110} \times \frac{72}{91} \times \frac{53}{72} \times \frac{34}{53} \cdot f(15, 19)$ (since $f(x,y) = f(y,x)$)
$= \frac{91}{110} \times \frac{72}{91} \times \frac{53}{72} \times \frac{34}{53} \times \frac{19}{34} \cdot f(15, 4)$
$= \frac{91}{110} \times \frac{72}{91} \times \frac{53}{72} \times \frac{34}{53} \times \frac{19}{34} \cdot f(4, 15)$
$= \frac{91}{110} \times \frac{72}{91} \times \frac{53}{72} \times \frac{34}{53} \times \frac{19}{34} \times \frac{15}{19} \cdot f(4, 11)$
$= \frac{91}{110} \times \frac{72}{91} \times \frac{53}{72} \times \frac{34}{53} \times \frac{19}{34} \times \frac{15}{19} \times \frac{11}{15} \cdot f(4, 7)$
$= \frac{91}{110} \times \frac{72}{91} \times \frac{53}{72} \times \frac{34}{53} \times \frac{19}{34} \times \frac{15}{19} \times \frac{11}{15} \times \frac{7}{11} \cdot f(4, 3)$
$= \frac{91}{110} \times \frac{72}{91} \times \frac{53}{72} \times \frac{34}{53} \times \frac{19}{34} \times \frac{15}{19} \times \frac{11}{15} \times \frac{7}{11} \cdot f(3, 4)$
$= \frac{91}{110} \times \frac{72}{91} \times \frac{53}{72} \times \frac{34}{53} \times \frac{19}{34} \times \frac{15}{19} \times \frac{11}{15} \times \frac{7}{11} \times \frac{4}{7} \cdot f(3, 1)$
$= \frac{91}{110} \times \frac{72}{91} \times \frac{53}{72} \times \frac{34}{53} \times \frac{19}{34} \times \frac{15}{19} \times \frac{11}{15} \times \frac{7}{11} \times \frac{4}{7} \cdot f(1, 3)$
$= \frac{91}{110} \times \frac{72}{91} \times \frac{53}{72} \times \frac{34}{53} \times \frac{19}{34} \times \frac{15}{19} \times \frac{11}{15} \times \frac{7}{11} \times \frac{4}{7} \times \frac{3}{4} \cdot f(1, 2)$
$= \frac{91}{110} \times \frac{72}{91} \times \frac{53}{72} \times \frac{34}{53} \times \frac{19}{34} \times \frac{15}{19} \times \frac{11}{15} \times \frac{7}{11} \times \frac{4}{7} \times \frac{3}{4} \times \frac{2}{3} \cdot f(1, 1)$
$= \frac{91}{110} \times \frac{72}{91} \times \frac{53}{72} \times \frac{34}{53} \times \frac{19}{34} \times \frac{15}{19} \times \frac{11}{15} \times \frac{7}{11} \times \frac{4}{7} \times \frac{3}{4} \times \frac{2}{3} \times 1$
$= \frac{2}{110} = \frac{1}{55}$

Alternatively The fact that $f(19, 91)$ turns out to be equal to $\frac{2}{19+91}$ would seem to suggest that, when $x = 19$ and $y = 91$, $f(x, y) = \frac{2}{x+y}$, and that there should therefore be an easier solution.
However, in an exam it is often best to take the direct route – as above – and to think about things more deeply afterwards!

You are told that $f(n, n) = n$, which contradicts the simple-minded guess $f(x, y) = \frac{2}{x+y}$ (since when $n \geq 2$, $n \neq \frac{1}{n} = \frac{2}{n+n}$).

However, simple calculations using (*) show:
$$f(0, n) = f(n, 0) = \frac{n}{2n} \cdot f(n, n) = 2n$$

$$f(1, n) = \frac{n}{n+1} \cdot f(1, n-1) = \frac{n}{n+1} \cdot \frac{n-1}{n} \cdot f(1, n-2) = \cdots = \frac{2}{n+1}$$

138

Similar calculations (and proof by induction) show that:
$$f(2, 2n-1) = \frac{2}{2n+1}, \quad f(2, 2n) = 4 \cdot \frac{2}{2n+2}$$
This may be enough to suggest the improved conjecture:
$$f(m, n) = (\text{hcf}(m, n))^2 \cdot \frac{2}{m+n}$$
Once you have guessed this general formula, it is relatively easy to prove that it is correct (by induction on $m + n$, using (*) and the fact that $\text{hcf}(m, n) = \text{hcf}(m, n - m)$).

24 C Suppose $N^2 - 1991$ is a perfect square.
$\therefore N^2 - 1991 = M^2$ with $N > M > 0$
$\therefore N^2 - M^2 = 1991$
$\therefore (N - M)(N + M) = 1991 = 11 \times 181$ (prime factorisation)

Now $0 < N - M < N + M$ (since $N > M > 0$), so there are just two possibilities:
(a) $N - M = 1$ and $N + M = 1991$, so $2N = 1 + 1991$, $N = 996$;
(b) $N - M = 11$ and $N + M = 181$, so $2N = 11 + 181$, $N = 96$.

25 A $\angle XPY = \angle YPZ = \angle ZPX = 120°$, and $\cos 120° = -\frac{1}{2}$, $\sin 120° = \frac{\sqrt{3}}{2}$

Using the cosine rule in $\triangle XPY$, $\triangle YPZ$, and $\triangle ZPX$:
$3^2 = l^2 + m^2 + lm$
$4^2 = m^2 + n^2 + mn$
$5^2 = n^2 + l^2 + nl$
$\therefore 3^2 + 4^2 + 5^2 = 2(l^2 + m^2 + n^2) + (lm + mn + nl)$

Equating areas:
$\text{area}(\triangle XYZ) = \frac{1}{2}(3 \times 4) = 6$
$= \text{area}(\triangle XPY) + \text{area}(\triangle YPZ) + \text{area}(\triangle ZPX)$
$= \frac{1}{2}lm \sin 120° + \frac{1}{2}mn \sin 120° + \frac{1}{2}ml \sin 120°$
$= \frac{\sqrt{3}}{4}(lm + mn + nl)$

$\therefore 8\sqrt{3} = lm + mn + nl$
$\therefore 2(l^2 + m^2 + n^2) = 50 - 8\sqrt{3}$

1990

1 B I am holding the picture and rotate it so that the side you can now see turns to face me.

Since my right hand is at the top and my left hand is at the bottom, the top edge rotates to become the edge on *my* right.

2 D Trial and error may suggest the solution $x = 5$ and $y = 3$ (since $5^3 + 3^3 = 125 + 27 = 152$).

> However, in mathematics calculation is always better than guessing. For example, when you are asked to solve simultaneous equations – as in this problem – it is often unclear how many different solutions to expect.

So let the two unknown integers be m and n.
$\therefore m + n = 8$ and $m^3 + n^3 = 152$
$\therefore n = 8 - m$
$\therefore 152 = m^3 + n^3 = m^3 + (8-m)^3$
$\quad = m^3 + (8^3 - 3 \times 8^2 \times m + 3 \times 8 \times m^2 - m^3)$
$\therefore 24m^2 - 192m + 360 = 0$
$\therefore m^2 - 8m + 15 = 0$
$\therefore (m-3)(m-5) = 0$
$\therefore m = 3$ (so $n = 5$), or $m = 5$ (so $n = 3$)

Alternatively You are only asked to find the product mn, so there is no need to calculate m and n separately.
$m^3 + n^3 = (m+n)(m^2 - mn + n^2)$
$\therefore m^2 - mn + n^2 = \dfrac{m^3 + n^3}{m+n} = \dfrac{152}{8} = 19$
$\therefore 8^2 = (m+n)^2 = m^2 + 2mn + n^2$
$\quad = (m^2 - mn + n^2) + 3mn$
$\quad = 19 + 3mn$
$\therefore mn = 15$

> Reference [42] in the resource list in Section B contains lots of work which shows how simple results in mathematics often emerge only when one is able to manipulate algebraic expressions sufficiently freely to be able to see easily such links as that between $m^2 - mn + n^2$, $(m+n)^2$ and $3mn$.
>
> There is an interesting discussion of the need for fluency in handling algebraic expressions in reference [32, Chapter 4, pages 82–102].

3 D The question is a little strange. However, you clearly have to choose an option (if there is one) in which the answer is *self-describing*. That is, you have to look for an option in which the given number word describes the number of letters in itself.

> For a glimpse of some of the interesting mathematics related to 'self-reference', see references [51, Chapter 3] and [23] in the resource list in Section B.

4 C $0.\dot{3} = \frac{1}{3}$; $\frac{1}{3} \times \frac{1}{3} = \frac{1}{9}$; $\frac{1}{9} = 0.\dot{1}$.

> For a careful analysis of the meaning of infinite decimals, the link between rational numbers and recurring decimals, and the arithmetic of infinite decimals, see [37, pages 70–136] in the list of resources in Section B.

5 A $\angle DAP = 60°$ ($\triangle ADP$ is equilateral)
$\therefore \angle PAB = 30°$
$AP = AD$ ($\triangle ADP$ is equilateral)
$ = AB$ (sides of the square $ABCD$)
$\therefore \triangle APB$ is isosceles
$\therefore \angle ABP = \frac{1}{2}(180° - \angle PAB)$
$ = 75°$
$\therefore \angle PBC = \angle ABC - \angle ABP = 90° - 75°$

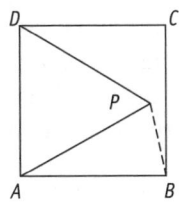

6 E Suppose a golden dollr has weight x grams, a silver nickl has weight y grams, and a silver dim has weight z grams.
$\therefore 7x = 13y$ and $7z = 13x$
$\therefore 100x = 65x + 35x$
$ = 5 \times (13x) + 5 \times (7x)$
$ = 5 \times 7z + 5 \times 13y = 35z + 65y$

> The above produces one solution to $100x = ay + bz$ with $a + b = 100$. This leaves unanswered (even unasked!) the question as to why – or whether – the answer is unique.

Suppose $100x = ay + bz$, with $a, b \geq 0$.

(a) Is it necessarily true that $a + b = 100$?
(b) Is $a = 65$, $b = 35$ in fact the only solution?

The answer to both questions is Yes.

Suppose $ay + bz = 100x = 65y + 35z$, for some integers $a, b \geq 0$.
$\therefore (65 - a)y = (b - 35)z$
$\therefore \dfrac{b - 35}{65 - a} = \dfrac{y}{z}$

Solutions to the National Mathematics Contest problems

From the question you know that $7x = 13y$ and $7z = 13x$.
∴ $13 \times 7x = 169y$ and $7 \times 13x = 49z$
∴ $\dfrac{y}{z} = \dfrac{49}{169}$
∴ $169(b - 35) = 49(65 - a)$
∴ 169 divides $65 - a$ and 49 divides $b - 35$ (since hcf(169, 49) = 1)
∴ Either:

(a) $65 - a = b - 35 = 0$, giving the solution found above; or
(b) $65 - a = 169k$ for some integer $k \ne 0$.

∴ $k \le -1$ (since a counts the number of silver nickls used, so $a \ge 0$)
∴ $b - 35 = 49k \le -49$, contradicting $b \ge 0$

7 A Take a 2D 'horizontal' cross-section of the round hole and the square peg.
If the hole has radius r, then the square peg has cross-section of side $r\sqrt{2}$.

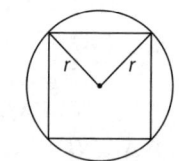

∴ Fraction of hole occupied by peg = $\dfrac{\text{area(square)}}{\text{area(circle)}}$

$= \dfrac{(r\sqrt{2})^2}{\pi r^2} = \dfrac{2}{\pi}$

8 C Let the four numbers be w, x, y, z in order.
∴ $\dfrac{w+x}{2} = 7, \dfrac{x+y}{2} = 2.3, \dfrac{y+z}{2} = 8.4$

∴ $\dfrac{w+z}{2} = \dfrac{w+x}{2} - \dfrac{x+y}{2} + \dfrac{y+z}{2}$
$= 7 - 2.3 + 8.4$

9 C Suppose the school enters N pupils.
∴ Amount paid $= 29 \times N$
$= 35 \times 8 + 25 \times (N - 8)$
∴ $4N = 35 \times 8 - 25 \times 8 = 10 \times 8$

10 D Suppose that the thickness of all coins is t.
∴ volume(Arkenstone) : volume(Baggins) $= \pi a^2 t : \pi b^2 t$
$= a^2 : b^2$

∴ $\dfrac{a^2}{b^2} = 2$

∴ $\dfrac{b}{a} = \dfrac{1}{\sqrt{2}} = \dfrac{\sqrt{2}}{2} \approx \dfrac{1.414}{2} = 0.707$

142

11 D In the left-hand column, S ≠ M
∴ M = S + 1   (since the largest possible carry is 1)
∴ S < S + 1 = M
∴ S < M + H

```
  S I X T H
+   F O R M
-----------
  M A T H S
```

So the only way the right-hand column can make sense is if M + H = S + 10.
∴ S + 10 = M + H
         = (S + 1) + H
         = S + (1 + H)
∴ 1 + H = 10

For more 'word sums', see reference [14, Chapter 8] in the resource list in Section B.

12 B ∠BID = ∠BAI + ∠ABI   (external angle of △ABI)
∠ABC = 135° = ∠HAB   (internal angle of regular octagon)
△ABH is isosceles   (since AB = AH)
∴ ∠ABI = ∠ABH = $\frac{1}{2}$(180° − ∠HAB) = $22\frac{1}{2}°$

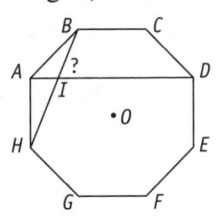

AD is parallel to BC.
∴ ∠BAD + ∠ABC = 180°
∴ ∠BAD = 180° − 135° = 45°
∴ ∠BID = ∠BAD + ∠ABI = 45° + $22\frac{1}{2}°$ = $67\frac{1}{2}°$

Alternatively Inscribe the regular octagon ABCDEFGH in a circle with centre O.
∴ ∠AOH = ∠BOC = $\frac{1}{8}$ × 360° = 45°
∴ ∠BOD = 2 × 45° = 90°
∴ ∠ABI = ∠ABH = $\frac{1}{2}$∠AOH = $22\frac{1}{2}°$
since the angle ∠ABH subtended by the chord AH at the point B on the circumference of the circle is equal to one half of the angle ∠AOH subtended by the same chord at the centre O.

∠BAI = ∠BAD = $\frac{1}{2}$∠BOD = 45°
since the angle ∠BAD subtended by the chord BD at the point D on the circumference is equal to one half of the angle ∠BOD subtended by BD at the centre O.
∴ ∠BID = ∠BAI + ∠ABI = 45° + $22\frac{1}{2}°$

Solutions to the National Mathematics Contest problems

13 A Decimal for $\frac{1}{7} = 0.\dot{1}4285\dot{7}$

$\frac{1}{7000} = \frac{1}{7} \times \frac{1}{1000}$

∴ Decimal for $\frac{1}{7000} = \frac{1}{1000} \times (0.\dot{1}4285\dot{7})$
$= 0.000\,\dot{1}4285\dot{7}$.

$7000 = 6 \times 1166 + 4 = 3 + 6 \times 1166 + 1$

Hence the 7000th decimal place is reached after passing the three initial 0s, 1166 complete repeating blocks of length 6, and then taking the very next digit – which must be the first digit of the next repeating block.

> For more detail about the link between rationals (like $\frac{1}{7}$) and recurring decimals, see references [28, Chapter II, Sections 1,2], [34, Chapter 12], [35, Chapter 13], [37, Chapters II.8 and II.9] and [46, Chapter 2] in the list of resources in Section B.
>
> The solution to Problem 13 is based on calculating the 7000th decimal place by working modulo 6 (since there are six digits in each block '142857'). For more about how to calculate modulo n see [13, Part I, Section 4.5], [28, Section 2 of the Supplement to Chapter I] and [49].

14 D To show in general that a statement is false, it is enough to find a single exception (or *counterexample*).

$1 + 2 + 3 = 6$ and $1 + 2 + 3 + 4 = 10$ are both even.
And although $1 + 2 + 3 + 4 + 5 = 15$ is odd, $2 + 3 + 4 + 5 + 6 = 20$ is even.
∴ The statement 'the sum of any N consecutive digits is always odd' is *not true* when $N = 3, 4$ or 5.

Let $N = 6$. The sum of any six consecutive integers can be written as:
$k + (k + 1) + (k + 2) + (k + 3) + (k + 4) + (k + 5)$
$= 6k + (1 + 2 + 3 + 4 + 5)$
$= 6k + 15$

which is always odd (since $6k = 2 \times (3k)$ is even, and 15 is odd).

15 B The only obvious strategy is to find the point of intersection P of two of the lines, and then to see whether P lies on the other lines.

To see where the first two lines $x + y = 5$ and $x = 2y + 1$ intersect, substitute $x = 2y + 1$ in the equation $x + y = 5$.
∴ $x + y = (2y + 1) + y = 5$
∴ $3y = 4$
∴ $y = \frac{4}{3}$, $x = \frac{11}{3}$

The point $P = (\frac{11}{3}, \frac{4}{3})$ does not satisfy $y = x - 2$ or $x = 3y - 1$.
∴ The odd line out is either **A** or **B**.

Therefore the point of intersection 'which lies on the other four lines' is the point Q where lines **C** and **D** meet:
$x = 3y - 1$ and $y = x - 2$
∴ $x = 3(x - 2) - 1$
∴ $2x = 7$
∴ $x = \frac{7}{2}, y = \frac{3}{2}$

It is easy to check that the point $Q = (\frac{7}{2}, \frac{3}{2})$ also lies on the line $x + y = 5$ (and on the line $y = 3x - 9$) but not on the line $x = 2y + 1$.

16 A Suppose $\boxed{\text{A B}}\,\boxed{\text{C A}}\,\boxed{\text{B C}}$ is any arrangement of the required kind.

If AB CA BC represented a number rather than a time, there would be 10 choices for each of the first three digits, and hence $10 \times 10 \times 10$ possible numbers. Counting possible times uses the same idea, but is more delicate.

The first two digits AB record the hours $00, 01, 02, \ldots, 23$.
The middle two digits CA record the minutes $00, 01, 02, \ldots, 59$.
The last two digits BC record the seconds $00, 01, 02, \ldots, 59$.

∴ The first digit A can be either a 0, or a 1, or a 2;
the third digit C can be 0, or 1, or 2, or 3, or 4, or 5;
the fifth digit B can be 0, or 1, or 2, or 3, or 4, or 5.

If the first digit $A = 0$ or 1, then the second digit B can take any value from 0 to 9; if $A = 2$, then B can only take values from 0 to 3.

(a) Suppose first that $A = 0$ or 1 (**two** choices).
∴ Second digit B = fifth digit B,
and fifth digit B can only take values 0–5 (**six** choices).
Also
sixth digit C = third digit C,
and third digit C can only take the values 0–5 (**six** choices).
Every such arrangement corresponds to a real time, so there are $2 \times 6 \times 6 = 72$ such times AB CA BC with $A = 0$ or 1.

(b) Now suppose that $A = 2$. Then the six conceivable choices 0–5 for the fifth digit B are constrained by the fact that the second digit B can only take the four values 0–3. Hence there are $1 \times 4 \times 6 = 24$ such times AB CA BC with $A = 2$.

Solutions to the National Mathematics Contest problems

17 C It is enough to notice that $f(5) = 2^5 = 32$.
∴ $f(f(5)) = f(32) = 2^{32} = 2^{4\times 8} = (2^4)^8 = 16^8$

Alternatively Check that the others all fail.
(a) $16^8 = (2^4)^8 = 2^{4\times 8} = 2^{32} = f(32)$. Hence neither **A** nor **B** is equal to 16^8.
(b) $f(3) = 2^3 = 8$, so $f(f(3)) = f(8) = 2^8 = 256$, so **D** is not equal to 16^8.
(c) $f(f(f(f(3)))) = f(f(2^8)) = f(f(256)) = f(2^{256}) = 2^{2^{256}} = (2^2)^{2^{254}} = 16^{2^{254}} > 16^8$, so **E** is not equal to 16^8.

18 C First count how many integers ⩽1990 have 3 as a factor.

1989 is the largest such multiple of 3, so there are exactly $\dfrac{1989}{3} = 663$ such multiples of 3.

Next count how many integers ⩽1990 have 5 as a factor.

1990 is clearly a multiple of 5, so there are exactly $\dfrac{1990}{5} = 398$ such multiples of 5.

Some integers are counted in both these sets – namely those integers which are multiples of both 3 and 5; i.e. those integers ⩽1990 which are multiples of 15. 1980 is the largest such multiple of 15, so there are exactly $\dfrac{1980}{15} = 132$ such multiples of 15.

∴ Number of integers ⩽1990 which have either 3 or 5 as a factor $\Big\} = 663 + 398 - 132 = 929$

∴ Number of integers ⩽1990 which do *not* have either 3 or 5 as a factor $\Big\} = 1990 - 929 = 1061$

In general, if there are M objects with property $\mathcal{A}$, N objects with property $\mathcal{B}$, and K objects having both properties (which are therefore included among the M objects with property $\mathcal{A}$ and among the N objects with property $\mathcal{B}$), then:

Total number of objects with either property $= M + N - K$

> This problem shows how important it is, when setting multiple-choice questions, to choose the numbers in the question and the five options with care. When solving unfamiliar problems, it is all too easy to mistake what should be an intermediate result as the final answer. In this instance, candidates who worked out '663 + 398 = 1061' and who noticed that this was one of the options, could easily think they had found the answer – and would get the available marks without doing the correct calculation!

The method of counting the number of objects which satisfy condition $\mathcal{A}$ or condition $\mathcal{B}$ by first adding the numbers for $\mathcal{A}$ and $\mathcal{B}$ (thereby counting those that satisfy *both* $\mathcal{A}$ and $\mathcal{B}$ *twice*) and then subtracting the number that satisfy both $\mathcal{A}$ and $\mathcal{B}$, is called the 'principle of inclusion/exclusion'. For more on this, see reference [47, Chapter 5] in the list of resources in Section B.

19 E *AE* and *BD* are altitudes, so $\angle AEB = \angle AEC = 90° = \angle BDC$
$\triangle ABE$ and $\triangle ACE$ are congruent – by the RHS congruence criterion, since:

$AB = AC$ (given)
AE is common
$\angle AEB = \angle AEC = 90°$ (given)

$\therefore BE = CE$ and $\angle CAE = \angle BAE = \theta$
$\therefore \angle ACE = 90° - \theta$ (since the angles of $\triangle ACE$ sum to 180°)
$\therefore \angle CBD = \theta$ (since the angles of $\triangle BCD$ sum to 180°)
$\therefore$ Triangles *ACE* and *BPE* are similar.

$\therefore \dfrac{PE}{BE} = \dfrac{CE}{AE}$

$\therefore \dfrac{PE}{AE} = \dfrac{PE}{BE} \times \dfrac{CE}{AE}$ (since $BE = CE$)

$\qquad = \tan\theta \times \tan\theta$

Alternatively Clearly $\tan\theta = BE/AE$. From $\angle CBD = \theta$, it follows that $\tan\theta = PE/BE$. Hence $PE/AE = \tan^2\theta$.

20 B You have to find all possible solutions of the equation:
$n^2 - m^2 = 60$, with $0 < m < n$
i.e. $(n-m)(n+m) = 2^2 \times 3 \times 5$

Now $n - m < n + m$
$\therefore 0 < n - m < \sqrt{60} < 8$

We consider each possible value of $n - m$ in turn:

(a) $n - m = 1$, $n + m = 60$, so $n = 61/2$ which is not an integer;
(b) $n - m = 2$, $n + m = 30$, so $n = \mathbf{16}$;
(c) $n - m = 3$, $n + m = 20$, so $n = 23/2$, which is not an integer;
(d) $n - m = 4$, $n + m = 15$, so $n = 19/2$, which is not an integer;
(e) $n - m = 5$, $n + m = 12$, so $n = 17/2$, which is not an integer;
(f) $n - m = 6$, $n + m = 10$, so $n = \mathbf{8}$.

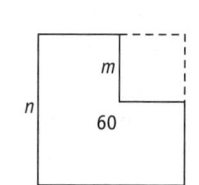

Solutions to the National Mathematics Contest problems

Alternatively One way to avoid considering cases which turn out to be impossible is to notice that the two factors $n - m$ and $n + m$ differ by $2m$, which is even. So these two factors have to be *both even or both odd*, i.e. they must have the same *parity*.

> The solution to Problem 20 highlights the difference between solving for *real* unknowns (where one should always take everything to one side to obtain an equation 'expression = 0'; and then factorise) and solving for *integer* unknowns (where it can be a good move to arrange the equation in the form 'expression = n', where n has very few factorisations, since a factorisation of the expression on the LHS then leaves very few possibilities. See reference [13, pages 8–9] in the resource list in Section B.

21 B $\dfrac{AB}{OA} = \dfrac{PQ}{OP}$ and $\dfrac{AB}{OB} = \dfrac{PQ}{OQ}$

$\therefore \dfrac{OA}{OP} = \dfrac{AB}{PQ} = \dfrac{OB}{OQ}$

$\therefore \dfrac{AB}{PQ} = \sqrt{\dfrac{OA}{OP} \times \dfrac{OB}{OQ}} = \sqrt{\dfrac{OA}{OQ} \times \dfrac{QB}{OP}} \times = \sqrt{3 \times 2}$

22 D Let the original pastry circle have centre O, radius $2R$ and hence area $4\pi R^2$.

Then each of the two medium-sized circles has diameter $2R$, so their combined area is $2 \times \pi R^2$.

It remains to calculate the radius r, and hence the area of each of the two small circles.

Let C be the centre of one of the medium-sized circles, D the centre of one of the small circles, and let OD meet the large circle at E.
Then in the right-angled triangle DOC:
$\quad OC = R$, $OD = 2R - r$ (since $OE = 2R$ and $DE = r$), and $CD = R + r$
$\therefore R^2 + (2R - r)^2 = (R + r)^2$
$\therefore 4R^2 = 6Rr$
$\therefore 2R = 3r$ (since $R \neq 0$)
$\therefore$ Area of pastry left unused $= 4\pi R^2 - (2\pi R^2 + \pi r^2)$
$\qquad\qquad\qquad\qquad\qquad\quad = 4\pi R^2 - (2\pi R^2 + 2\pi(\tfrac{2}{3}R)^2) = \tfrac{10}{9}\pi R^2$

$\therefore$ Fraction of pastry left unused $= \dfrac{\tfrac{10}{9}}{4} = \tfrac{10}{36} = \tfrac{5}{18}$

148

23 A Since a is not an exact multiple of x, the job requires $\left[\dfrac{a}{x}\right]$ whole-width strips (each of length b), and an additional part-width strip (also of length b).

24 E The only obvious approach is to try to deduce each of the given options from the given equation $b^3 = b + 1$.

Let b satisfy the given equation $b^3 = b + 1$.
Observe first that $b \ne 0$ (since $0 \ne 0 + 1$).

Multiply both sides by b.
$\therefore b^4 = b^2 + b$ (so **A** is true)
$ = b^2 + (b^3 - 1)$ (so **C** is true)
$\therefore b^4 + b^3 = [b^2 + (b^3 - 1)] + b^3$
$ = 2b^3 + b^2 - 1$
$ = 2(b + 1) + b^2 - 1$
$ = b^2 + 2b + 1$
$ \ne b^2 + 1$ (since $b \ne 0$)

Hence **E** is false.
$b^4 = b^2 + b$ (by **A**)
$\therefore b^5 = b^3 + b^2$
$ = (b + 1) + b^2$
$ = (b^2 + b) + 1$
$ = b^4 + 1$ (so **B** is true)

$(b - 1)(b^2 + b + 1) = b^3 - 1 = b = (b - 1) + 1$
$\therefore b^2 + b + 1 = \dfrac{b^3 - 1}{b - 1} = \dfrac{b - 1}{b - 1} + \dfrac{1}{b - 1} = 1 + \dfrac{1}{b - 1}$ (so **D** is true)

> You should avoid the temptation to test particular values without thinking very carefully. For example, the fact that $b = 1$ satisfies **E**, but not the original equation $b^3 = b + 1$, does *not* tell you that **E** is false. To see why not, suppose you were given a sixth option:
> **F**: $b^3(b - 1) = (b + 1)(b - 1)$
> Then **F** would be true, even though it is satisfied by $b = 1$.

Solutions to the National Mathematics Contest problems

25 E x men working x hours a day for x days dig x metres of tunnel.
∴ 1 man working x hours a day for x days digs 1 metre of tunnel.
∴ 1 man working 1 hour a day for x days digs $\dfrac{1}{x}$ metres of tunnel.
∴ 1 man working 1 hour a day for 1 day digs $\dfrac{1}{x^2}$ metres of tunnel.
∴ y men working 1 hour a day for 1 day dig $\dfrac{y}{x^2}$ metres of tunnel.
∴ y men working y hours a day for 1 day dig $\dfrac{y^2}{x^2}$ metres of tunnel.
∴ y men working y hours a day for y days dig $\dfrac{y^3}{x^2}$ metres of tunnel.

Alternatively
x men working x hours a day for x days dig x metres.
∴ $y = \dfrac{y}{x} \cdot x$ men working $y = \dfrac{y}{x} \cdot x$ hours a day for $y = \dfrac{y}{x} \cdot x$ days
dig $\left(\dfrac{y}{x}\right)^3 \cdot x$ metres.

26 C It is tempting to try to guess the answer by trying a few conveniently chosen values of x and y. For example:
If $x = y = 1$, then $S = 2$ and $P = 1$, so $S - P = 1$.
If $x = 0$ and $y = 1$, then $S = 1$ and $P = 0$, so $S - P = 1$.
If $x = -1$ and $y = 1$, then $S = 0$ and $P = -1$, so $S - P = 1$.
If $x = -3$ and $y = 1$, then $S = -2$ and $P = -3$, so $S - P = 1$.

There is nothing wrong with doing this as long as you realise:
(a) that the results will be dependent on the values you choose, so may be misleading (if $x = 0$ and $y = 2$, then $S - P = $ __!);
(b) the only mathematical way to solve a mathematical problem is to calculate, rather than to guess.

In general:
$S - P = (x + y) - xy$
$\qquad = -(xy - x - y + 1) + 1$
$\qquad = -(x - 1)(y - 1) + 1$
Now $x - 1 \leq 0$ (since $x \leq 1$) and $y - 1 \geq 0$ (since $y \geq 1$)
∴ $(x - 1)(y - 1) \leq 0$
∴ $-(x - 1)(y - 1) \geq 0$
∴ $-(x - 1)(y - 1) + 1 \geq 1$

27 E Let $p = \frac{3}{5}$ and $q = 1 - p = \frac{2}{5}$.

Steffi wins as soon as she is two points ahead.

For this to happen after N points have been played since arriving at deuce, N must equal $2k + 2$ for some $k \geq 0$ (since if Boris wins k points, Steffi must win $k + 2$ points).

Moreover, the score must then return to deuce after two points, after four points, ..., after $2k$ points, with Steffi winning the final two points.

There are exactly two ways to get from each deuce to the next deuce (namely 'Boris wins a point, then Steffi wins one' or 'Steffi wins a point, then Boris wins one'); hence there are exactly 2^k such sequences.

∴ Probability(Steffi wins from deuce after $2k + 2$ points)
$$= 2^k \times p^{k+2} \times q^k$$

∴ Probability(Steffi wins from deuce)
$$= p^2 + 2p^3q + 2^2p^4q^2 + 2^4p^5q^3 + \ldots$$
$$= \frac{p^2}{1 - 2pq} \quad \text{(since } -1 < 2pq < 1\text{)}$$
$$= \frac{(\frac{3}{5})^2}{1 - 2 \cdot (\frac{3}{5}) \cdot (\frac{2}{5})} = \frac{9}{13}$$

Alternatively Let x be the probability that Steffi wins from deuce. After two points, Steffi may have won (with probability $\frac{9}{25}$) or Boris may have won (with probability $\frac{4}{25}$).
If neither of these occurs, then they will be back at deuce again (with probability $\frac{12}{25}$), so the probability that Steffi wins *from here* is x.

∴ x = probability that Steffi wins from deuce
  = probability(Steffi wins immediately, i.e. after just two points)
  + probability(game returns to deuce after two points, and Steffi wins from there)
$= \frac{9}{25} + \frac{12}{25}x$

For a more realistic approach to modelling a tennis match, see reference [25, Chapter 2] in the list of resources in Section B.

28 B The turtle traces out the first five edges AB, BC, CD, DE, EF of a regular 18-gon $ABCDEFG\ldots PQR$.

Let Z be the circumcentre of this regular 18-gon, and let $r = ZA$ be the circumradius.

Then each side such as AB subtends an angle $\frac{360°}{18} = 20°$ at the centre Z.

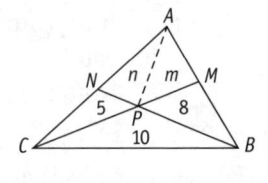

Solutions to the National Mathematics Contest problems

Let the perpendicular from Z to AB meet AB at the point Y.
$\therefore \angle AZY = 10°$
$\therefore \sin 10° = \dfrac{YB}{ZB} = \dfrac{5}{r}$
$\therefore r = \dfrac{5}{\sin 10°}$

Let the perpendicular from Z to AF meet AF at the point X.
$\therefore \angle AZF = 5 \times 20° = 100°$
$\therefore \angle AZX = 50°$
$\therefore \sin 50° = \dfrac{AX}{ZA} = \dfrac{AX}{r}$
$\therefore AF = 2 \times AX = 2 \times r \sin 50° = \dfrac{10 \sin 50°}{\sin 10°}$

29 E $a = \dfrac{xy}{x+y}$, $b = \dfrac{yz}{y+z}$, $c = \dfrac{zx}{z+x}$, with $a, b, c \neq 0$

$\therefore \dfrac{1}{a} = \dfrac{x+y}{xy} = \dfrac{1}{y} + \dfrac{1}{x}$, and similarly $\dfrac{1}{b} = \dfrac{1}{z} + \dfrac{1}{y}$, $\dfrac{1}{c} = \dfrac{1}{x} + \dfrac{1}{z}$

$\therefore \dfrac{1}{a} + \dfrac{1}{c} - \dfrac{1}{b} = \dfrac{2}{x}$

$\therefore \dfrac{bc + ab - ac}{abc} = \dfrac{2}{x}$

$\therefore x = \dfrac{2abc}{ab + bc - ac}$

30 A Let the triangle be ABC, and let CM and BN cross at the point P.
Join AP and let triangles AMP, ANP have areas m and n respectively.
$\therefore m + n = x$

$\dfrac{5+n}{23+x} = \dfrac{\text{area}(APC)}{\text{area}(ABC)} = \dfrac{PN}{BN}$
$\qquad\qquad = \dfrac{\text{area}(PNC)}{\text{area}(BNC)}$
$\qquad\qquad = \dfrac{5}{15} = \dfrac{1}{3}$

$\dfrac{8+m}{23+x} = \dfrac{\text{area}(APB)}{\text{area}(ACB)} = \dfrac{PM}{CM}$
$\qquad\qquad = \dfrac{\text{area}(PMB)}{\text{area}(CMB)}$
$\qquad\qquad = \dfrac{8}{18} = \dfrac{4}{9}$

∴ $3(5 + n) = 23 + x = 23 + m + n$
and $9(8 + m) = 4(23 + m + n)$
∴ $m = 12, n = 10$

Alternatively The same approach yields the equations:
$$\frac{n}{5} = \frac{x+8}{5+10} \text{ and } \frac{m}{8} = \frac{x+5}{8+10}$$
∴ $x = n + m = 5\left(\frac{x+8}{5+10}\right) + 8\left(\frac{x+5}{8+10}\right)$
∴ $x = 22$

1989

1 D Right-hand column sum = $8 + 9 + 4 = 21$
Let the entry in the centre square be x.
∴ Middle row sum = $5 + x + 9 = 14 + x = 21$
∴ $x = 7$
∴ Entry in bottom left square = $21 - (8 + 7) = 6$
∴ Bottom row sum = $6 + n + 4 = 21$
∴ $n = 11$

> For more on magic squares see reference [29, Chapter VII] or [33, Chapter 14] in the list of resources given in Section B.

2 E $6 = 5 + 1$
$= 4 + 2 = 4 + 1 + 1$
$= 3 + 3 = 3 + 2 + 1 = 3 + 1 + 1 + 1$
$= 2 + 2 + 2 = 2 + 2 + 1 + 1 = 2 + 1 + 1 + 1 + 1$
$= 1 + 1 + 1 + 1 + 1 + 1$

> These are called the eleven 'partitions of 6'. The number of partitions of n is denoted by $p(n)$: thus $p(6) = 11$. For more about partitions, see references [47, Chapter 6] and [36, pages 94–96] in the list of resources in Section B.

3 A Total length of bottle top plus brush = $y + z$
∴ Distance from table top to brush tip = $x - (y + z)$

Solutions to the National Mathematics Contest problems

4 D A If $\triangle ABC$ is equilateral, let L, M, N be the mid-points of AB, BC, CA respectively.
Then $LM = \frac{1}{2}AC = \frac{1}{2}BA = \frac{1}{2}BC$, so $LM = BL = BM$.
Similarly, $MN = CM = CN$ and $NL = AN = AL$.
∴ LMN, ALN, BML, CNM are all equilateral triangles.
Hence **A** is true.

B Let ABC be an isosceles triangle with $AB = AC$.
Let the perpendicular from the apex A to the base BC meet BC at M.
Then in triangles AMB and AMC: $AB = AC$ (given),
$\angle AMB = \angle AMC = 90°$ (by construction) and AM is common.
∴ $\triangle AMB$ and $\triangle AMC$ are congruent (by the RHS congruence criterion).
Hence **B** is true.

Statements **C**, **D** and **E** all depend on the same configuration.
Let $ABCD$ be any parallelogram with diagonals AC and BD crossing at O.
∴ $\angle BAC = \angle DCA$ (alternate angles)
$\angle BCA = \angle DAC$ (alternate angles)
and $AC = CA$
∴ $\triangle ABC$ and $\triangle CDA$ are congruent (by the ASA congruence criterion)
∴ $AB = CD$, $\angle BAO = \angle DCO$ and $\angle ABO = \angle CDO$ (alternate angles)
∴ $\triangle ABO$ and $\triangle CDO$ are congruent (by the ASA congruence criterion)

Similarly, $\triangle ADO$ and $\triangle CBO$ are congruent.

However, $\triangle ABO$ and $\triangle ADO$ are congruent only if $AB = AD$, i.e. only when $ABCD$ is a rhombus.
Hence **C** and **E** are both true (since a square is a special rhombus), but **D** is false.

5 A 110, 112, 114, 116, 118, 120 are all even.
$111 = 3 \times 37$
113 is prime (you only need to check for prime divisors $p \leqslant \sqrt{113} < 11$: dividing by $p = 2$ leaves remainder 1; dividing by $p = 3$ leaves remainder 2; dividing by $p = 5$ leaves remainder 3; dividing by $p = 7$ leaves remainder 1).
$115 = 5 \times 23$
$117 = 3 \times 39$
$119 = 7 \times 17$

In general, prime numbers become fewer and further between as you move to larger and larger numbers: there are 25 prime numbers between 1 and 100, but only 21 between 101 and 200, and just 14 between 901 and 1000. But there is no simple decreasing pattern: there are 16 prime numbers between 1001 and 1100, 8 between 4801 and 4900, and 16 between 4901 and 5000. One can, however, prove some remarkable results about the way prime numbers are distributed: see references [14, Chapter 28], [28, Section 1 of the Supplement to Chapter I; Section 4 of the Supplement to Chapter VIII; Chapter IX, Sections 1 and 2] and [36, Chapter 5] in the list of resources in Section B.

6 C Old cost = $\frac{55}{6}$p each
New cost = $\frac{61}{7}$p each
Price difference (in pence) = $\frac{55}{6} - \frac{61}{7}$
$$= \frac{7 \times 55 - 6 \times 61}{42} = \frac{385 - 366}{42} = \frac{19}{42}$$

7 D Region $x = \frac{1}{3}(\Delta LMN)$
$= \frac{1}{12}(\Delta ABC)$
Region $y = \frac{1}{2}(\Delta ALN)$
$= \frac{1}{8}(\Delta ABC)$
∴ Shaded region in question $= (\frac{1}{12} + \frac{1}{8})(\Delta ABC)$
$= \frac{5}{24}(\Delta ABC)$

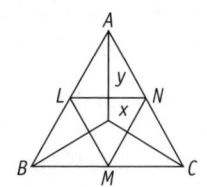

8 B Number of 17-year-olds expected from the East = 1500
Total number of 17-year-olds expected to enter (in thousands)
$$= 2.5 + 3.6 + 1.5 + 0.4$$
$$= 8.0$$
∴ Required percentage $= \frac{1500}{8000} \times 100 = \frac{150}{8} \approx 19$

9 A Let a, b, c, d be any four consecutive digits.
∴ $a + b + c = 15 = b + c + d$ (given)
∴ $a = d$ (i.e. every third digit is the same)
∴ The given values 7, x, 5 determine all twelve entries.
∴ Sum of three consecutive entries $= 5 + 7 + x = 15$
∴ $x = 3$

Solutions to the National Mathematics Contest problems

10 E You have to identify the *smallest* such integer. So you have little choice but to start with the smallest of the given integers, and factorise each one in turn.

Strictly speaking, you should check 100 and 101:
$100 = 2^2 \times 5^2$ ✗
101 is prime ✗
$102 = 2 \times 51 = 2 \times 3 \times 17$ ✗
103 is prime ✗
$104 = 2 \times 2 \times 2 \times 13$ ✗
$105 = 5 \times 3 \times 7$ ✗
$106 = 2 \times 53$ ✓

Much of modern cryptography is based on a clever use of integers which are equal to the product of two *very large* prime numbers. For details, see reference [41, Chapter 6, pages 274 – 79] in the list of resources in Section B.

11 B It is easy to check that four of the options can occur as the units digit of a triangular number:

A $1 + 2 + 3 + 4 = 10$
C $1 + 2 + 3 + 4 + 5 = 15$
D $1 + 2 + 3 = 6$
E $1 + 2 + 3 + 4 + 5 + 6 + 7 = 28$

It is less easy to prove:
Claim 2 never occurs as the units digit of a triangular number.
Proof 1 Consider the units digits of the first 21 triangular numbers
$T_n = 1 + 2 + 3 + \cdots + n = \dfrac{n(n+1)}{2}$:

n	0 1 2 3 4 5 6 7 8 9 10 11 12 13 14 15 16 17 18 19 20
Units digit of $1 + 2 + 3 + \cdots + n$	0 1 3 6 0 5 1 8 6 5 5 6 8 1 5 0 6 3 1 0 0

Notice that $T_{20} = 210$ has the same units digit as $T_0 = \mathbf{0}$.
$T_1 = T_0 + \mathbf{1}$, and $T_{21} = T_{20} + \mathbf{21}$
∴ T_{21} has the same units digit as T_1
Similarly, T_{22} has the same units digits as T_2, and so on.
Hence 2 never occurs as the units digit of a triangular number.

Proof 2 Work mod 5 to show that $T_n = \dfrac{n(n+1)}{2}$ is never $\equiv 2 \pmod{5}$.

$n \pmod 5 \equiv$	0	1	2	3	4
$T_n \pmod 5 \equiv$	0	1	3	1	0

12 C Let the original price of the article be £P.

$\therefore$ Increased price $= £\left(\dfrac{100+x}{100}\right) \times P$

$\therefore$ Decreased price $= £\left(\dfrac{100-y}{100}\right) \times \left(\dfrac{100+x}{100} \times P\right)$

$\qquad = £P$

$\therefore \left(\dfrac{100-y}{100}\right) \times \left(\dfrac{100+x}{100}\right) = 1$

$\therefore \dfrac{x}{100} - \dfrac{y}{100} = \dfrac{xy}{100^2}$

$\therefore \dfrac{x-y}{xy} = \dfrac{1}{100}$

$\therefore \dfrac{1}{y} - \dfrac{1}{x} = \dfrac{1}{100}$

13 C You are clearly meant to look for some unexpected structure in the sequence (rather than calculate 46 terms!).

If $x_1 = 4$, then $x_2 = 3 - \tfrac{3}{4} = \tfrac{9}{4}$

$\therefore x_3 = 3 - \dfrac{3}{\tfrac{9}{4}} = 3 - \tfrac{12}{9} = \tfrac{15}{9} = \tfrac{5}{3}$

$\therefore x_4 = 3 - \dfrac{3}{\tfrac{5}{3}} = 3 - \tfrac{9}{5} = \tfrac{6}{5}$

$\therefore x_5 = 3 - \dfrac{3}{\tfrac{6}{5}} = 3 - \tfrac{15}{6} = \tfrac{3}{6} = \tfrac{1}{2}$

$\therefore x_6 = 3 - \dfrac{3}{\tfrac{1}{2}} = 3 - 6 = -3$

$\therefore x_7 = 3 - \dfrac{3}{-3} = 3 + 1 = 4 = x_1$

Since the value of x_{n+1} depends only on the value of x_n, the sequence simply repeats: $x_7 = x_1$, so $x_8 = x_2$, and so on.

$\therefore x_{46} = x_{(7 \times 6 + 4)} = x_4$

Solutions to the National Mathematics Contest problems

14 D You are told that:
  Some plonks are plinks.
  All plinks are plunks.
  ∴ Some plonks are plunks (so III is false).

To say that 'some plonks are plinks' means that there is *at least one* plonk that is also a plink.
The very same individuals are at the same time 'plinks that are also plunks'.
∴ Some plonks are plunks (so I is true).

The only remaining options which might conceivably be correct are **B** and **D**.

The two given statements in the question:
  Some plonks are plinks.
  All plinks are plunks.
use different names to refer to plonks and plinks. It may be tempting to infer that, since they have different names, they could not possibly refer to the same set of individuals. This would be a serious error! Mathematics is only possible because interesting objects frequently have more than one name (e.g. $a^2 - b^2 = (a+b)(a-b)$).

In this question, the given information 'some plonks are plinks' is still true if all plinks are plonks and all plonks are plinks.
∴ II is not *necessarily* true.

> For books of excellent logic puzzles, see references [20], [22], [23] and [24] in the list of resources given in Section B. For shorter sets of logic puzzles, see [35] and [25, Chapters 5 and 12].

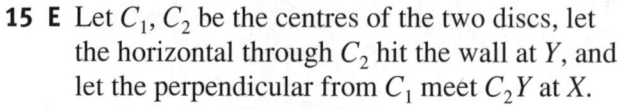

15 E Let C_1, C_2 be the centres of the two discs, let the horizontal through C_2 hit the wall at Y, and let the perpendicular from C_1 meet C_2Y at X.

∴ $\cos 30° = \dfrac{C_2X}{C_1C_2} = \dfrac{C_2X}{3+5}$

∴ $C_2X = 8 \times \dfrac{\sqrt{3}}{2} = 4\sqrt{3}$

∴ $C_2Y = 3 + 4\sqrt{3}$

∴ Distance moved by $C_2 = (3 + 4\sqrt{3}) - 5$

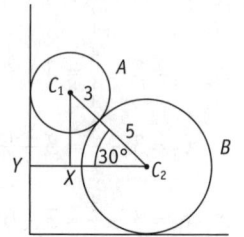

158

16 C Any path from S to F must start by crossing one of the three square faces which meet at S to one of the opposite sides – say to the point P.
∴ The shortest path from S to P is the straight line segment SP.

The the shortest path from P to F is the straight line segment PF.

The total length $SP + PF$ is shortest precisely when, if you unfold these two faces and lay them flat, S, P, and F all lie in a straight line, i.e. when P is the mid-point of the unfolded edge.
∴ $(SP + PF)^2 = SF^2 = SX^2 + XF^2 = 1^2 + 2^2$

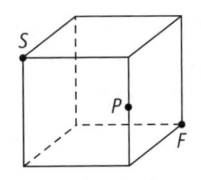

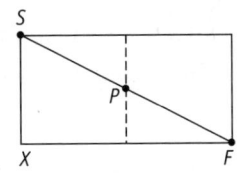

> The shortest path joining two points on a surface is called a 'geodesic'. For more information about geodesics on simple surfaces, see reference [52, Chapter 7] in the list of resources in Section B.

17 D Let the sequence be:
$$u_1 = a, u_2 = a + d, u_3 = a + 2d, \ldots, u_{58} = a + 57d, \ldots$$
All terms are positive integers (given).
∴ a and d must be positive integers.
$s_{10} = a + (a + d) + (a + 2d) + \cdots + (a + 9d)$
$= (2a + 9d) \times 5 = 10a + 45d$

Suppose $s_{10} = u_{58}$.
∴ $10a + 45d = a + 57d$
∴ $3a = 4d$

Since a and d are integers, 4 is a factor of the RHS.
∴ 4 must also be a factor of the LHS.
∴ a is a multiple of 4.
∴ Smallest possible value of $a = 4$ (with $d = 3$)

18 B Let θ be the angle of incline of the first path.
∴ $\tan \theta = \frac{3}{4}$, so $\sin \theta = \frac{3}{\sqrt{3^2 + 4^2}} = \frac{3}{5}$

Let β be the angle of incline of the second path.
∴ $\tan \beta = \frac{5}{12}$, so $\sin \beta = \frac{5}{\sqrt{5^2 + 12^2}} = \frac{5}{13}$

Solutions to the National Mathematics Contest problems

Let the vertical height climbed be h.
∴ Length of path of gradient $\frac{3}{4} = \frac{5}{3}h$
and length of path of gradient $\frac{5}{12} = \frac{13}{5}h$
∴ Total distance walked $= \frac{5}{3}h + \frac{13}{5}h = \frac{64}{15}h$
∴ Uphill fraction of total distance covered $= \dfrac{\frac{5}{3}h}{\frac{64}{15}h} = \dfrac{25}{64}$

19 E $1989 = 9 \times 13 \times 17$ with $n = 9$
∴ Next integer of the form $n(n + 4)(n + 8) = 10 \times 14 \times 18$
$= 2520$

20 C If the sectors were all equal, you might have to make allowance for the fact that some apparently different colourings (such as black–white–black–white and white–black–white–black) look exactly the same if you rotate one of them.
Since the sectors are all unequal, this problem does not arise.

No two adjacent sectors have the same colour.
∴ At least two colours must be used.

(a) Suppose first that exactly two colours – say black and white – are used.
Then there are just **2** ways to colour the sectors, namely B–W–B–W and W–B–W–B.
There are $\binom{4}{2} = \mathbf{6}$ ways to choose two colours from four.
∴ Number of colourings with two colours $= 6 \times 2 = 12$

(b) Suppose next that exactly three colours are used.
∴ One of these three colours is used for two (opposite) sectors.
There are **3** ways to choose the repeated colour, **2** ways to choose the pair of opposite sectors, and then **2** ways to colour the remaining two sectors using the second and third colours.
There are also $\binom{4}{3} = \mathbf{4}$ ways to choose three colours from four.
∴ Number of colourings with three colours $= 4 \times 3 \times 2 \times 2 = 48$

(c) Finally suppose that exactly four colours are used. Then the four sectors can be coloured in $4! = 24$ ways.

∴ Total number of possible colourings $= 12 + 48 + 24 = 84$

For more on the basic art of counting, see reference [47, Chapters 1, 2] in the list of resources in Section B; see also [14, Chapters 15, 17, 19] and [34, Chapters 13, 19].

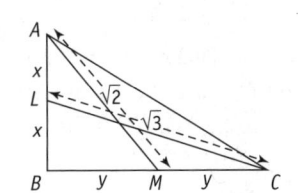

21 C Let M be the mid-point of BC.

∴ $BM = 5$ and $\angle AMB = 90°$, $\angle BAM = \dfrac{\alpha}{2}$

∴ $AM = \sqrt{13^2 - 5^2} = 12$

∴ $\sin\left(\dfrac{\alpha}{2}\right) = \dfrac{5}{13}$, $\cos\left(\dfrac{\alpha}{2}\right) = \dfrac{12}{13}$

∴ $\sin \alpha = 2 \sin\left(\dfrac{\alpha}{2}\right) \cos\left(\dfrac{\alpha}{2}\right) = 2 \cdot \dfrac{5}{13} \cdot \dfrac{12}{13} = \dfrac{120}{169}$

Alternatively Drop the perpendicular BD from B to AC (of length h, say). Let $CD = x$

∴ $\sin \alpha = \dfrac{h}{13}$

$h^2 + x^2 = 10^2$ and $h^2 + (13-x)^2 = 13^2$

∴ $169 - 26x + 10^2 = 13^2$

∴ $x = \dfrac{50}{13}$

∴ $h^2 = 100 - \dfrac{2500}{169} = \dfrac{14\,400}{169} = \left(\dfrac{120}{13}\right)^2$

∴ $h = \dfrac{120}{13}$

22 A Let the triangle be ABC with a right angle at B, with AM the median of length $\sqrt{2}$ and CL median of length $\sqrt{3}$.
Let $AB = 2x$, $BC = 2y$

∴ $4x^2 + y^2 = 2$ and $x^2 + 4y^2 = 3$

∴ $5(x^2 + y^2) = 5$

∴ $x^2 + y^2 = 1$

∴ $AC^2 = AB^2 + BC^2 = (2x)^2 + (2y)^2$
$= 4(x^2 + y^2) = 4$

23 E The most direct approach is to 'equate coefficients' in the identity:
$x^9 + 512 = (x+2)(a_8 x^8 + a_7 x^7 + a_6 x^6 + \ldots + a_2 x^2 + a_1 x^1 + a_0)$
Coefficient of x^9 on LHS = 1; on RHS = a_8:   ∴ $a_8 = 1$
Coefficient of x^8 on LHS = 0; on RHS = $a_7 + 2a_8 = a_7 + 2$:   ∴ $a_7 = -2$
And so on.

A more instructive approach is to realise that $2^9 = 512$.
$\therefore (-2)^9 = -512$
$\therefore -2$ is a root of $x^9 + 512$
$\therefore x + 2$ is a factor of $x^9 + 512$
$\therefore x^9 + 512 = (x + 2)(x^8 - 2x^7 + 4x^6 - 8x^5 + 16x^4 - 32x^3 + 64x^2 - 128x + 256)$
$\therefore a_8 + a_7 + a_6 + a_5 + a_4 + a_3 + a_2 + a_1 + a_0$
$= 1 - 2 + 4 - 8 + 16 - 32 + 64 - 128 + 256 = 171$

Alternatively Put $x = 1$ in the given equation.
$\therefore 1 + 512 = (1 + 2) \times (a_8 + a_7 + a_6 + a_5 + a_4 + a_3 + a_2 + a_1 + a_0)$
$\therefore a_8 + a_7 + a_6 + a_5 + a_4 + a_3 + a_2 + a_1 + a_0 = \dfrac{513}{3}$

For more on properties of polynomials, see reference [42] in the list of resources in Section B.

24 D Let the perpendicular from A to BC meet BC at M and PQ at N.
$\therefore AM = 3 \cdot PS$ (given)
$\therefore AN = 2 \cdot PS$

Let area($\triangle PSB$) = a, and area($\triangle QRC$) = b
$\triangle ANP$ and $\triangle PSB$ are similar with $AN = 2 \cdot PS$.
$\therefore$ area($\triangle ANP$) = $4a$, area($\triangle AMB$) = $9a$
$\therefore$ area($PNMS$) = $4a$

$\triangle ANQ$ and $\triangle QRC$ are similar with $AN = 2 \cdot QR$.
$\therefore$ area($\triangle ANQ$) = $4b$, area($\triangle AMC$) = $9b$
$\therefore$ area($QNMR$) = $4b$

$\therefore \dfrac{\text{area}(PQRS)}{\text{area}(ABC)} = \dfrac{4a + 4b}{9a + 9b} = \dfrac{4}{9}$

Alternatively Let $PS = MN = QR = w$, $BS = x$, $RC = y$
$\therefore AM = 3w$, $BM = 3x$, $CM = 3y$
$\therefore SM = 2x$, $MR = 2y$
$\therefore$ area($PQRS$) = $(2x + 2y)w = 2w(x + y)$
area($\triangle ABM$) = $\tfrac{1}{2} \cdot 3x \cdot 3w$, area($\triangle AMC$) = $\tfrac{1}{2} \cdot 3y \cdot 3w$
$\therefore$ area($\triangle ABC$) = area($\triangle ABM$) + area($\triangle AMC$) = $\tfrac{9}{2} \cdot w(x + y)$

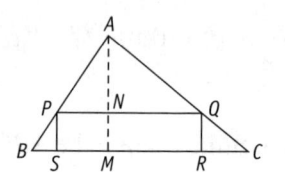

25 B I $y = |x+1|$ consists of two straight sections: $y = x+1$ when $x \geq -1$, and $y = -(x+1)$ when $x < -1$.

II $x^2 - y^2 = 0$ may be rewritten as $(x-y)(x+y) = 0$, and so is satisfied precisely when either $x + y = 0$ or $x - y = 0$ (two straight lines).

III $x^2 + xy = 2x + 2y$ many be rewritten as $(y+x)(x-2) = 0$, and so is satisfied precisely when either $y + x = 0$ or $x = 2$ (two straight lines).

IV $y^2 = |x|$ consists of two parabolic sections: $y^2 = x$ when $x \geq 0$ and $y^2 = -x$ when $x < 0$.

26 E Number $a + b$ points on a circle:
$$1, 2, 3, \ldots, a-1, a, a+1, \ldots, a+b-1, a+b$$
Then the chords crossed by the chord joining $a + b$ to a are precisely the $(a-1) \times (b-1)$ chords joining the $a-1$ points $\{1, 2, 3, \ldots, a-1\}$ (i.e. those points on one side of the chord joining 1 to a) to the $b-1$ points $\{a+1, a+2, \ldots, a+b-1\}$ (i.e. those points on the other side of the chord joining $a + b$ to a).

Suppose all the chords joining the n points $1, 2, 3, \ldots, n$ on a circle have already been drawn, producing exactly C_n crossing points inside the circle.

If a new point $n + 1$ is then added, and the new chords '$(n+1)1$', '$(n+1)2$', ..., '$(n+1)n$' are drawn, the observation in the previous paragraph allows one to write down a simple recurrence relation giving the total number of crossing points C_{n+1} with $n + 1$ points:

C_{n+1} = (number of old crossing points for n points) + (number of new crossing points created by $(n+1)$th point)
$= C_n + [0 \cdot (n-1) + 1 \cdot (n-2) + 2 \cdot (n-3) + \cdots + (n-1) \cdot 0]$

Clearly, $C_3 = 0$ and $C_4 = 1$
$\therefore\ C_5 = 1 + (0.3 + 1.2 + 2.1 + 3.0) = 5$
$C_6 = 5 + (0.4 + 1.3 + 2.2 + 3.1 + 4.0) = 15$
$C_7 = 15 + (0.5 + 1.4 + 2.3 + 3.2 + 4.1 + 5.0) = 35$
$C_8 = 35 + (0.6 + 1.5 + 2.4 + 3.3 + 4.2 + 5.1 + 6.0) = 70$
$C_9 = 70 + (0.7 + 1.6 + 2.5 + 3.4 + 4.3 + 5.2 + 6.1 + 7.0) = 126$
$C_{10} = 126 + (0.8 + 1.7 + 2.6 + 3.5 + 4.4 + 5.3 + 6.2 + 7.1 + 8.0)$
$= 210$

Alternatively Each crossing point arises from two chords AC and BD, and hence from four points A, B, C, D. Conversely, each choice of four points A, B, C, D on the circle corresponds to just one pair of crossing chords AC, BD.

So with ten points on the circle, the number of such crossing points is equal to $\binom{10}{4}$, the number of ways of choosing four points from ten.

> For a recurrence relation similar to the one above for C_{n+1}, see reference [47, Chapter 11] in the list of resources in Section B; for a more intuitive introduction to recurrence relations, see [14, Chapters 15, 17, 19].

27 C $\triangle AHK$ and $\triangle BLC$ are isosceles right-angled triangles with $AH = BC = 1$.

$\therefore HK = LC = \dfrac{1}{\sqrt{2}}$

$\therefore$ Shaded square has side $= 1 - 2 \times \left(1 - \dfrac{1}{\sqrt{2}}\right) = \sqrt{2} - 1$

$\therefore$ Shaded square has area $= (\sqrt{2} - 1)^2 = 3 - 2\sqrt{2}$

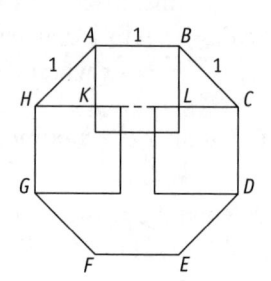

28 B Notice that 6 cannot be written as the sum or difference of two squares. Hence **A** is false.

Every *odd* integer can be expressed as the difference of two successive squares:

$(m+1)^2 - m^2 = 2m + 1$

Every *even* integer $2m$ can be obtained by subtracting 1^2 from $2m + 1$:

$(m+1)^2 - m^2 - 1^2 = 2m$

So the smallest value of k is 3.

> For interesting properties of sums of squares, see references [32, pages 38–42] and [36, pages 146–47] in the list of resources in Section B.

29 D (a) $h(2, 1) = g(2, h(2, 0)) = g(2, 1)$
$\qquad\qquad\qquad\qquad\quad = f(2, g(2, 0)) = f(2, 0) = 2$
(b) $h(2, 2) = g(2, h(2, 1)) = g(2, 2)$
$\qquad\qquad\qquad\qquad\quad = f(2, g(2, 1))$
$\qquad\qquad\qquad\qquad\quad = f(2, 2) = f(2, 1) + 1$
$\qquad\qquad\qquad\qquad\qquad\quad = (f(2, 0) + 1) + 1 = 4$
(c) $g(2, 3) = f(2, g(2, 2))$
$\qquad\qquad\quad = f(2, 4) = f(2, 3) + 1$
$\qquad\qquad\qquad\quad = (f(2, 2) + 1) + 1 = (4 + 1) + 1 = 6$
(d) $f(2, 6) = f(2, 5) + 1$
$\qquad\qquad\quad = (f(2, 4) + 1) + 1 = (6 + 1) + 1 = 8$
(e) $h(2, 3) = g(2, h(2, 2))$
$\qquad\qquad\quad = g(2, 4) = f(2, g(2, 3))$
$\qquad\qquad\qquad\quad = f(2, 6) = 8$

Alternatively It is easy to show that $f(n, m) = n + m$.
$g(n, 0) = 0$ (given); $g(n, 1) = f(n, g(n, 0)) = n$; $g(n, 2) = f(n, g(n, 1))$ $= f(n, n) = 2n$; and in general $g(n, m) = n \cdot m$ (by induction on m).
$h(n, 0) = 1$ (given); $h(n, 1) = g(n, h(n, 0)) = g(n, 1) = n$; $h(n, 2) = g(n, h(n, 1)) = g(n, n) = n^2$; and in general $h(n, m) = n^m$.
$\therefore h(2, 3) = g(2, h(2, 2)) = g(2, 4) = 8$

30 C At most, one of a, b can be negative (since their sum $a + b \geq 2$).
Hence if $a < 0$, then $b > 0$; but then $\dfrac{3b+1}{a} < 0$, which is impossible (since $\dfrac{3b+1}{a}$ is a positive integral power of 2). Hence $a > 0$.
Similarly $b > 0$, so a and b are both positive rationals.
Let $\dfrac{3b+1}{a} = 2^r$ and $\dfrac{3a+1}{b} = 2^s$, with r, s positive integers.
$\therefore 3a + 1 = 2^s b$ and $3b + 1 = 2^r a$
$\therefore a = \dfrac{3 + 2^s}{2^{r+s} - 9}, \ b = \dfrac{3 + 2^r}{2^{r+s} - 9}$
$\therefore 2^{r+s} - 9 > 0$ (since a is a positive)
$\therefore r + s \geq 4$

On the other hand:
$2 \leq a + b$ (given)
$= \dfrac{3 + 2^s}{2^{r+s} - 9} + \dfrac{3 + 2^r}{2^{r+s} - 9} = \dfrac{6 + 2^s + 2^r}{2^{r+s} - 9}$
$\therefore 2 \times 2^{r+s} - 18 \leq 6 + 2^s + 2^r$
$\therefore 2^{r+s} + (2^{r+s} - 2^r - 2^s + 1) \leq 25$
$\therefore 2^{r+s} + (2^r - 1)(2^s - 1) \leq 25$
$\therefore r + s \leq 4$ (since $2^r - 1 \geq 0$ and $2^s - 1 \geq 0$)

Hence $r + s = 4$, so there are exactly three possible solutions:
(a) $(r, s) = (1, 3)$, whence $(a, b) = (\tfrac{5}{7}, \tfrac{11}{7})$;
(b) $(r, s) = (2, 2)$, whence $(a, b) = (1, 1)$;
(c) $(r, s) = (3, 1)$, whence $(a, b) = (\tfrac{11}{7}, \tfrac{5}{7})$.

Solutions to the National Mathematics Contest problems

1988

1 B Let the cube have side s.
∴ $AB = AC = BC = s\sqrt{2}$
∴ $\triangle ABC$ is equilateral.

2 C B $4^{15} = (2^2)^{15} = 2^{2 \times 15} = 2^{30}$
  C $8^{11} = (2^3)^{11} = 2^{3 \times 11} = 2^{33}$
  D $16^8 = (2^4)^8 = 2^{4 \times 8} = 2^{32}$
  E $32^6 = (2^5)^6 = 2^{5 \times 6} = 2^{30}$

3 D $1 = 1, 2 = 2, 3 = 2 + 1$ can all be paid.
4 cannot be paid.
$5 = 5, 6 = 5 + 1, 7 = 5 + 2, 8 = 5 + 2 + 1$ can all be paid.
9 cannot be paid.
$10 = 10, 11 = 10 + 1, 12 = 10 + 2, 13 = 10 + 2 + 1$ can all be paid.
14 cannot be paid.
$15 = 10 + 5, 16 = 10 + 5 + 1, 17 = 10 + 5 + 2, 18 = 10 + 5 + 2 + 1$ can all be paid.
19 cannot be paid.
$20 = 20$ can be paid.

4 C Palindromes between 100 and 1000 have the form '*aba*'.
There are nine choices for a (since $a \geq 1$) and 10 choices for b.

5 B Notice that precisely two of the points P, Q, R, S, T, U have an odd number of lines namely P and Q.

When you leave the starting point you use up *just one edge* to go out; and when you arrive at the finishing point you use *just one edge* to come in. On every other occasion, when you visit one of the points P, Q, R, S, T, U you use up one edge coming in and one edge going out, i.e. you use up *two edges* each time you pass through a vertex. So only the starting and finishing points can have an odd number of lines.

Since there are two points with an odd number of lines (namely P and Q), one of these has to be the starting point and the other has to be the finishing point.
And since any path can be drawn 'backwards', either of them can be the starting point.

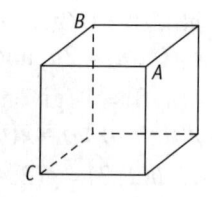

The study of such properties of configurations of points and lines is known as 'graph theory'; a path which traces every line exactly once is called an 'Eulerian path'. For a beginner's guide, see reference [48, Sections 2.2 and 2.3] in the list of resources in Section B; see also [29, Chapter 9], [32, pages 143–44] and [52, Chapter 12].

6 D $a + b + c + d = (a + b - c) + (b + c - d) + (c + d - a) + (d + a - b)$
$= 6 + 6 + 6 + 6$

7 A Suppose $x \geq 0$
$\therefore 0 = x^2 - 3|x| + 2 = x^2 - 3x + 2$
$\therefore 0 = (x - 2)(x - 1)$
$\therefore x = 2$ or $x = 1$ (**two** solutions)

Suppose $x < 0$
$\therefore 0 = x^2 - 3|x| + 2 = x^2 + 3x + 2$
$\therefore 0 = (x + 2)(x + 1)$
$\therefore x = -2$, or $x = -1$ (**two** solutions)

8 E $W := (5, 6)$ is a corner of the square and $C := (2, 1)$ is the centre of the square.

$\therefore \overrightarrow{CW} = \begin{pmatrix} 5 \\ 6 \end{pmatrix} - \begin{pmatrix} 2 \\ 1 \end{pmatrix} = \begin{pmatrix} 3 \\ 5 \end{pmatrix}$

$\therefore$ Length $CW = \sqrt{3^2 + 5^2} = \sqrt{34}$

$\therefore$ The corner of the square opposite W is length CW in the opposite direction: i.e. at $\begin{pmatrix} 2 \\ 1 \end{pmatrix} - \overrightarrow{CW} = \begin{pmatrix} 2 \\ 1 \end{pmatrix} - \begin{pmatrix} 3 \\ 5 \end{pmatrix} = \begin{pmatrix} -1 \\ -4 \end{pmatrix} = Q$.

The vertices W, Q of the square lie on a diagonal with gradient $= \frac{5}{3}$. The other two vertices of the square lie on the other diagonal. The two diagonals of a square are perpendicular; hence the other diagonal has gradient $-\frac{3}{5}$, and passes through $C := (2, 1)$, so has equation $y = -\frac{3}{5}x + \frac{11}{5}$. Hence $R := (5, -4)$ is not a vertex of the square.

Substituting shows that $P := (-3, 4)$ lies on the line $y = -\frac{3}{5}x + \frac{11}{5}$.
Moreover:
$\overrightarrow{CP} = \begin{pmatrix} -3 \\ 4 \end{pmatrix} - \begin{pmatrix} 2 \\ 1 \end{pmatrix} = \begin{pmatrix} -5 \\ 3 \end{pmatrix}$

$\therefore CP = \sqrt{(-5)^2 + 3^2} = \sqrt{34} = CW$
Hence $P := (-3, 4)$ is a vertex of the square.

Solutions to the National Mathematics Contest problems

9 B Let the radii of the small and large circles be r and R respectively.
Let $AB = 2s$
$\therefore BM = s$
$\angle OBM = \angle BAM = 30°$
$\therefore \triangle BOM$ and $\triangle ABM$ are similar
$\therefore \dfrac{r}{R} = \dfrac{OM}{OB} = \dfrac{BM}{BA} = \dfrac{s}{2s} = \dfrac{1}{2}$
$\therefore \pi r^2 : \pi R^2 = 1 : 4$

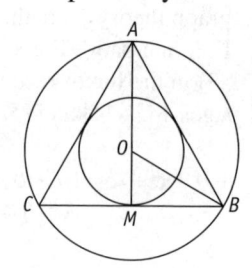

Alternatively $\angle BOM = 60°$. So $\frac{1}{2} = \cos BOM = \dfrac{OM}{OB} = \dfrac{r}{R}$.

10 E d dogs eat s kg of steak in m minutes.

$\therefore$ 1 dog eats $\dfrac{s}{d}$ kg of steak in m minutes.

$\therefore$ 1 dog eats $\dfrac{s}{dm}$ kg of steak in 1 minute.

$\therefore$ s dogs eat $\dfrac{s^2}{dm}$ kg of steak in 1 minute.

$\therefore$ s dogs eat $\dfrac{s^2}{m}$ kg of steak in d minutes.

11 D $EC = \sqrt{1^2 + 2^2} = \sqrt{5} = 1 \times \sqrt{5}$
$CA = \sqrt{1^2 + 2^2} = \sqrt{5} = 1 \times \sqrt{5}$
$EA = \sqrt{1^2 + 3^2} = \sqrt{10} = \sqrt{2} \times \sqrt{5}$
$\therefore \triangle ECA$ is an isosceles right-angled triangle with hypotenuse EA.
$\therefore \angle AEC = 45°$

12 A Opposite angles of a cyclic quadrilateral sum to 180°.
$(3x + 2y) + (4x + 5y) = 180$
$\therefore 7(x + y) = 180$
$\therefore x + y = \dfrac{180}{7}$ (1)
$(5x + 3y) + (6y - 8x) = 180$
$\therefore 9y - 3x = 180$
$\therefore 3y - x = 60$ (2)
Add (1) and (2):
$4y = \dfrac{180}{7} + 60$
$\therefore y = 15 + \dfrac{45}{7} = \dfrac{150}{7}, x = \dfrac{180}{7} - y = \dfrac{30}{7}$

168

13 E Any axis of rotational symmetry l must pass through the centre of the cube.

(a) If such an axis passes through (the centre and) a vertex of the cube, then it must pass through the opposite vertex. Hence there are four such axes l through vertices, corresponding to the four pairs of opposite vertices.

(b) If an axis of rotational symmetry l meets an edge e of the cube *not* at a vertex, then the edge must rotate wholly onto itself. Hence l must pass through the mid-point of e (and the centre of the cube, which guarantees that l will then be perpendicular to e, and that l will also pass through the mid-point of the edge opposite e). Hence there are six such axes l corresponding to the six pairs of opposite edges in the cube.

(c) Any other axis of rotational symmetry l passes through no vertex and meets no edge of the cube; hence l meets some face F at an internal point. Since that face must rotate wholly onto itself, the axis l must pass through the centre of the face (and the centre of the cube, which guarantees that l is then perpendicular to the face F, and that l will also pass through the centre of the face opposite F). Hence there are three such axes l corresponding to the three pairs of opposite faces in the cube.

14 D Suppose that $3^x \times 3^y = 3^{x+y}$

∴ $3^{x+y} = 3^{xy}$

∴ $x + y = xy$

∴ $xy - x - y + 1 = 1$

∴ $(x-1)(y-1) = 1$

Factorising one side of an equation when the other side is non-zero is usually a bad move. But here you are told that x and y are *integers*; so the above factorisation tells you that $x - 1$ and $y - 1$ are integers whose product is equal to 1. Hence there are just two solutions:

either $x - 1 = y - 1 = 1$, or $x - 1 = y - 1 = -1$

∴ $x = y = 0$, or $x = y = 2$ (**two** solutions: $(x, y) = (0, 0)$ or $(2, 2)$)

Suppose next that $2^x + 2^y = 2^{x+y}$. One of the difficulties which any solution has to confront is that x or y could be *negative* integers.

(a) If $x = y$, then $2 \cdot 2^x = 2^{x+x}$, so $x = y = 1$ (**one** solution: $(x, y) = (1, 1)$)

(b) If $x < y$, then $1 + 2^{y-x} = 2^y$ with $y - x > 0$. Then 2^{y-x} is a positive integral power of 2, so the LHS is a positive integer. Hence the RHS is an integer, so $y \geq 0$.

Now you know that $1 + 2^{y-x}$ and 2^y are both integers it is enough to notice that $1 + 2^{y-x}$ is odd (since $y - x > 0$).

∴ 2^y must also be odd.
∴ $y = 0$
∴ $2^{y-x} = 0$, which is impossible.
Hence there are no solutions if $x < y$.
(c) Similarly $y < x$ gives rise to no solutions.

15 C Suppose Mum took t hours to finish her 9 km.

∴ Mum ran at $\dfrac{9}{t}$ km/h.

∴ Dad ran at $\left(\dfrac{9}{t} + \dfrac{3}{2}\right)$ km/h (given)

and took $\left(t - \dfrac{1}{15}\right)$ h to finish.

∴ Dad's speed $= \dfrac{9}{t} + \dfrac{3}{2} = \dfrac{9}{t - \frac{1}{15}}$

∴ $(18 + 3t)\left(t - \dfrac{1}{15}\right) = 18t$

∴ $3t^2 - \dfrac{t}{5} - \dfrac{6}{5} = 0$

∴ $15t^2 - t - 6 = 0$
∴ $(5t + 3)(3t - 2) = 0$
∴ $t = \frac{2}{3}$ (since $t > 0$)

16 A The two 'largest possible equal circles' pass through, and are tangent at, the centre C of the square.
Let the circles be of radius r, let their centres be at X and Y, let A be the corner of the square nearest X and B be the corner nearest Y.
∴ $AB = \sqrt{2}$
$XP = PA = r$
∴ $XA = r\sqrt{2} = YB$
$XY = XC + CY = 2r$
∴ $\sqrt{2} = AB = AX + XY + YB$
$= r\sqrt{2} + 2r + r\sqrt{2} = 2r(\sqrt{2} + 1)$

∴ $r = \dfrac{\sqrt{2}}{2(\sqrt{2} + 1)} = \dfrac{1}{\sqrt{2}(\sqrt{2} + 1)} = \dfrac{1}{2 + \sqrt{2}}$

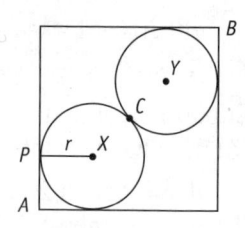

170

17 E When solving *equations* you are only allowed to cancel common factors if they are non-zero. When solving *inequalities* you have to be more careful, since you can then only cancel *positive* factors.

Suppose $x(x-1)^2 < (x-1)x^2$ (*)

(a) To ensure that the factors x and $(x-1)$ are both positive, one must restrict attention at first to values of $x > 1$. Then the given inequality simplifies to $(x-1) < x$, which is valid for all $x > 1$. Hence every $x > 1$ is a solution of the inequality (*).

(b) If $x = 0$ or 1, then both sides of (*) are 0 so the inequality is not satisfied.

(c) If $0 < x < 1$, then $x > 0$ and $1 - x > 0$.
   $\therefore$ One may cancel the (positive) common factor x on each side of (*) to get $(x-1)^2 < (x-1)x$.
   $\therefore$ One may then rewrite this as $(1-x)^2 < -(1-x)x$ and then cancel the (positive) common factor $(1-x)$ on each side to get $1 - x < -x$; that is, $1 < 0$ – which is false.
   Hence there are no solutions with $0 < x < 1$.

(d) If $x < 0$, then $-x > 0$ and $1 - x > 0$, so one may rewrite (*) as
$$-(-x)(1-x)^2 < -(1-x)(-x)^2$$
One may then cancel the (positive) common factors $-x$ and $(1-x)$ to get $-(1-x) < -(-x)$; i.e. $x - 1 < x$, which is valid for all $x < 0$. Hence every $x < 0$ is a solution of the inequality (*).

Alternatively Take everything to one side and simplify: x satisfies the inequality $x(x-1)^2 < (x-1)x^2$ precisely when:
   $(x-1)x^2 - x(x-1)^2 > 0$
$\therefore$ $(x-1)x[x - (x-1)] > 0$
$\therefore$ $(x-1)x > 0$
The product $(x-1)x$ is positive precisely when both factors are positive or both factors are negative, i.e. when $x > 1$ or $x < 0$.

Notice that the two-part condition:
   $x > 0$ and $x < 1$ (1)
and the two-part condition:
   $x > 0$ or $x < 1$ (2)
have quite different meanings: $x = 2$ satisfies (2) but not (1). Condition (1) is often written, by convention, in the shortened form $0 < x < 1$.

Solutions to the National Mathematics Contest problems

> When the two conditions $x > 0$ and $x < 1$ are combined in this way, the missing word 'and' is understood, i.e.:
>
> x is assumed to satisfy <u>both</u> of the conditions.
>
> So if you need to refer to:
>
> 'all real numbers x which satisfy either $x < 0$ <u>or</u> $x > 1$'
>
> you must *never* invent your own private shorthand by writing this in the form $1 < x < 0$.

18 B You may have found this a strangely awkward problem. Though there are masses of things you can calculate, it is easy to get in a mess. The key idea is to look for some way of combining the two pieces of given information: '$AB = BC = 3$' and 'area $= 6$'.

Start by using the second piece of information to find $\cos \angle AOB$. Then use the cosine rule in $\triangle ABC$.

Let the radius of the circle be r.

$6 = \text{area}(OABC) = \text{area}(\triangle AOB) + \text{area}(\triangle BOC) = 2 \times \text{area}(\triangle AOB)$

$\therefore \text{area}(\triangle AOB) = 3$

$\qquad = \frac{1}{2} \cdot r \cdot r \cdot \sin AOB$

$\therefore \sin AOB = \dfrac{6}{r^2}$

$\therefore \cos AOB = \sqrt{1 - \dfrac{36}{r^4}} \qquad (*)$

A simple observation involving cyclic quadrilaterals now shows that $\angle ABC = 180° - \angle AOB$.

The angle subtended by the chord AC at the centre O is equal to $2 \times \angle AOB$.

$\therefore$ Angle subtended by AC on the circumference below O is $\angle AOB$.

$\therefore$ Angle subtended by AC at B is $180° - \angle AOB$ (opposite angles in a cyclic quadrilateral add to $180°$).

Let BO and AC meet at X. The cosine rule in $\triangle ABC$ then gives:

$AC^2 = 3^2 + 3^2 - 2 \cdot 3 \cdot 3 \cdot \cos(180° - \angle AOB)$

$\therefore (2 \cdot AX)^2 = 18 + 18 \cos AOB$

$\therefore \left(\dfrac{12}{r}\right)^2 = 18 + 18\sqrt{1 - \dfrac{36}{r^4}}$

$\therefore \sqrt{r^4 - 36} = 8 - r^2$

$\therefore r^4 - 36 = r^4 - 16r^2 + 64$

$\therefore 16r^2 = 100$

$\therefore r = \frac{5}{2}$ (since $r > 0$)

Alternatively
(a) Let $BX = b$, $AX = a$, $\angle BAC = \theta$. Then $\angle BOC = 2\theta = \angle AOB$.
In $\triangle BAX$, $\sin \theta = b/3$, and $\cos \theta = a/3$, so
$\sin 2\theta = 2 \cdot \sin \theta \cdot \cos \theta = 2ba/9$.
In $\triangle AOX$, $\sin 2\theta = a/r = 2 \cdot \sin \theta \cdot \cos \theta = 2ba/9$, so $2br = 9$.
area $(\triangle AOB) = \frac{1}{2} \cdot OB \cdot AX = \frac{1}{2}ra = 3$, so $ar = 6$.
In $\triangle ABX$, $a^2 + b^2 = 3^2$, so $(6/r)^2 + (9/2r)^2 = 9$, i.e. $r^2 = 25/4$.

(b) Let M be the mid-point of AB. $\triangle AOB$ is isosceles, so $\triangle OMB$ is a right-angled triangle; hence $OM = \sqrt{r^2 - \frac{9}{4}}$.
$\therefore 6 = \text{area}(AOBC) = \text{area}(\triangle AOB) + \text{area}(\triangle BOC)$
$\qquad = 2 \times \frac{1}{2} \cdot 3 \cdot \sqrt{r^2 - \frac{9}{4}}$
$\therefore \sqrt{r^2 - \frac{9}{4}} = 2$, so $r = \frac{5}{2}$

19 A This is a classic problem with a hidden surprise. Notice that the distance BC is not given. This would seem to suggest that there cannot be enough information to calculate h. Hence **E** is a reasonable first guess. But it is wrong!

$\triangle ABC$ and $\triangle EFC$ are similar.
$\therefore \dfrac{AB}{BC} = \dfrac{EF}{FC}$
$\therefore \dfrac{FC}{BC} = \dfrac{h}{x}$
$\triangle DCB$ and $\triangle EFB$ are similar.
$\therefore \dfrac{DC}{BC} = \dfrac{EF}{BF}$
$\therefore \dfrac{BF}{BC} = \dfrac{h}{y}$
$\therefore 1 = \dfrac{BF}{BC} + \dfrac{FC}{BC} = \dfrac{h}{y} + \dfrac{h}{x}$
$\therefore xy = h(x + y)$

20 B The expression $p^r \cdot q^q \cdot r^p$ only involves the three numbers p, q, r. So it must take its smallest value when p, q, r are as small as possible. Since p, q, r are distinct primes, they must therefore be 2, 3 and 5 – in some order.

(a) The smallest given option $2700 = 2^2 \times 3^3 \times 5^2$ does not have the required form.
(b) The second smallest given option $21\,600 = 2^5 \times 3^3 \times 5^2$ does have the required form.

However, it is worth looking a little more closely at the mathematics behind the problem.

Claim If three distinct positive real numbers p, q, r are substituted (in all possible orders) for x, y, z in the expression $x^z y^y z^x$, the value will be smallest when $x < y < z$ or $z < y < x$.

Proof Suppose $a < b < c$, and show $a^b b^a c^c > a^c b^b c^a$ and $a^a b^c c^b > a^c b^b c^a$.
$$c^{c-a} = c^{c-b} \cdot c^{b-a}$$
$$> a^{c-b} \cdot b^{b-a}$$
$\therefore a^b b^a c^c > a^c b^b c^a$.
$$a^{c-a} = a^{c-b} \cdot a^{b-a}$$
$$< b^{c-b} \cdot c^{b-a}$$
$\therefore a^c b^b c^a < a^a b^c c^b$ **QED**

Consequence The three smallest primes p, q, r are 2, 3, 5. Hence the smallest possible value of $p^r q^q r^p$ is $2^5 3^3 5^2$.

21 D Let $SP = SQ = SR = r$
$SR^2 = ST^2 + TR^2$ (Pythagoras in $\triangle STR$)
$\therefore RT = \sqrt{r^2 - 1}$
$PR^2 = PT^2 + TR^2$ (Pythagoras in $\triangle PTR$)
$\therefore 12^2 - (r+1)^2 + (r^2 - 1)$
$\quad = 2r^2 + 2r$
$\therefore r^2 + r - 72 = 0$
$\therefore (r+9)(r-8) = 0$
$\therefore r = 8$ (since $r > 0$)

22 B Let 'abc' be an unknown three-digit integer which is equal to 12 times the sum of its digits.
$\therefore 100a + 10b + c = 12(a + b + c)$
$\therefore 88a - 11c = 2b$
$\therefore 11(8a - c) = 2b$
11 is a factor of the LHS, so 11 must be a factor of the RHS.
$\therefore b = 0$ (since $0 \leq b \leq 9$)
$\therefore 8a = c$
$\therefore a = 1$ and $c = 8$ (since $1 \leq a \leq 9$ and $0 \leq c \leq 9$)

23 C $y = kx$ and $y = kx + 1$ are parallel; and $x = ky$ and $x = ky + 1$ are parallel. Hence the quadrilateral is a parallelogram $OABC$ with the origin O as one vertex. The second pair of lines is obtained from the first by interchanging x and y, i.e. by reflecting in the line $y = x$. Hence $OA = OC$, so the parallelogram is a rhombus.

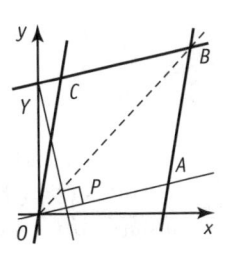

This shows that there are lots of ways of calculating the required area.

area($OABC$) = (length of base OA) × (distance PY between lines OA and CB)

A is the point where $y = kx$ and $x = ky + 1$ meet, so $A := \left(\dfrac{1}{1-k^2}, \dfrac{k}{1-k^2}\right)$

$\therefore OA^2 = \left(\dfrac{1}{1-k^2}\right)^2 + \left(\dfrac{k}{1-k^2}\right)^2$

$\therefore OA = \dfrac{\sqrt{1+k^2}}{1-k^2}$

The perpendicular to $y = kx + 1$ through the point $Y := (0, 1)$ has gradient $-\dfrac{1}{k}$, and so has equation $y = -\left(\dfrac{1}{k}\right)x + 1$ and meets the line $y = kx$ at the point $P := \left(\dfrac{k}{k^2+1}, \dfrac{k^2}{k^2+1}\right)$.

$\therefore OP^2 = \left(\dfrac{k}{k^2+1}\right)^2 + \left(\dfrac{k^2}{k^2+1}\right)^2$

$OY^2 = OP^2 + PY^2$

$\therefore PY^2 = 1 - \dfrac{k^2(1+k^2)}{(k^2+1)^2} = 1 - \dfrac{k^2}{k^2+1} = \dfrac{1}{k^2+1}$

$\therefore PY = \sqrt{\dfrac{1}{k^2+1}}$

$\therefore$ Required area $= OA \times PY = \dfrac{1}{1-k^2}$

Alternatively

(a) $y = kx + 1$ and $x = ky + 1$ meet on $y = x$ at $B := \left(\dfrac{1}{1-k}, \dfrac{1}{1-k}\right)$, and

$y = kx + 1$ and $x = ky$ meet at $C := \left(\dfrac{k}{1-k^2}, \dfrac{1}{1-k^2}\right)$.

∴ area(rhombus($OABC$)) = $\frac{1}{2}(OB \times AC)$

$$= \frac{1}{2} \times \sqrt{2\left(\frac{1}{1-k}\right)^2} \times \sqrt{2\left(\frac{1-k}{1-k^2}\right)^2} = \frac{1}{1-k} \times \frac{1}{1-k}$$

(b) It is easy, and instructive, to show that the parallelogram with vertices $O := (0, 0)$, $A := (a, b)$, $C := (c, d)$, and $B := (a+c, b+d)$ has area($OABC$) = $ad - bc$. In this case:

$$A := \left(\frac{1}{1-k^2}, \frac{k}{1-k^2}\right), C := \left(\frac{k}{1-k^2}, \frac{1}{1-k^2}\right)$$

∴ area($OABC$) = $\left(\frac{1}{1-k^2}\right)^2 - \left(\frac{k}{1-k^2}\right)^2 = \frac{1}{1-k^2}$

24 D The regular octahedron contains three squares – each being the 'equator' corresponding to one of the three pairs of opposite 'poles'. Each of these three squares can be labelled $ABCD$ (in order) in eight ways: there are four vertices to choose for A, then two vertices to choose for B – namely the two vertices of the square which are joined to A; C and D are then are determined.

Once the letters A, B, C, D have been used to label a square $ABCD$, the remaining two vertices can be labelled E, F in two ways.
∴ Total number of such labellings of the octahedron
= (number of ways to choose a square)
× (number of ways to label each square)
× (number of ways to label the remaining two vertices)
= 3 × 8 × 2

Alternatively

(a) There are six choices for A. And there are four edges at each vertex so there are four choices for B; then C and D are determined. The two remaining vertices may then be labelled in two ways – either EF or FE.

(b) Begin by labelling E and F: there are six choices for E, and F is then determined (as the vertex opposite E). The square $ABCD$ can then be labelled in 4 × 2 ways.

25 C | The key is to factorise the algebraic expression.
$$n^3 - 10n^2 - 84n + 840 = n^2(n-10) - 84(n-10)$$
$$= (n^2 - 84)(n - 10)$$
The only way the LHS can equal a prime p is if one of the factors on the RHS is equal to ± 1, and the other is equal to $\pm p$.

Case 1 $\quad n - 10 = 1$
$\quad\quad\quad\therefore\quad n = 11$ and $n^2 - 84 = 121 - 84 = 37 = p$ is prime.

Case 2 $\quad n - 10 = -1$
$\quad\quad\quad\therefore\quad n = 9$ and $n^2 - 84 = -3 = -p$ with $p = 3$ is prime.

Case 3 $\quad n^2 - 84 = \pm 1$ is impossible (since neither 85 nor 83 is a square).

26 E $\triangle AEF$ and $\triangle ABC$ are similar and $AE : AB = 2 : 3$ (given).
$\therefore EF : BC = 2 : 3$
$\triangle EFG$ and $\triangle CBG$ are similar and $EF : CB = 2 : 3$
$\therefore \text{area}(\triangle EFG) : \text{area}(\triangle CBG) = 2^2 : 3^2$.
Let $\triangle EFG$ have area $4a$. Then $\triangle CBG$ has area $9a$.
$$\therefore \quad \frac{9a + \text{area}(\triangle EGB)}{4a + \text{area}(\triangle EGB)} = \frac{\text{area}(\triangle ECB)}{\text{area}(\triangle EFB)} = \frac{BC}{EF} = \frac{3}{2}$$
$\therefore \text{area}(\triangle EGB) = 6a$
$\quad\quad\quad\quad\quad\quad = \text{area}(\triangle FGC)$
$$\therefore \quad \frac{25a + \text{area}(\triangle AEF)}{\text{area}(\triangle AEF)} = \frac{\text{area}(\triangle ABC)}{\text{area}(\triangle AEF)} = \left(\frac{AB}{AE}\right)^2 = \left(\frac{3}{2}\right)^2 = \frac{9}{4}$$
$\therefore \text{area}(\triangle AEF) = 20a$
$$\therefore \quad \frac{\text{area}(\triangle ABC)}{\text{area}(\triangle EFG)} = \frac{45a}{4a}$$

27 C | A flexible combination of arithmetic and algebra is enough to show that four of the given options can occur.

A $1^{10} = 01$
B $25^2 = 625$, so all higher powers of 25 end in ...25
D $49^2 = (50 - 1)^2 = 2500 - 100 + 1 = 2401$
$\quad\therefore 7^{10} = 49^5 = (50 - 1)^2 \times (50 - 1)^2 \times 49$
$\quad\quad\quad = 2401 \times 2401 \times 49$, which ends in ...49
E $76^2 = (80 - 4)^2 = 6400 - 2 \times 320 + 16 = 5776$, so all higher powers of 76 end in ...76.

It is a bit more subtle to show that ...36 cannot occur.

Solutions to the National Mathematics Contest problems

Claim $n^{10} \equiv 36 \pmod{100}$ has no solutions.
Proof Suppose $n^{10} \equiv 36 \pmod{100}$
$\therefore n^{10} - 6^2 \equiv 0 \pmod{100}$
$\therefore (n^5 - 6)(n^5 + 6) \equiv 0 \pmod{100}$
$\therefore (n^5 - 6)(n^5 + 6) \equiv 0 \pmod{25}$

However, the only possible fifth powers (mod 25) are $0, \pm 1, \pm 7$. Hence $(n^5 - 6)(n^5 + 6) \equiv 0 \pmod{25}$ has no solutions. $((n^5 - 6)(n^5 + 6)$ can be divisible by 5, but never by 25: for example, if $n^5 \equiv 1 \pmod{25}$, then $n^5 - 6 \equiv -5$, but $n^5 + 6 \equiv 7$.)

28 D At first sight this may seem rather hard. If so, take a deep breath and think a bit harder.

One approach is to choose particular points which are special to each graph (e.g. **A**: $(\frac{1}{2}, \frac{1}{2})$, **B**: $(0.9, 1)$, **C**: $(1, 2)$, **E**: $(\frac{1}{2} + \varepsilon, 1 - \varepsilon)$ with ε small and positive) and show that they do not satisfy the given equation.

A slightly more satisfying approach is to observe that:

$$|2y - 1| = \begin{cases} 2y - 1 & \text{when } y \geq \frac{1}{2} \\ -(2y - 1) & \text{when } y < \frac{1}{2} \end{cases}$$

$$|2y + 1| = \begin{cases} 2y + 1 & \text{when } y \geq -\frac{1}{2} \\ -(2y + 1) & \text{when } y < -\frac{1}{2} \end{cases}$$

$$|x| = \begin{cases} x & \text{when } x \geq 0 \\ -x & \text{when } x < 0 \end{cases}$$

Hence the correct graph should have corners at $y = \pm \frac{1}{2}$, and at $x = 0$.

In fact, if you change the scale on the y-axis, setting $X = x$, $Y = 2y$, then the values $y = \pm \frac{1}{2}$ correspond to $Y = \pm 1$, and the equation given in the question takes the form:

$$(|Y - 1| + |X - 0|) + (|Y - (-1)| + |X - 0|) = 4 \qquad (*)$$

The expression $|Y - 1| + |X - 0|$ represents the distance from the point $F_1 := (0, 1)$ to the point $P := (X, Y)$ using the *Taxicab distance* 'along and up' (as in an American city like New York). Similarly, the expression $|Y + 1| + |X - 0|$ represents the distance from the point $F_2 := (0, -1)$ to the point P. So equation (*) describes the locus of points P such that $PF_1 + PF_2 = 4$ (constant). This is the *focus–focus* definition of an *ellipse*; but since the definition of distance has changed, so has the shape of an ellipse!
For further details, see reference [51, pages 194–202] in the list of resources in Section B.

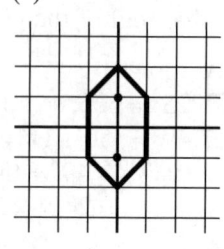

29 A Let O be the centre of the circle, and let r be the its radius.

$\therefore \angle CDO = \alpha$, $\angle COD = \pi - 2\alpha$

$\therefore$ area(sector ODC) $= \dfrac{\pi - 2\alpha}{2\pi} \times \pi r^2$,

area($\triangle ODC$) $= \tfrac{1}{2} \times r^2 \sin(\pi - 2\alpha)$

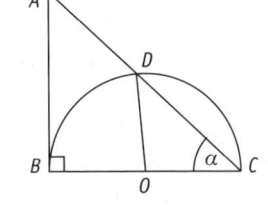

$\therefore$ area of region bounded by segment DC and arc DC
= area(sector ODC) − area($\triangle ODC$)
$= r^2 \left(\dfrac{\pi}{2} - \alpha - \dfrac{\sin 2\alpha}{2} \right)$

$AB = 2r \cdot \tan \alpha$ and area(sector OBD) $= \dfrac{2\alpha}{2\pi} \times \pi r^2$

$\therefore$ area of region bounded by segment AB and arc BD
= area($\triangle ABC$) − area(sector OBD) − area($\triangle ODC$)
$= 2r^2 \tan \alpha - r^2 \alpha - \tfrac{1}{2}r^2 \sin 2\alpha$
$= r^2 \left(2 \tan \alpha - \alpha - \dfrac{\sin 2\alpha}{2} \right)$

Suppose these two regions have the same area.

$\therefore \dfrac{\pi}{2} - \alpha - \dfrac{\sin 2\alpha}{2} = 2 \tan \alpha - \alpha - \dfrac{\sin 2\alpha}{2}$

$\therefore \tan \alpha = \dfrac{\pi}{4}$

Alternatively The fact that the two given areas are equal means that $\triangle ABC$ and the semicircle on BC have equal areas.

$\therefore \tfrac{1}{2} \cdot 2r \cdot 2r \tan \alpha = \tfrac{1}{2}\pi r^2$

$\therefore \tan \alpha = \pi/4$

30 C Suppose $f(x)f(y) = f(x+y) + xy$ for all real values of x and y.

$\therefore f(0)^2 = f(0)$

$\therefore$ Either $f(0) = 0$, or $f(0) = 1$.

Suppose first that $f(0) = 0$.

$\therefore f(x)f(0) = f(x+0) + x \cdot 0$

$\therefore 0 = f(x)$ for all values of x

But '$f(x) = 0$ for all x' does not satisfy the given functional equation (e.g. when $x = y = 1$, we must have $f(1) \cdot f(1) = f(2) + 1$).

Hence we may conclude that $f(0) = 1$.

$\therefore f(1)f(-1) = f(0) - 1 = 0$

$\therefore$ Either (a) $f(1) = 0$, or (b) $f(-1) = 0$.

(a) Suppose first that $f(1) = 0$.
$\therefore \ 0 = f(x-1)f(1)$
$f((x-1)+1) + (x-1) \cdot 1 = f(x) + x - 1$
$\therefore \ f(x) = -x + 1$ for all values of x
You should now check that the function $f(x) = -x + 1$ satisfies the given functional equation:
$f(x)f(y) = (-x+1)(-y+1) = xy - x - y + 1$
$f(x+y) + xy = [-(x+y) + 1] + xy = xy - x - y + 1$

(b) Suppose next that $f(-1) = 0$.
$\therefore \ 0 = f(x+1)f(-1)$
$= f((x+1)-1) + (x+1) \cdot (-1) = f(x) - x - 1$
$\therefore \ f(x) = x + 1$ for all values of x
Now check that $f(x) = x + 1$ satisfies the given functional equation:
$f(x)f(y) = (x+1)(y+1) = xy + x + y + 1$
$f(x+y) + xy = [(x+y) + 1] + xy = xy + x + y + 1$